1 Peter

Reformed Expository Commentary

A Series

Series Editors

Richard D. Phillips

Philip Graham Ryken

Testament Editors

Iain M. Duguid, Old Testament

Daniel M. Doriani, New Testament

1 Peter

Daniel M. Doriani

P&R
PUBLISHING
P.O. BOX 817 • PHILLIPSBURG • NEW JERSEY 08865-0817

ISBN: 978-1-59638-469-9 (cloth)
ISBN: 978-1-62995-040-2 (ePub)
ISBN: 978-1-62995-041-9 (Mobi)

Printed in the United States of America

Library of Congress Cataloging-in-Publication Data

Doriani, Daniel M., 1953-
  1 Peter / Daniel M. Doriani.
      pages cm. -- (Reformed expository commentary)
  Includes bibliographical references and index.
  ISBN 978-1-59638-469-9 (cloth)
  1. Bible. Peter, 1st--Commentaries. I. Title. II. Title: First Peter.
  BS2795.53.D67 2014
  227'.92077--dc23
                                    2013048513

I dedicate this book to my friends at Central Presbyterian Church, especially its elders and deacons. I thank them for granting me a study leave to complete the work, for their friendship, and for their desire to exemplify the godly shepherd of 1 Peter 5.

CONTENTS

Contents

ACKNOWLEDGMENTS

I thank Jo Durham and Andrew Allen for timely editorial and research assistance. Rick Phillips's comments strengthened and clarified the book at many points. Walker Cosgrove offered invaluable assistance for the segment on the Crusades. In ways that each one knows, Clay Smith, Robbie Griggs, Bryan Chapell, Iain Duguid, and Phil Ryken helped me to think through the issues or the presentation. My daughters Abby and Beth and my beloved wife, Debbie, became assistant editors at essential points. I especially thank Tom and Sue Hays, whose home on the South Carolina coast offered a blessed setting for a gentle launch of the final push toward completion. Their porch is the one of the finest places in God's good world for blessed meditation that leads to action.

Series Introduction

In every generation there is a fresh need for the faithful exposition of God's Word in the church. At the same time, the church must constantly do the work of theology: reflecting on the teaching of Scripture, confessing its doctrines of the Christian faith, and applying them to contemporary culture. We believe that these two tasks—the expositional and the theological—are interdependent. Our doctrine must derive from the biblical text, and our understanding of any particular passage of Scripture must arise from the doctrine taught in Scripture as a whole.

We further believe that these interdependent tasks of biblical exposition and theological reflection are best undertaken in the church, and most specifically in the pulpits of the church. This is all the more true since the study of Scripture properly results in doxology and praxis—that is, in praise to God and practical application in the lives of believers. In pursuit of these ends, we are pleased to present the Reformed Expository Commentary as a fresh exposition of Scripture for our generation in the church. We hope and pray that pastors, teachers, Bible study leaders, and many others will find this series to be a faithful, inspiring, and useful resource for the study of God's infallible, inerrant Word.

The Reformed Expository Commentary has four fundamental commitments. First, these commentaries aim to be *biblical*, presenting a comprehensive exposition characterized by careful attention to the details of the text. They are not exegetical commentaries—commenting word by word or even verse by verse—but integrated expositions of whole passages of Scripture. Each commentary will thus present a sequential, systematic treatment of an entire book of the Bible, passage by passage. Second, these commentaries are unashamedly *doctrinal*. We are committed to the Westminster Confession of Faith and Catechisms as containing the system of doctrine taught in the Scriptures of the Old and New Testaments. Each volume will teach, promote, and defend the doctrines of the Reformed faith as they are found in the Bible. Third, these commentaries are *redemptive-historical* in their orientation. We believe in the unity of the Bible and its central message of salvation in Christ. We are thus committed to a Christ-centered view of the Old Testament, in which its characters, events, regulations, and institutions are properly understood as pointing us to Christ and his gospel, as well as giving us examples to follow in living by faith. Fourth, these commentaries are *practical*, applying the text of Scripture to contemporary challenges of life—both public and private—with appropriate illustrations.

The contributors to the Reformed Expository Commentary are all pastor-scholars. As pastor, each author will first present his expositions in the pulpit ministry of his church. This means that these commentaries are rooted in the teaching of Scripture to real people in the church. While aiming to be scholarly, these expositions are not academic. Our intent is to be faithful, clear, and helpful to Christians who possess various levels of biblical and theological training—as should be true in any effective pulpit ministry. Inevitably this means that some issues of academic interest will not be covered. Nevertheless, we aim to achieve a responsible level of scholarship, seeking to promote and model this for pastors and other teachers in the church. Significant exegetical and theological difficulties, along with such historical and cultural background as is relevant to the text, will be treated with care.

We strive for a high standard of enduring excellence. This begins with the selection of the authors, all of whom have proved to be outstanding communicators of God's Word. But this pursuit of excellence is also reflected in a disciplined editorial process. Each volume is edited by both a series editor and a testament editor. The testament editors, Iain Duguid for the Old Testament and Daniel Doriani for the New Testament, are accomplished pastors and respected scholars who have taught at the seminary level. Their job is to ensure that each volume is sufficiently conversant with up-to-date scholarship and is faithful and accurate in its exposition of the text. As series editors, we oversee each volume to ensure its overall quality—including excellence of writing, soundness of teaching, and usefulness in application. Working together as an editorial team, along with the publisher, we are devoted to ensuring that these are the best commentaries that our gifted authors can provide, so that the church will be served with trustworthy and exemplary expositions of God's Word.

It is our goal and prayer that the Reformed Expository Commentary will serve the church by renewing confidence in the clarity and power of Scripture and by upholding the great doctrinal heritage of the Reformed faith. We hope that pastors who read these commentaries will be encouraged in their own expository preaching ministry, which we believe to be the best and most biblical pattern for teaching God's Word in the church. We hope that lay teachers will find these commentaries among the most useful resources they rely on for understanding and presenting the text of the Bible. And we hope that the devotional quality of these studies of Scripture will instruct and inspire each Christian who reads them in joyful, obedient discipleship to Jesus Christ.

May the Lord bless all who read the Reformed Expository Commentary. We commit these volumes to the Lord Jesus Christ, praying that the Holy Spirit will use them for the instruction and edification of the church, with thanksgiving to God the Father for his unceasing faithfulness in building his church through the ministry of his Word.

Richard D. Phillips
Philip Graham Ryken
Series Editors

PREFACE

This book is the product of a long relationship with 1 Peter. When I first read Peter's epistle as a new Christian, it seemed like a distillation of the whole of Christian theology and much of the Christian life. His epistle presents Jesus as both Redeemer and Exemplar of the holy life. It offers the broadest principles for Christian living, grounds them in the work of Christ past, present, and future, and then presents norms for life in the family, at work, and in society at large. Peter's guidance is perfect for Christians who hope to engage their culture in uncertain times. It holds out hope that a beautiful life will be noticed, that no one will harm those who do good, and that we can do good because Jesus has given us life and gifts that we can use to serve others. On the other hand, Peter banishes triumphalism. We are aliens here, he warns, and must expect to attract unwarranted hostility, as Jesus did.

As a seminary professor, I surveyed Peter fourteen times, but never had the occasion to probe its depths. I finally had the opportunity to explore 1 Peter in a series of sermons for Central Presbyterian Church, where I was senior pastor until my recent return to Covenant Seminary. As always, the blessed members of the church and my many good friends there listened well, thanked me, and asked questions that made me study more thoroughly. I thank them for the kingdom-mindedness that led them to grant me the study leave that let me conclude the work.

1 Peter

GRACE-DRIVEN DISCIPLESHIP
IN A DIFFICULT AGE

1

STRANGERS IN A STRANGE LAND

1 *Peter* 1:1—2

Peter, an apostle of Jesus Christ, to God's elect, strangers in
the world, scattered throughout Pontus, Galatia, Cappadocia,
Asia and Bithynia, who have been chosen according to the
foreknowledge of God the Father, through the sanctifying work
of the Spirit, for obedience to Jesus Christ and sprinkling by his
blood: Grace and peace be yours in abundance. (1 Peter 1:1–2)

THE AUTHOR: THE APOSTLE PETER

The unanimous tradition of the early church declares that the apostle
Peter wrote his first epistle while living in Rome, late in his life, around
A.D. 65.[1] If that is correct, then Peter wrote from a lifetime of wisdom and
conviction. He experienced everything, not least the trials and suffering that
he describes in his letter. He also walked with Jesus every day for roughly
three years. Yet Peter drew on more than experience when he wrote his
epistles. He was an apostle, God's ambassador, chosen by Jesus to see his

---

1. Peter writes from "Babylon," which is code for "Rome" (1 Peter 5:13); church tradition places
Peter in Rome, where he died in the mid-60s.

deeds, hear his words, and declare what it all means. Peter was at ease with this authority. He did not trumpet his credentials. Rather, he assumed that he had the right to describe God's salvation and explain its significance.

Peter addressed his epistle to people and churches that he calls "God's elect." They lived in regions east of Rome, in "Pontus, Galatia, Cappadocia, Asia and Bithynia" (1 Peter 1:1).

Since Peter identifies himself as "an apostle of Jesus Christ" (1 Peter 1:1), he invites us to read his letter through the lens of his experience as disciple and apostle. The Gospels name Peter as one of "the Twelve" (Mark 10:32; 14:10) and as a member of the inner three, "Peter, James and John" (5:37; 9:2; 14:33). Peter was, at a minimum, the most outspoken among the twelve disciples. At most, he was their spokesman, and in some sense their leader. He articulated their best thoughts, thoughts given by God himself. He confessed Jesus: "You are the Christ, the Son of the living God" (Matt. 16:16). But Peter also blurted out the disciples' worst errors. He even dared to rebuke Jesus—on the very day that he confessed Jesus' deity—for saying that he must go to the cross (16:21–22). He asked pointed questions (19:23–27), made rash vows ("I will never disown you," Mark 14:31), and failed to keep them, above all by denying Jesus three times (John 18:15–27).

After the resurrection, Jesus commissioned the apostles to make disciples of the nations (Matt. 28:18–20). Despite Peter's failures, Jesus reinstated him as an apostle and commanded Peter to feed his sheep (John 21:15–17). At Pentecost, Peter proclaimed Jesus' resurrection, and three thousand repented, believed, and were baptized. That marked the birth of the church as we know it (Acts 2:22–41). When Peter preached again, the church exploded with additional disciples (4:4; 5:14). Peter performed signs, testified to Christ, solved problems, and rebuked sin within the infant Jerusalem church. Before Paul took the lead, Peter inaugurated the mission to the Gentiles (Acts 10).

Peter did betray Jesus, but even his failures fascinate us and illumine both the man and the message. It is fitting that Peter, who betrayed the Lord and received the grace of forgiveness, both opens and closes his epistle by offering his churches the grace of God. His letter begins, "Grace and peace be yours in abundance" (1 Peter 1:2). And he closes, "I have written to you briefly, encouraging you and testifying that this is the true grace of God. Stand fast in it" (5:12). Knowing Peter's history, we understand that his talk of grace is no mere formula. Peter denied Jesus three times, insisting, with oaths, that he did not even know Jesus. He did this despite warnings, despite vows to the contrary, and at the hour of Jesus' greatest need. Yet Peter repented, in tears, and received forgiveness and reinstatement as an apostle (Luke 22:62; John 21:15–17). Because he knew the depth of his need and because he understood the perfection of Jesus' offer, Peter loved the grace of God.

Peter's need of grace was most acute when he denied Jesus during the trial. It is moving, therefore, that Peter wrote his letter to help God's elect as they "suffer grief in all kinds of trials" (1 Peter 1:6). Yet trials bring more than misery and temptation. When we endure trials, when we remain loyal in hardship, according to Peter, it proves our faith genuine (1:6–7), and that brings us glory when Christ is revealed. So suffering can create confidence. If we are willing to suffer for Jesus, it shows that we truly belong to him (4:1) and stand fast with him (5:12). We stand fast when we remain holy in a corrupt age (1:14–16; 4:1–4) and when we remain loyal to Jesus through persecution (4:12–16).

THE AUDIENCE: BELIEVERS WHO ARE STRANGERS IN THEIR OWN LAND

Peter wrote for everyone, but especially for believers, God's elect. He explicitly addressed a group of churches scattered through a wide swath in the northeast of the Roman Empire: "To God's elect, strangers in the world, scattered throughout Pontus, Galatia, Cappadocia, Asia and Bithynia" (1 Peter 1:1–2). These named areas represent millions of people across an area of roughly the size of Turkey or America's Southwest from Texas to California (about 750,000 square miles). In short, this is a universal letter, not a local letter.

Peter reminded his people of their status, privileges, and responsibilities. The church is God's elect, "who have been chosen according to the foreknowledge of God the Father, through the sanctifying work of the Spirit, for obedience to Jesus Christ and sprinkling by his blood" (1 Peter 1:2). The elect are redeemed by the triune God. The Father chose them according to his foreknowledge. The Spirit sanctifies them for obedience to the Son, who sprinkled them with his blood and so atoned for their sins. In God's name, Peter blesses his readers: "Grace and peace be yours in abundance" (1:2).

So Peter opens with his great themes: the work of the triune God who elects, gives grace, commands and empowers holiness, and leads us to a mission. The first hint of that mission arrives in the salutation. Peter identifies us as "God's elect, strangers in the world" (1 Peter 1:1). More literally, we are "elect exiles of the dispersion" (1:1 ESV). The church is privileged by God; we are his chosen ones. Yet at the same time, and for the same reason, the church is disadvantaged in society. Because believers are God's chosen people, we are "strangers" or "exiles" in our own world. The word *stranger* or *exile* (*parepidemos*) denotes a temporary resident, a traveler whose stay is measured in weeks or a few months.[2] The term *alien* (*paroikos*), used in 1 Peter 2:11, is similar but suggests a long-term resident. It could describe an immigrant from a distant place who has lived in another land for several years, started a career, and found a home.[3] Both terms signify that the person originally belonged elsewhere.

Peter wants believers to realize that we never fully belong in this world. Strangers have no permanent residence. Aliens cannot hold positions of power and rarely enjoy full privileges. This is essential to a Christian's identity. People in Reformed and Calvinist churches have committed to engage the culture rather than fleeing from it, and rightly so. Yet we must remember that we are exiles and therefore will never be completely at home in this world.

Most commentators believe Peter's audience consists primarily of Gentiles, not Jews. Peter's people "were redeemed from the empty way of life handed down . . . from your forefathers" (1 Peter 1:18). For years, they did "what pagans choose to do" (4:3). Their neighbors thought it "strange" when they abandoned their former life of dissipation (4:4). Their lifestyle was manifestly different from the conduct of others in the empire. So most of Peter's people did not grow up in the covenant. God's election, salvation, and subsequent sanctification estranged them from their native culture.

The life of John Adams is illustrative. Adams was a Massachusetts farmer and lawyer. The Constitutional Congress named Adams as its ambassador to France. He was not successful. He was too fiery, too much the unyield-

---

2. Peter H. Davids, *The First Epistle of Peter* (Grand Rapids: Eerdmans, 1990), 95.
3. J. Ramsey Michaels, *1 Peter*, Word Biblical Commentary 49 (Nashville: Thomas Nelson, 1988), 6–9; Johannes Louw and Eugene Nida, *Greek-English Lexicon of the New Testament: Based on Semantic Domains*, 2nd ed. (New York: United Bible Societies, 1998–99), 1:133.

ing crusader, to suit the cool and venial French court. Adams was a great American, but in France he was a stranger in a strange land.[4] Travelers often experience the same sense of estrangement. Whether we know the language or not, we feel out of place when we first visit a new land. The food, the conception of time, and sundry unwritten rules of conduct conspire to surprise and unsettle us. Similarly, the first visit to any established group, whether social, spiritual, professional, or intellectual, can easily leave the newcomer feeling out of place.

These are the experiences of strangers and aliens. Peter understood that life. He knew Greek, he had once had a good income as a fisherman, and he had traveled widely in the Roman Empire before settling in Rome itself. But he was a Jew from Galilee, a backwater of the empire. When he first traveled to Jerusalem, he marveled at its sights (Mark 13:1). We can imagine how Rome impressed him. Since Galilee had been Hellenized to a degree, he was familiar with elements of Greco-Roman culture. Still, a wholly Gentile world had to seem strange at times to an observant Jew (Acts 10:14).

In fact, because Peter had followed Jesus from the beginning, he had become an outsider even within Israel. After he became a disciple, he left his business and family to wander through Galilee and Judea with Jesus (Luke 5:1–11). When the authorities began to question Jesus, Peter and the other disciples were implicated (e.g., Matt. 12:1ff.; John 18:1–27). After Jesus' ascension, Peter became even more controversial. He performed miracles like the miracles of Jesus and did so in his name (Acts 4:2, 13). As the church grew, the authorities threatened, beat, and jailed Peter (Acts 4, 5, 12). Peter fit neither in Rome nor in Israel, and he tells the believers in the church that his lot will be theirs. They, too, will be outsiders and aliens.

But we must not think Peter resented his status. He knew his identity and savored his call. He knew that every disciple of Jesus will, in part at least, be an outsider, stranger, and exile in the wider world.

Peter wrote his epistle to Christians scattered through five provinces of the eastern empire, provinces that encompassed many peoples and languages. But Peter ignored race, ethnicity, and language and defined the churches by their status as God's elect. He said that Jesus had sprinkled us with his blood and so atoned for our sin. We are sanctified by the Spirit, that we

4. David McCollough, *John Adams* (New York: Simon & Schuster, 2001).

may believe the gospel, obey Jesus, and experience God's grace and peace (1 Peter 1:1–2).

Exiles live between two worlds. When a couple has a baby, they remain in their old world, with the same marriage, skills, friends, and interests. Yet their baby places them in a new world, with a new schedule and a powerful new interest in the eating, sleeping, crawling, and babbling of their child. They meet other parents, who become new friends and advisers. The new world of parenting will partially alienate them from their former world, since they have less in common with their childless friends, whether single or married. But the change from pagan polytheist to Christian is greater than the changes wrought by parenthood. As strangers and exiles, we will never perfectly fit in with, never fully belong to, pagan society. We *feel* like aliens in our own world because we are—at least partially so.

We need to grasp the right lessons from this. Peter says that we are aliens, but he never tells us to alienate ourselves from this world by abandoning it or cursing it. God did not abandon his creation; he sent his Son to redeem and restore it and fully renew it one day. Since God's ways are our model, we should remain engaged with this world. Historically, the Reformed or Calvinistic branch of Christendom has engaged the culture. We hope to form, reform, and transform it, not abandon it. We admire Calvin not only for his theology but also for his social action. For example, an infectious plague swept through Italy and Switzerland during Calvin's day, in the sixteenth century. Showing admirable courage, Cardinal Borromeo of Milan stayed in his city to feed and pray for those who were dying. Yet we may admire Calvin more, not because he was braver, but because he was wiser. "Calvin acted better and more wisely, for he not only cared incessantly for the spiritual needs of the sick, but at the same time introduced hitherto unsurpassed hygienic measures whereby the ravages of the plague were arrested."[5]

Nor was Calvin's cultural engagement limited to the traditional sphere of works of mercy. In sixteenth-century Europe, the growth of market economies led to a sharp increase in the cost of living and a simultaneous drop in

---

5. Abraham Kuyper, *Calvinism: Six Stone Foundation Lectures* (Grand Rapids: Eerdmans, 1943), 120. See also Cornelius Plantinga, *Engaging God's World* (Grand Rapids: Eerdmans, 2002); Lee Hardy, *The Fabric of This World* (Grand Rapids: Eerdmans, 1990); Gene Edward Veith, *God at Work: Your Christian Vocation in All of Life* (Wheaton, IL: Crossway, 2002).

the value of labor. Calvin spoke prophetically against a rising aristocracy that exploited the poor by depriving them of fair wages.[6] We are prone to admire Calvin for his cultural engagement, but is this the way that God expects his exiles to act?

Scripture holds two ideas in tension. We are, simultaneously, exiles in this world and agents of change within it. Because we are exiles, we resist conformity to the patterns of this age. God told his people, living in the shadow of Babylon, that great city of wealth and decadent pleasures, "Come out of her, my people, so that you will not share in her sins, so that you will not receive any of her plagues." Clearly, we must flee the corrupt world, for judgment will fall upon it (Rev. 18:4). Yet we are reformers, constantly ready to engage society. Jesus notes that his disciples are "in the world" but that "they are not *of* the world any more than I am of the world." He continues, "My prayer is not that you take them out of the world but that you protect them from the evil one" (John 17:11–15). As we so often notice, Jesus called his disciples "the salt of the earth"—retarding its decay—and "the light of the world" (Matt. 5:13–14).

So, then, we are engaged exiles. A few years ago, I shared a long meal with the brilliant, crusading atheist Christopher Hitchens. His book title, *God Is Not Great: How Religion Poisons Everything*, reveals his conviction.[7] Hitchens's tone was occasionally brutish but generally cordial (it helped that my agnostic dissertation adviser had been a friend of his). Through our long conversation, I came to understand atheism better and, as he listened to me and another theologian at the table, he came to understand Christianity better. Since his main ideas about Christianity came from European Catholicism, liberal Protestantism, and the atheist's list of "repulsive things we found in the Bible," we were able to blunt many of his objections to biblical Christianity. We cleared up serious misconceptions and introduced him to essential tenets of the faith. At times it seemed that we were making progress. Yet Hitchens remained a devoted atheist. A radical individualist and libertarian, he despised the very concept of a sovereign, all-powerful

6. Calvin had a view of "fair wages"—one formed both by an older cultural consensus and by theological convictions. See William P. Brown, "Calvin and Qoheleth Meet after a Hard Day's Night," in *Reformed Theology: Identity and Ecumenicity II*, ed. Wallace Alston and Michael Welker (Grand Rapids: Eerdmans, 2007), 75–76.

7. Christopher Hitchens, *God Is Not Great: How Religion Poisons Everything* (New York: Warner Books, 2007).

God who calls humans to worship him and render an account for their lives. He hated biblical notions of grace and called the atonement barbaric. He raged at the idea that hell awaits those who deny God, but found heaven offensive, too. He had no desire to spend eternity "groveling" before a deity. Therefore, no matter how cordial and instructive our discussion was, there was no ultimate rapprochement, for he believed the God of the Bible to be a cosmic despot. We would always be exiles if Hitchens hosted a table, unless the Spirit renewed him.

In a similar sense, Peter's people were aliens in the empire. Their beliefs and practices were, and inevitably remained, radically at odds with their culture. In certain lands, Christianity is now so widespread that it obtains general tolerance, possibly even respect. But Christians are "aliens" and will never perfectly fit into secular society. We will never be able to laugh at every joke or enjoy every entertainment and pastime.

No one likes to be excluded. Everyone cringes or bristles when things we hold dear are mocked or dismissed, even if the manner is polite. But exclusion is not necessarily an evil. If we detest cigar smoke, we should not mind if we are banned from a cigar club, with its pointless discussion of the virtues of Cuba's soil and climate, and its constant pollution of lips, lungs, and clothes. So, too, there are groups, however attractive they initially seem, to which a wise disciple will not want to belong. There are jokes that make people laugh, even though they are more cruel than funny, so that a noble person should not be amused. There are entertainments that are novel and exciting at first, but degrading and enslaving in the end. It is a gain, not a loss, to stand outside such groups, with their humorless jokes and wearisome entertainments.

The first Christians knew they were outsiders, for their beliefs and practices stood in radical conflict with their culture. Today, wherever Christianity is most widespread, it gets tolerance, if not respect. But we must neither attempt nor expect to fit perfectly into secular society. The life of the exile is not necessarily onerous, since we join God's exiled community. Peter promises that although the redeemed are aliens now, we will have a better home and "an inheritance that is imperishable, undefiled, and unfading" (1 Peter 1:3–4 ESV). That initiates the theme of the next passage. But before we consider that, we need an overview of the main message of 1 Peter and of its structure, that is, the way its message unfolds.

The Themes and Goals of 1 Peter

The twelve apostles wrote just eight of the twenty-seven books of the New Testament;[8] long tradition says that Peter stood behind a ninth, Mark's gospel. Among these nine books, we see a tendency to state the purpose of the book at the beginning (Mark 1:1) or the end (Matt. 28:18–20; John 20:31; 1 John 5:13). Indeed, we can see theme statements at both the beginning and the end of 1 Peter.

Grace

As Peter begins, he tells his people that they have been chosen by the Father, sanctified by the Spirit, and sprinkled by the blood of Jesus Christ (1 Peter 1:1–2). He gives us grace; we owe him obedience (1:2). We praise him for his great mercy, for our new birth, and for the hope of an eternal inheritance, shared with Christ (1:3–4, 7).

As Peter closes, he appeals to his readers, "exhorting and declaring that this is the true grace of God. Stand firm in it" (1 Peter 5:12 ESV). The word *this* in the phrase "this is the true grace of God" is crucial. Since it comes at the end of the epistle, "this . . . grace" seems to refer to the whole letter, with its message of hope and salvation in the gospel. Throughout this epistle, Peter is a good steward "of God's varied grace" (4:10 ESV). That grace begins with Jesus' atonement (1:2, 18–21) and continues with assurance that Jesus is our Shepherd and Overseer, even in suffering (2:25). Further, while Satan prowls and brothers through the world suffer, "the God of all grace" pledges to restore, strengthen, and establish his people (5:8–11). "This . . . grace" then begins with Jesus' substitutionary atonement for sins (1:17–21; 2:24; 3:18–22), includes God's promise of protection in suffering in the present, and promises glory with Christ in the future (1:6–9).

Therefore, although suffering is never far from Peter's mind, it is not the focus of Peter's attention. Rather, Jesus "suffered once for sins, the righteous for the unrighteous, that he might bring us to God" (3:18 ESV). Jesus suffered for "the salvation of your souls," shedding his blood as a "lamb without blemish" (1:9, 19). By this sacrifice, the true members of Peter's churches "were ransomed from the futile ways inherited from your forefathers" (1:18 ESV).

---

8. The eight books are Matthew, John, 1–2 Peter, 1–3 John, and Revelation.

11

The suffering of the churches is an inevitable result of their new life, but not the core of that life. Rather, because Peter's people are now the new people of God (1 Peter 1:1; 2:4–10), they must break with the pagan ways they inherited from their fathers (1:14, 18). Because of this break, they will seem strange, perhaps even evil, to their former friends (2:12; 4:1–4). A willingness to suffer the consequences of their faith shows that they are united to Christ and brings the promise of eternal life with him (1:3–9; 4:13; 5:1, 4, 10). In the day that I write this, anyone who declares that God wants marriage to unite one man and one woman will be called a bigot and a hater. Other ages have other flash points. Disciples need to be willing to clash with their culture in order to align with Christ.

Faithfulness in Suffering

That said, suffering is prominent in 1 Peter. In the apostolic era, neither the empire nor the Jewish establishment settled on a policy of systematic persecution of the church. Nonetheless, persecution was always a possibility, since believers refused to worship the emperor. Christians followed a crucified Jew (hence a condemned man) who claimed, in a way that could sound threatening to established powers, to be Lord of Israel. This helps to explain why trials and suffering are a topic in every chapter of 1 Peter (1:6–9; 2:18–25; 3:13–18; 4:12–19; 5:9), and the strength of the warnings seems to grow sharper as the epistle progresses. Compare the warnings of chapters 3 and 4:

> Who is going to harm you if you are eager to do good? But even if you should suffer for what is right, you are blessed. . . . Always be prepared to give an answer to everyone who asks you to give the reason for the hope that you have. (1 Peter 3:13–15)

> Dear friends, do not be surprised at the painful trial you are suffering, as though something strange were happening to you. But rejoice that you participate in the sufferings of Christ. (4:12–13)

In the first passage, persecution is possible. In the second, it seems certain. Clearly, Peter wants to tell his readers that trouble is coming, but he eases them into it. Chapter 3 states, "It could happen. Be ready in case it does."

Chapter 4 warns, "It will happen, so don't be surprised when it does, and see it in light of your union with Christ." Peter therefore aims to teach believers how to live as faithfully as possible in an often-hostile world.

The path of faithfulness is clear. We remain holy in a sinful age (1 Peter 1:18; 2:9; 4:3–4). We follow the norms of behavior that make life work in every society (2:20; 3:8–12). And we are always ready to endure persecution and so to follow Jesus' example (2:21–23; 3:13–18; 4:12–16).

Note on the Structure of 1 Peter

It is good also to observe the structure of Peter's epistle. After his opening greeting (1 Peter 1:1–2), Peter praises God for granting believers new birth into a living hope (1:3–9), described in Scripture (1:10–12). God calls his people to a life of holiness that is grounded in the redemptive work of Christ. Because God is holy, we are holy. Because Jesus ransomed us and we tasted his goodness, we put away sin (1:13–2:3). Because we are God's chosen, a holy nation, we abstain from sin and live honorably, even if slandered (2:4–12).

Holiness manifests itself socially, in submission to governors and masters (1 Peter 2:13–25). While wives still submit to husbands, husbands honor their wives, that they may live together in grace (3:1–7). We can ordinarily expect to live well, experiencing God's favor, if we are loving and honest and seek peace (3:8–13). Nonetheless, it is possible to suffer for doing good (3:13–17). Jesus did so when he suffered for us and liberated us from death (3:18–22).

Jesus' example arms us for opposition from the Gentiles (1 Peter 4:1–6). Nonetheless, the disciple is not combative. He is self-controlled, loving, hospitable, and eager to use God's gifts to administer God's grace (4:7–11). This is necessary if we hope to face the trials that will come to those who share in Christ, to whom we entrust ourselves (4:12–19). While individual believers seek to endure and do good, the elders of the church lead by setting an example and by watching over all (5:1–5). While Peter is glad to advise people in their specific callings, the great principles of life are the same for all: we humble ourselves before God, cast our cares on him, resist Satan, and stand firm in God's grace (5:6–14).

So, then, let us plunge into the riches of the work of Peter, eyewitness and apostle of Christ, and servant of God's elect.

2

A Sure and Living Hope

1 Peter 1:3–9

Praise be to the God and Father of our Lord Jesus Christ! In his
great mercy he has given us new birth into a living hope through
the resurrection of Jesus Christ from the dead. (1 Peter 1:3)

once wrote a short story and everyone seemed to like it, but I
have no contacts in fiction, so I have *faint hope* that it will ever
be published. I have *a middling hope* of visiting Hawaii someday.
I would like to hike its isolated trails, yet it seems far away, commercial-
ized, and expensive. But if I say I *hope* my wife will always love me, I mean
something quite different. That hope is strong and personal, and a great
deal rests on it. Even if I shiver at the weight of saying, "I hope she *always*
loves me," I am not troubled with doubts, because I know her.

In a similar vein, Peter begins with a strong and personal hope. It rests
on the God he knows. His hope rests in God's election (1 Peter 1:1), God's
foreknowledge (1:2), and God's power (1:5). Peter also names Jesus Christ
five times in his first seven verses. He tells us to praise Jesus and obey him
(1:2–3). Our hope is "living," that is, imperishable and undying (cf. Rom.
6:9). It depends on Jesus' blood (1 Peter 1:2), Jesus' resurrection (1:3), and
Jesus' second appearance (1:7).

After he describes God's character and work, Peter moves swiftly to blessing and praise. "Blessed be God" was a common phrase in Jewish devotion, but Peter's focus on Jesus makes it a Christian blessing (see 1 Peter 1:3 ESV). Peter gives us several reasons to bless God. We were *chosen* by God the Father, *sanctified* by God the Spirit, and *sprinkled clean* by the blood of Jesus, the Son. Because of the triune God's work, Peter can tell us, "May grace and peace be multiplied to you" (1:2 ESV). Peter knows that God has blessed his people, but he also says that God is blessed—and, he hints, we may bless him, too, as we see the present hope and future inheritance that God has granted us (1:3–5).

This hope was essential, since Peter's churches, scattered through the region now called Asia Minor, suffered all kinds of trials (1 Peter 1:6). These fiery trials tested and refined their faith, but also provoked fear (3:14; 4:12). Peter assures his people that God's power will shield them. They will pass these tests, prove their faith genuine, and gain honor when their salvation is complete (1:7–9).

BLESSED BE OUR LORD GOD

The NIV translates Peter's first words as "Praise" be to God (1 Peter 1:3a), while the ESV says "Blessed" be God. It is easy to defend both choices. The word that Peter uses, *eulogētos*, means "blessed." Yet Peter does not bless God in the way that God blesses us. God *gives us* his blessing, but we *declare* that God is the Blessed One. Full of knowledge and strength (1:2, 5), he gives us grace, mercy, and life (1:2–3). When we say these things, we *praise* God. God doesn't *need* our blessing, so in one sense we cannot bless him. As Hebrews 7:7 notes, the greater blesses the lesser. God doesn't need to hear nice words in order to feel better about himself or to stay motivated to do good. Rather, it is good *for us* to declare God's excellence.

In verse 3, Peter cites Jesus' full title, "our Lord Jesus Christ," which appears about thirty-five times in eleven different books of the New Testament.[1] Working backward, *Christ* means that he is the promised Messiah. *Jesus* means that he is Savior; in Hebrew, *Joshua/Jesus* means "Yahweh saves." *Lord* means that he rules all things. Beyond all that, he is *ours*, and we are

---

1. There is some doubt about the numbers because of variant readings in the original text.

his. So he is the Lord and *our* Lord. He is God's Anointed, and Yahweh saves through him.

Our Hope and Inheritance

Peter's praise mentions both the quality and the certainty of God's salvation: "In his great mercy he has given us new birth into a living hope through the resurrection of Jesus Christ from the dead, and into an inheritance that can never perish, spoil or fade" (1 Peter 1:3b–4a). The opening verses of Peter are steeped in covenantal language. Peter has already said that God elects and has foreknowledge of his people. His *mercy* (*hesed* in the Old Testament, *eleos* in the LXX[2] and New Testament) is closely linked to God's covenant name and covenant-making deeds. He shows mercy (*hesed* is also translated "steadfast love") to thousands who love him (Ex. 20:6; Deut. 5:10). When he reveals himself to Moses, he says that he is "the compassionate and gracious God, slow to anger, abounding in love [*hesed*] and faithfulness" (Ex. 34:6).

In his mercy, Peter continues, "he has given us new birth" (1 Peter 1:3). "Give new birth" translates one Greek verb (*anagennaō*) that appears only in 1 Peter. The term echoes Jesus' teaching of Nicodemus, Israel's teacher, that he had to be born anew and born of the Spirit if he hoped to see God's kingdom (John 3:1–10). Nicodemus and Peter, Jews and Gentiles, you and I—all need God's Spirit to breathe life into our dead souls. Pastors need to believe this, and to say it, to move believers to gratitude and to move unbelievers to humble themselves and receive this rebirth.

In his mercy, God has given us three things: a living hope (1 Peter 1:3), an inheritance (1:4), and salvation (1:5). All three follow our new birth. Our hope rests not in teachings, nor even in a teacher, but in the Redeemer who rose from the dead.

Through his death, Jesus bore our sins (1 Peter 2:24), and through his resurrection, we obtain "an inheritance that is imperishable, undefiled, and unfading, kept in heaven for you" (1:4 ESV). The resurrection of Jesus gives us hope because it proves that death is not the last word. Death could not hold him (Acts 2:24), and it cannot hold us if we are united to him by faith (Rom. 5:21–6:9). An inheritance is a *gift* based on a relationship, not

2. The Septuagint (LXX) is the oldest translation of the Hebrew Old Testament in Greek. It was completed around 100 B.C.

a wage for a performance. Because the gift rests on the Father's grace and covenant, and because God keeps *us* safe, our inheritance is safe. In language that is almost poetic in the original, Peter says that this inheritance is "imperishable, undefiled, and unfading." Nothing can spoil our inheritance. It is "untouched by death, unstained by evil, unimpaired by time; it is compounded of immortality, purity and beauty."[3] Nothing can jeopardize it and nothing can ruin it.[4]

Nothing can keep this inheritance from us, and, Peter declares, nothing can keep us from it. Our inheritance is "kept in heaven for you, who by God's power are being guarded through faith for a salvation ready to be revealed in the last time" (1 Peter 1:4b–5 ESV). The symmetry is perfect. God keeps the inheritance for us, and he keeps us for the inheritance. He keeps the treasure for us, *and* he guards us so that we will properly enjoy it.[5]

Suppose someone's fortieth birthday is at hand. Family and friends plan a surprise party. The celebrants have everything ready at the chosen venue. But if it is a surprise, someone has to deliver the birthday girl to the appointed place at the ordained time. Peter says that God plays both roles in this vignette. He prepares the perfect party *and* he brings us to the party. Philippians promises that God "who began a good work in you will carry it on to completion until the day of Christ Jesus" (Phil. 1:6).

The Westminster Confession perhaps offers the finest description of the assurance that believers should have that the Lord will grant them eternal life in chapter 17, "Of the Perseverance of the Saints":

17.1. They, whom God has accepted in His Beloved, effectually called, and sanctified by His Spirit, can neither totally nor finally fall away from the state of grace, but shall certainly persevere therein to the end, and be eternally saved.

17.2. This perseverance of the saints depends not upon their own free will, but upon the immutability of the decree of election, flowing from the free

3. F. W. Beare, *The First Epistle of Peter*, 3rd ed. (Oxford: Blackwell, 1970), 83–84.

4. *Inheritance* is a common concept in Scripture. Believers can inherit the kingdom, the promise, the land, the earth, and salvation. An inheritance is a settled and sanctioned possession, whether it comes from family or from God. See J. Ramsey Michaels, *1 Peter*, Word Biblical Commentary 49 (Nashville: Thomas Nelson, 1988), 20–21.

5. The Greek verbs are different. The first, *tēreō*, means "to keep" or "guard." The second, *phroureō*, means "to guard" or "watch over." Clearly, their meanings are close.

and unchangeable love of God the Father; upon the efficacy of the merit and intercession of Jesus Christ, the abiding of the Spirit, and of the seed of God within them; and the nature of the covenant of grace: from all which arises also the certainty and infallibility thereof.

Peter teaches that God keeps both us and the inheritance until salvation is "ready to be revealed in the last time" (1 Peter 1:5). Although he knows there is more, Paul typically stresses that the "mystery" of salvation has *already been revealed* (e.g., Eph. 3:8–12; Col. 1:25–27). Peter stresses that there is *more to be revealed* (1 Peter 1:5, 7). Both are true. Similarly, John calls our attention to eternal life as a present possession (John 3:36; 4:36; 5:24; etc.), while Peter tells us that eternal life is coming. Again, both are true and necessary perspectives. Life is here, but there is much more to come.

Joy in Suffering

At that moment, the Christians of Asia Minor were suffering grief, but Peter teaches that the prospect of an inheritance, secured by God, still brings joy. We can celebrate because we know that the salvation that is already ours will one day be revealed in full: "In this you greatly rejoice, though now for a little while you may have had to suffer grief in all kinds of trials" (1 Peter 1:6). This suffering is brief—"for a little while"—from the perspective of eternity, even if pain can seem to last forever when we are immersed in it.

Peter says that his people "had to suffer." He says this because suffering is a logical result of conversion. It is "the wake following behind salvation's boat."[6] It was predictable because following God entails abandoning "the gods" whose worship was part of the glue that united Roman society. It was foreseeable because Christian morality clashed with pagan morality.

Peter doesn't quite say that suffering is inevitable, but he says that it is no surprise (1 Peter 4:12). In the quasi-Christianized societies of the West, when belief in one God is common and Christian ethics have some influence on social ethics, suffering is not certain. But in most places and times, Christian beliefs and practices are exceptional, not normal. If we tell the world that its ideas are false and its practices dangerous, as we must, the world will not be pleased, and that displeasure readily leads to opposition.

---

6. Scot McKnight, *1 Peter*, NIV Application Commentary (Grand Rapids: Zondervan, 1996), 74.

If, while living in a non-Christian culture, we face no opposition, we are probably too interested in fitting in and getting along. When worldviews clash, we don't have the right to sit in silence. When we push against a misguided world, the world will push back, hard. We should expect it and rejoice in it, as Jesus says:

> Blessed are those who are persecuted because of righteousness,
>   for theirs is the kingdom of heaven.

> Blessed are you when people insult you, persecute you and falsely say all kinds of evil against you because of me. Rejoice . . . , because great is your reward in heaven, for in the same way they persecuted the prophets who were before you. (Matt. 5:10–12)

Peter describes our trials in five ways in 1 Peter 1:6–7. First, when compared to eternity, they are brief in duration; they last "a little while." Second, they are varied in form; there are "all kinds." Third, they have a kind of necessity; "you . . . had to suffer." Fourth, suffering proves that our faith is real; "these have come so that your faith—of greater worth than gold, which perishes even though refined by fire—may be proved genuine" (1:7a). Fifth, suffering will "result in praise, glory and honor when Jesus Christ is revealed" (1:7b). Because suffering has a limit and a purpose, we can still rejoice in it.

Peter's comment about gold is a parenthesis that explains how trials "prove" our faith. First, gold and faith are both proved by fire. Literal fire tests gold, and the metaphorical fire of adversity tests men and their faith (see Ps. 66:10; Prov. 17:3; James 1:2–4; etc.).[7] "Just as men used fire to distinguish true gold from counterfeit [and alloyed or imperfect metals], so God uses trials to distinguish genuine faith from superficial profession."[8] Second, while gold was the most precious metal to the ancients, faith has greater value. Like every other created thing, gold is perishable (1 Peter 1:7, 18), but our faith is imperishable, since God preserves us in it (1:5).

---

7. Writing around Peter's time, Seneca said, "Fire tests gold, affliction tests strong men" in his work *Epistles on Providence*, 5.10. Ecclesiasticus, a widely read collection of intertestamental Jewish wisdom, said, "Gold is tested in the fire, and those found acceptable [to God], in the furnace of humiliation" (Ecclus. 2:5 NRSV).

8. Alan M. Stibbs, *The First Epistle General of Peter* (London: Tyndale, 1959), 78.

Peter's teaching about suffering questions us. Do you see it as he does? Or do you withdraw and complain that life is unfair? There *is* a time to flee persecution: when no one is listening, when the opposition or abuse is unrelenting, when there is important work to do elsewhere, and (most important) when we have no obligations or vows *so that we are free to leave* (see Matthew 10:23 in context). But on most occasions, we are not free to leave. In that case, do we do all we can to avoid pain, or do we endure, knowing that our willingness to endure proves that our faith is real?

When our relationships are deeper, our minds sharper, our bodies stronger, our self-discipline stiffer, our emotions healthier, and our contributions well received, it is easy to give thanks. But if you suffer trials, take heart; God is guarding your inheritance.[9] Many trials come from the outside, when people wrong us or when disease and disaster wound us. Other trials come from within—self-doubt, irrational fear, loss of passion. Trials are fiery, and we should never pretend otherwise. They hurt, sometimes so badly that despair assails us. But Peter encourages us that we can rejoice as trials prove our faith real. All things lead to praise when Jesus is revealed and completes his salvation. That coming salvation transforms our present experience, offering us hope even in the worst of times.

These claims can sound like religious jargon, but anyone who has immersed himself in life long enough has tasted the bitter pains that life hurls at humans. Again, it can sound like rhetoric, but it was not rhetoric for Peter. He walked with Jesus and suffered arrest and threats for the crime of telling the truth about him. To be sure, we can deceive others and deceive ourselves with vapid talk of joy, but it is good and right to have peace at 3 A.M. when troubles interrupt our sleep.

When we persevere and our faith is proved, the result is "praise, glory and honor when Jesus Christ is revealed" (1 Peter 1:7b). This praise could be God's, since he always merits praise, even for completing his redemption. Or it could be the praise that God bestows on the faithful on judgment day (Matt. 25:19–23; Rom. 2:29). Since Peter has his eye on the coming of salvation and the revelation of Christ "in the last time," it seems that Peter means the praise God confers to us, for our faith and justice in this age.

---

9. The grammatically attentive reader will notice that this section, like others, shifts from first-person *we*-language to second-person *you*-language. Peter normally speaks in the second person, but he shifts to the first-person plural in 1 Peter 1:3; 2:24; 4:17.

Jesus, the Object of Our Faith and Source of Our Blessing

First Peter 1:3–9 is one complex sentence with each part connecting to the one before. In the Greek text, Peter links verses 7 and 8 with the relative pronoun *whom*, referring to Jesus. It works this way: Peter mentions Jesus' future coming at the end of 1:7 and then turns to his current absence in 1:8. Peter addresses "the discrepancy between [the] present experience of suffering and [the] anticipated future glory."[10] Peter saw Jesus with his own eyes and touched him with his hands, but his people have not done so and will not do so until the day that Jesus is revealed. Peter states, "Though *you have not seen him*, you love him; and *even though you do not see him now*, you believe in him and are filled with an inexpressible and glorious joy" (1:8).[11]

No passage better explains the challenge of believing in Jesus without seeing him than the account of Thomas and the risen Christ in John 20. Late on the day of his resurrection, Jesus appeared to his disciples, minus Judas, who had killed himself, and minus Thomas, who was away for unstated reasons. The ten were so glad to see Jesus, and when Thomas rejoined them, they told him, "We have seen the Lord!" (20:25). Thomas refused to believe them and swore, "Unless I see in his hands the mark of the nails, and place my finger into the mark of the nails, and place my hand into his side, I will never believe" (20:25b ESV).

A week later, Jesus appeared to the disciples again, and this time Thomas was present. In essence, Jesus told Thomas something like this: "I've been listening. Your brash skepticism stands on the cusp of unbelief, but I know you and will yield to your foolish demand." So then Jesus said, "Put your finger here, and see my hands; and put out your hand, and place it in my side. Do not disbelieve, but believe" (John 20:27 ESV).

John doesn't mention whether Thomas took up the invitation to touch his wounds or not, but Thomas certainly saw Jesus. It was all he needed, and the braggadocio of unbelief melted away. He repented and confessed, "My Lord and my God!" (John 20:28). Important as Jesus' encounter with

---

10. Paul J. Achtemeier, *1 Peter* (Minneapolis: Fortress, 1996), 102.

11. The two finite verbs, translated "love" and "are filled with . . . joy," could be either indicatives or imperatives, since the forms are identical in the present, second-person plural, but it is best to take them as indicatives, since Peter is still describing his people's situation. Commands begin in 1 Peter 1:13.

Thomas was, John's account looks past Thomas himself and sees the generations coming after him. Knowing that future disciples would not see his flesh, as Thomas had, Jesus told Thomas, "Because you have seen me, you have believed; blessed are those who have not seen and yet have believed" (20:29).

So Jesus looked past Thomas and saw *us*. He envisioned the day when all who believe must do so without the evidence that Thomas enjoyed. The skeptical member of later generations has roughly the position that Thomas had in John 20:25. He had *heard* that Jesus was alive, but had not *seen* him. Jesus calls Thomas a poor guide for those who have not seen. Thomas had enough reason to believe. He had the testimony of his trusted friends, yet he refused it. The Lord graciously granted Thomas the evidence that he wrongly demanded. Still, the Lord corrected him when he said, "Blessed are those who have not seen and yet have believed" (20:29 ESV). Jesus speaks this blessing to us, as we trust the testimony of the apostles, yield to the Spirit's persuasion, and believe.

As we believe, Peter concludes, we "are filled with an inexpressible and glorious joy" (1 Peter 1:8b). As Alan Stibbs observes, "Peter's readers had not seen Jesus during His earthly life, as Peter himself had done, yet they were giving Him the responsive love of their hearts in living fellowship."[12] Because this joy has its origin in God, not man, it is "inexpressible," that is, it defies perfect human expression.

This joy rests on confidence in God's continuing direction, Peter explains, "for you are receiving the goal of your faith, the salvation of your souls" (1 Peter 1:9). The translation "souls" could mislead us. On most occasions, the Greek word *psuchē* could just as easily be translated "life." The definitive Greek-English lexicon offers three definitions for *psuchē*. First, it is "life on earth in its animating aspect"; second, it is the "seat and center of the inner human life"; and third, it is "an entity with personhood."[13] In other words, the soul stands for the whole person, not the spirit or reason in contrast to the body. In Scripture, a human is a psychosomatic unity. The goal of redemption is not the liberation of the disembodied soul from this wretched life, as Greeks thought. It is a new creation, which the whole

---

12. Stibbs, *First Epistle General of Peter*, 79.
13. Frederick W. Danker, ed., *A Greek-English Lexicon of the New Testament and Other Early Christian Literature*, 3rd ed. (Chicago: University of Chicago Press, 2000), 1098–99.

person enjoys forever, with both a new spirit and a new body, one much like the resurrection body of Jesus.

When I was in third and fourth grades, I attended a Sunday school class that made me think I didn't want to be a Christian. I heard that if I believed in God, I could go to heaven when I died and be like an angel, sitting on a cloud, playing a harp, and singing all day. I knew I wasn't supposed to think this way, but I wanted no part of my teacher's cloud-harp heaven. What boy would? What man or woman should? The gospel story says more than "Jesus is alive." It says that Jesus is alive in flesh and blood, chewing fish, shaking hands, slapping backs, and looking better than ever! His resurrection body is a foretaste of our resurrected bodies, which we will enjoy as embodied spirits, living in a renewed, sin-free creation. Peter does not say that we will go up to heaven, but that we have started to receive and will one day fully receive comprehensive salvation. That promise gives us hope and joy in affliction.

The first sentences of 1 Peter introduce us to his essential themes. Christians are God's elect, yet strangers in the world. Because we are outsiders, Peter knows we will face trouble. Indeed, the only way to avoid trouble is to live as pagans do, or to hide our lifestyle, or to eviscerate our message so that it ceases to offend. In other words, the way to live without trouble is to remove our nerves and spine. That might be a sad thought, since our culture is our home. We care about it and at least hope to make it a better place. But there are limits. So many of the values of our age stand opposed to God's truth. Still, it can grieve us when we realize that we will never exactly fit in our world.

Peter counters this sobering reality with God's promises and a call to claim them. Through Christ we have life, and no force from without or within can destroy it. Even when we face trials, we take heart because they demonstrate that our allegiance to God is genuine, especially when we persevere through them.

It is interesting that Peter mentions the cardinal Christian virtues in our passage. He says that our new birth gives us a living *hope* (1 Peter 1:3), that we receive God's protection through *faith* (1:5), and that we *love* Jesus even if we have never seen him (1:8). Still, as important as our hope, love, and faith may be, our attention stays with Jesus. He has conquered death, he protects us, and nothing can rob us of joy now or keep us from sharing his glory when he returns.

3

THE AUTHORITY OF PETER
AND HIS EPISTLE

1 Peter 1:10–12

*Concerning this salvation, the prophets, who spoke of the grace
that was to come to you, searched intently and with the greatest
care, trying to find out the time and circumstances to which
the Spirit of Christ in them was pointing when he predicted the
sufferings of Christ and the glories that would follow. It was
revealed to them that they were not serving themselves but you,
when they spoke of the things that have now been told you by
those who have preached the gospel to you by the Holy Spirit
sent from heaven. Even angels long to look into these things.*
(1 Peter 1:10–12)

PETER REFLECTS ON THE CHARACTER OF SCRIPTURE

Although Peter's first epistle has no publication date, conservative scholars
agree that Peter was an older man, living in Rome around A.D. 62–65, when
he wrote his first epistle, as we noted in chapter 1.[1] Peter wrote, therefore,

---

1. Again, "Babylon" is code for "Rome" (1 Peter 5:13).

from a lifetime of wisdom and conviction. He had experienced everything, including the trials and suffering described in the letter. As a younger man, he had walked with Jesus every day for three years. Nonetheless, as Peter writes, he does not cite his experience as the source of his knowledge and authority. He does not promote himself as a man who has seen it all from the beginning. He first cites his God-given role as an apostle: "Peter, an apostle of Jesus Christ, to God's elect" (1 Peter 1:1). Jesus appointed the apostles to "be with him" (Mark 3:14), to put his words into their ears (as the original of Luke 9:44 reads), and to witness everything from Jesus' baptism to his resurrection (Acts 1:22). Jesus chose Peter to witness his deeds, to remember his words, and to declare what everything signified. He was God's authoritative spokesman and representative.[2]

Peter is at ease with this authority. He does not remind his readers of his years with the Lord, or of the singular events he witnessed. He knows that the Holy Spirit speaks through him, but he makes the point subtly in 1 Peter 1:12, implicitly counting himself among "those who have preached the gospel to you by the Holy Spirit." Still, Peter knows that Jesus has commissioned him to present the story of Christ and its implications. In 1:10–12, he explains how God speaks and why God's prophets (and apostles) speak with his authority.

The first segment of Peter states the theme of all Scripture: "In his great mercy [God] has given us new birth into a living hope through the resurrection of Jesus Christ from the dead" and an imperishable inheritance (1 Peter 1:3–4). Peter closes the unit by saying, "The goal of your faith [is] the salvation of your souls" (1:9). Logically, Peter could have moved directly to his next theme, the holy conduct of his people. Instead, he pauses to explain the role of Scripture in their salvation. Historically speaking, most of the people reading 1 Peter first heard of Jesus through Peter or another preacher who had a connection to the apostolic band. Yet these men did not speak on their own authority. They "preached the gospel to you by the Holy Spirit sent from heaven" (1:12). Peter wanted to prepare his readers to grow through Scripture, both from the Old Testament and from the New Testament accounts of the suffering and glory of Christ (1:11).

2. Herman N. Ridderbos, *Redemptive History and the New Testament Scriptures*, 2nd rev. ed. (Phillipsburg, NJ: Presbyterian and Reformed, 1988), 12–41.

Paul knew that his writings were authoritative. He said things such as: "This is the rule I lay down in all the churches" (1 Cor. 7:17b; cf. 15:3ff.). He said that if anyone preaches a gospel that differs from the one he preached, "let him be eternally condemned!" (Gal. 1:8–9; cf. 1 Tim. 1:15). John knew that the Spirit guided him to remember, understand, and record the words and deeds of Jesus (John 2:22; 12:16; 14:26; 20:30–31). Writing around A.D. 65–68, Paul quotes a saying of Jesus that is recorded in Luke, and already calls it "Scripture." He says, "For the Scripture says, . . . 'The worker deserves his wages'" (1 Tim. 5:18; see Luke 10:7). So Peter joins John and Paul as New Testament writers who attest to the divine origin of their books and letters.

First Peter 1:10–12 also says several things about the character of Scripture: "Concerning this salvation, the prophets, who spoke of the grace that was to come to you, searched intently and with the greatest care, trying to find out the time and circumstances to which the Spirit of Christ in them was pointing when he predicted the sufferings of Christ and the glories that would follow." First, salvation is the theme of Scripture: "Concerning this salvation, the prophets . . . spoke" (1:10).

Second, God called and appointed spokesmen to record his Word—the prophets in the Old Testament ("the prophets, who spoke") and the apostles such as Peter in the New Testament. Paul agrees, saying, "The mystery of Christ . . . has now been revealed to his holy apostles and prophets by the Spirit" (Eph. 3:4–5 ESV). If the prophets "searched intently," they longed to discover what the Spirit was saying. Like Luke, who "carefully investigated" the life of Christ (Luke 1:3), the prophets were (ordinarily) active, not passive, agents of revelation. To be sure, the Lord sometimes told his prophets to write down exactly what he said (Isa. 30:8; Jer. 30:2; 36:2, 28; Ezek. 43:11; Hab. 2:2). Indeed, God himself rewrote the Decalogue on two stone tablets (Ex. 34:1). The Lord can use any means he wishes to ensure that we receive his inspired Word, but this passage accents the active participation of the prophets.

Third, Scripture's theme is God's grace, given for humanity. The prophets "spoke of the grace that was to come to you" (1 Peter 1:10).

Fourth, the Word came by the inspiration of God's Spirit and yet in such a way that the prophets and apostles were active, too. The prophets "searched intently and with the greatest care" (1:10). Yet God directed them, for the prophets were "trying to find out the time and circumstances to which the Spirit of Christ in them was pointing" (1:11).

Fifth, while the prophets understandably inquired after the *timing* of God's work, Peter stresses the *content* of God's work and message, which he summarizes as "the sufferings of Christ and the glories that would follow" (1 Peter 1:11). Peter returns to the suffering and glory of Christ in 2:21–24; 4:13; 5:1; and 5:9. Of course, the Gospels also describe Jesus' birth, teachings, encounters, travels, and miracles. But the suffering and glory, especially the death and resurrection, of Christ are central to his work and to our relationship with him. Peter commands believers to "rejoice that you participate in the sufferings of Christ, so that you may be overjoyed when his glory is revealed" (4:13). In his suffering on the cross, Jesus bore our sin and offered us forgiveness (2:20–25; Luke 24:25–27, 45–47). "He suffered death, so that by the grace of God he might taste death for everyone" (Heb. 2:9). Further, Peter's churches were in travail and needed to identify with Christ in his suffering. If they did so, they could endure and so share in his glory. We must stand "firm in the faith, because you know that your brothers throughout the world are undergoing the same kind of sufferings. And the God of all grace, who called you to his eternal glory in Christ, after you have suffered a little while, will himself restore you and make you strong, firm and steadfast" (1 Peter 5:9–10).

For Jesus, this "eternal glory in Christ" began with his resurrection (1 Peter 5:10; 1:3). It continued in his ascent to heaven (3:22) and in his present reign at the right hand of the Father, where all powers are subject to him (3:22b). Peter's churches will share in that glory (5:1, 9).

So, then, the prophets foretold this salvation, Jesus accomplished it, and the Spirit led Peter and the apostles to describe it. The pattern is *prediction* of salvation, the *fulfillment* of salvation, and the *interpretation* of saving events. Like all the rest of Scripture, Peter's letter provides moral guidance, but it isn't essentially a moral guide. Scripture contains a great many things, but in essence it describes our creation in God's image, our rebellion and its catastrophic consequences, and then God's plan for restoration, announced by the prophets, and accomplished in the life, death, and resurrection of Jesus. Before him we must repent, and in him we must believe. Every other theme is secondary.

This leads to an interpretive key for reading the Old Testament. God reveals his plan of redemption gradually, not instantaneously. God even reveals parts of his ethical will gradually (Matt. 19:3–9). The Lord revealed his redemptive plan and his ethical norms step by step so that his people had time to grow into them. Christian leaders can learn from this: if we hope to persuade or change others, we, too, may wish to introduce new ideas and laws gradually, so that our people have time to comprehend and truly accept them.

The prophets did not discover everything they longed to know. Yet they acquiesced in God's decision to reveal what he chose, for "it was revealed to them that they were not serving themselves but you, when they spoke of the things that have now been told you by those who have preached the gospel to you by the Holy Spirit sent from heaven. Even angels long to look into these things" (1 Peter 1:12). What angels and prophets never fully saw had now been revealed. Peter further describes the nature of Scripture in his second epistle:

> Above all, you must understand that no prophecy of Scripture came about by the prophet's own interpretation. For prophecy never had its origin in the will of man, but men spoke from God as they were carried along by the Holy Spirit. (2 Peter 1:20)

So Peter teaches that Scripture is at once the work of prophets who "searched intently" and the Word of God, "for prophecy never had its origin in the will of man." Rather, "men spoke from God" (that is, the Father) as the Holy Spirit carried them along. At times, God delivered oracles to the prophets, who wrote what they saw and heard (Isa. 13:1; 15:1; 17:1). But ordinarily the Bible's human authors did not simply take dictation. Scripture has a dual authorship. Luke, drawing on "eyewitnesses and servants of the word," could write an orderly account of the work of Christ because he "carefully investigated everything from the beginning" (Luke 1:2–3). Similarly, Paul wrote "with the wisdom that God gave him," straining with all his skills to apply his gospel to the challenges of his churches. Yet the Spirit so guided his work that Peter casually notes that Paul's letters, like "the other Scriptures," can be hard to understand (2 Peter 3:15–16).

So Peter agrees with the prophets and with Paul that Scripture is "inspired" or, more accurately, "God-breathed" (*theopneustos*), as Paul says in 2 Timothy 3:16. When we say that Scripture is God-breathed, we mean that our sixty-six books are the very words of the triune God. *Scripture* is a collective term for what we call the Old and New Testaments (Matt. 26:54–56; Luke 24:27–45; John 5:39; Acts 17:2, 11; Rom. 1:2; 15:4; 1 Cor. 15:3–4).

Paul notes that Scripture is "useful for teaching, rebuking, correcting and training in righteousness, so that the man of God may be thoroughly equipped for every good work" (2 Tim. 3:16–17). Paul asserts that *all* Scripture does these four things—history and prophecy, doctrinal and moral instruction, even the genealogies. The four uses of Scripture fall into two classes—creed and conduct. Scripture teaches what to believe and how to behave. The word *teaching* is *didaskalia*, which in Paul almost always means "doctrinal instruction." *Rebuking, elegmon,* belongs to a word family that commonly has the sense of correcting or pointing out a mistake, whether moral or doctrinal. Thus, training in the truth will lead to correction of false ideas. But doctrine is practical, too, and false teaching leads to sin. So Scripture also corrects wrongdoing. It trains us in righteousness and prepares us for good works.[3]

We say that Scripture is *inspired* because it proceeds from the mouth of God, through the agency of the Holy Spirit, and from the work of his chosen apostles and prophets. Because God is truth and always tells the truth, his "word is truth" (John 17:17). If it is true, it contains no errors. It is *inerrant*. Because God stands behind his Word, it will never fail. It is *infallible*. God pledges that his Word is the truth about himself and his salvation, and the guide to the church's faith and practice.

As all Christian leaders know, these traits make it essential to read Scripture in public worship and in private, as a guide to daily life. Leaders might not realize that most people, even in the church, read the Bible sporadically. Many hardly read the Bible outside of worship services. Sadly, even many church leaders read the Bible only occasionally. Christian leaders tend to address this through straight exhortations: "You need to read the Bible more!" We should extol the virtues of reading and

3. B. B. Warfield, *The Inspiration and Authority of Scripture* (Philadelphia: Presbyterian and Reformed, 1948), 234–39, 299; Daniel M. Doriani, *Putting the Truth to Work: The Theory and Practice of Biblical Application* (Phillipsburg, NJ: P&R Publishing, 2001), 55–57, 213ff.

meditation, but we should also teach people how to read and meditate more fruitfully.

Leaders should also read and expound the Bible in public worship. We can use biblical texts for confessions of faith, confessions of sin, and assurances of pardon. We can sing the Scriptures, including the Psalms. We can have Old Testament and New Testament readings. Sermons should feature the reading and exposition of Scripture. Pastors, as a corollary, can preach through books of the Bible, lest they focus unduly on favorite topics and miss the whole counsel of God (Acts 20:27).

Finally, let's remember that however valuable private reading and public teaching are, disciples also grow through study and discussion in small groups. We should be thankful that we have so many ways to hear or read excellent teaching, but we also need to seek the truth actively. For many people, the best way to do that is in a small group. Jesus and the apostles followed this practice.

Peter mentions the Spirit twice, so let's remember that he illumines minds and opens hearts to his truth. Pastors see this in surprising ways. We study, plan, and prepare to preach, but most of us also diverge from our notes at times. Sometimes a thought comes to us spontaneously, and we say it, with surprising results. One day a man strode up to me and said, "Five years ago you said something that changed my life. I was such a hypocrite; I'm not sure if I was a Christian or not, but I certainly wasn't serious. So thank you." As he told me what I had said, I was dumbfounded. The lesson he shared seemed both true and important, but I was sure I had not said it, and told him so: "What you say is certainly true and I believe it, but it's not the kind of thing I would say in public. I'm truly happy for you, but you must be thinking of someone else."

He looked at me strangely, and then began to quote my sermon line by line: "You said A, then B, then C, then D—the words God used to change my life." Suddenly, I realized that he was right! I remembered the week, when the topic that led to "the words that changed his life" had been in my thoughts. It wasn't in my notes, but it had been on my mind, and the Spirit nudged me to say what his receptive heart needed to hear. So our words become more than we plan, yet what he intends.

No teacher living today has a status like that of the apostles. Jesus chose and trained them, and the Spirit moved in them. Peter followed Jesus, but after the resurrection, Peter also studied, ministered, and spoke with other apostles (Gal. 2:1–10). In this way, he spent years preparing to write. Yet alongside Peter's human activities, the Spirit kept pointing him to Christ and carried him along so that his errors fell away as he wrote (1 Peter 1:11; 2 Peter 1:21). Peter wrote *what* he knew, yet he wrote *better* than he knew.

The Reliability of the New Testament

The Bible doesn't ask us to accept these claims as a matter of blind faith. There are reasons to believe that the Bible is reliable, reasons that should gain the respect of any open-minded person, especially if he is trained in evaluating historical evidence. A wide literature shows how historical remains, such as stone inscriptions and archaeological artifacts, verify the Bible's historical accounts. Evangelicals have written masterly defenses of the reliability of the Gospels and Acts.[4]

Scripture shows that Jesus prepared Peter, the disciples, and other New Testament writers for their work. Jesus appointed the apostles to "be with him" and to witness everything (Mark 3:14; Matt. 17:5; Acts 1:22). Some people treasured events and remembered them (Luke 2:19; 22:61; 24:8). Others did careful research. Luke knew many accounts of Jesus' life. He consulted "those who from the first were eyewitnesses and servants of the word," and then "carefully investigated everything from the beginning" (Luke 1:1–4). Similarly, Paul studied for fourteen years in Arabia and consulted with no one before he became the apostle to the Gentiles (Gal. 1:15–2:10). John relates that Jesus performed "many . . . miraculous signs in the presence of his disciples" (John 20:30; see also 21:25). His gospel did not hold them all, but they present enough evidence "that you may believe that Jesus is the Christ, the Son of God, and that by believing you may have life in his name" (20:31). Finally, Peter said, "We did not follow cleverly invented stories when we told you about the power and coming of our Lord Jesus Christ, but we were eyewitnesses of his majesty" (2 Peter 1:16).

4. To mention just a few, see Craig S. Keener, *The Historical Jesus of the Gospels* (Grand Rapids: Eerdmans, 2009), a densely detailed study of the reliability of the Gospels. At a slightly more popular level, see companion works by Craig Blomberg, *The Historical Reliability of the Gospels*, 2nd ed. (Downers Grove, IL: IVP Academic, 2007), and *The Historical Reliability of John's Gospel* (Downers Grove, IL: InterVarsity Press, 2002). For Acts, see note 10 below.

But as we affirm the reliability of the New Testament, we have more than the claims of the apostles. There are objective, historical reasons to believe that the apostles recorded events accurately. We can consider five of them.

First, we can trust their record of Jesus' words because memorization was essential to education in Israel (and other lands). Jewish students were expected to memorize every word of their teachers. Teachers repeated their main ideas again and again until students knew them by heart. Since the ancients lacked opportunity to retrieve data from the sources we have today, they developed superior skill in memorization. Jesus' disciples treasured his words, and because he was an itinerant preacher, they heard his teachings many times. Beyond that, Israelites sometimes took notes on the teachings of their rabbis.[5]

Second, ancient Greeks and Romans had standards for historical writing. Herodotus, called the father of history, was roundly criticized, five hundred years before the New Testament, for putting unsubstantiated fables and tales into his accounts. Around 400 B.C., Thucydides said that he confined himself to factual reports of contemporary political and military events, based on firsthand eyewitness accounts, although he admitted that he sometimes summarized the main points of a speech as best he could.

Both secular people and believers knew the difference between history and fabrication. An elder was deprived of his office for embellishing the history of Peter, even though the embellishment was edifying. In his treatise *On Baptism*, Tertullian asked whether women could baptize in an emergency. Those who answer in the affirmative claim *The Acts of Paul*, an "edifying" Christian novel, as evidence, since a woman teaches and baptizes in that document. Tertullian says, "But if the writings which wrongly go under Paul's name, claim [this] example as a license for women's teaching and baptizing, let them know that, the [leader] who composed that writing . . . if he were augmenting Paul's fame" was convicted of fabricating events. The leader confessed that "he had done it from love of Paul" and was yet removed from office.[6] Clearly, early Christians were aware of fabrication, guarded against it, and punished it, even if the content was orthodox and the author well intended.

In the ancient church, most people spoke Greek. Since the New Testament is in Greek, there was no need for a translation; everyone understood

5. E. E. Ellis, *Prophecy Hermeneutic* (Grand Rapids: Eerdmans, 1978), 242–47.
6. Tertullian, *On Baptism*, trans. S. Thelwall, in *Ante-Nicene Fathers*, ed. Alexander Roberts and James Donaldson, 9 vols. (Grand Rapids: Eerdmans, 1979–85), 3:677.

the original. One day a preacher spoke on Mark's account of the lame man whose friends brought him to Jesus, ultimately lowering him through a hole in the roof so that he lay on his stretcher before Jesus. The word used for this stretcher in Mark 2 is a common one—*krabbatos*. The preacher substituted a more literary or elegant Greek word—*skimpeus*—for the original. Immediately someone within the congregation called out, "Are you superior to the one who said *krabbatos*?" So the church had great interest in accuracy.[7]

Third, some events are unforgettable. Memorable events emblazon themselves on the minds of witnesses. I will never forget walking my daughters down the aisle for their weddings, nor the look on my own bride's face as we took our vows. I remember my dissertation defense; I recall the time that a group of policemen accused me of murder and pulled their guns on me. I even remember my teammates jumping on me when I got the winning hit with two outs in the last inning of a Little League baseball game—and a great deal more besides. You, my reader, also have dozens of indelible memories. Think, then, of the disciples when Jesus calmed the storm at sea, when Jesus called the risen Lazarus, still wrapped in graveclothes, out of his tomb with the thunder of command. Imagine the moment they saw the risen Christ. These events burned themselves into the disciples' memories. They could never forget them. Yet even if one disciple did forget something, he could consult the others.

Fourth, living witnesses had a role. The New Testament names little-known Roman officials such as Pilate and Gallio, whose identities are verified by secular accounts, but they also name ordinary people. The four Gospels cite specific events that occurred in named towns. For example, Jesus healed blind Bartimaeus, who used to beg outside Jericho on the road to Jerusalem (Mark 10:46). When Jesus raised Lazarus, he was in a small town near Jerusalem named Bethany (John 11:1). When Jesus stumbled under the cross, Simon of Cyrene, father of Alexander and Rufus, carried it for him (Mark 15:21). As Richard Bauckham argues in his meticulous study, these are real people, known to the church, known in their towns.[8] The Gospels would have been instantly discredited if fabricated stories reached such towns as Jericho and Bethany where the Gospels say they occurred. But the Gospels were not discredited.

---

7. Eta Linnemann, *Is There a Synoptic Problem? Rethinking the Literary Dependence of the First Three Gospels*, trans. Robert Yarbrough (Grand Rapids: Baker, 1992), x.

8. Richard Bauckham, *Jesus and the Eyewitnesses: The Gospels as Eyewitness Testimony* (Grand Rapids: Eerdmans, 2006), 39–66. A meticulously detailed work.

No, they were received as Scripture everywhere they went.[9] The book of Acts also gives officials specific titles and places them in known cities.[10]

Fifth, the witnesses sealed their testimony with their lives. It is true that people will die for a lie. This happens most readily when people are duped. Sometimes a person will die for what he or she knows to be a lie—if that lie brought the person great benefits. But the disciples gained no earthly benefits from their testimony to Jesus. They suffered every kind of abuse, and almost all eventually died for their testimony. Yet the disciples staked their lives to Jesus to the end. None moved on to a second career. None recanted to save his skin. They all lived and died for their testimony about Jesus because they knew it was true.

I hope you believe the Bible is God's Word, the sure guide to faith and life. But even if you don't, there are reasons to believe it is reliable, reasons to warrant a careful reading. Yet Scripture can be hard to understand, as Peter himself says when describing Paul's letters. How can we gain from reading Scripture?

HOW SHOULD WE READ THE BIBLE?

First, we read the Bible *seriously*. This means that we take the Bible literally when it expects us to do so, but we read it metaphorically when appropriate. Peter expects us to take it literally when he reports that Jesus performed miracles, died on the cross, and rose again. The Bible also uses metaphors. Second Chronicles 16:9 says that "the eyes of the LORD range throughout the earth." This does not mean that God literally has eyes that rapidly run over the land. Jesus uses hyperbole: "If your right hand causes you to sin, cut it off and throw it away" (Matt. 5:30). We see no battalions of one-handed Christians. But we do take our sin seriously, and take action to remove it from our lives.

Second, we read *holistically*. That is, we don't snatch isolated statements from the Bible and find meaning that the authors never intended. We let

9. Bruce Metzger, *The Canon of the New Testament: Its Origin, Development and Significance* (New York: Oxford University Press, 1987).

10. See Colin Hemer, *The Book of Acts in the Setting of Hellenistic History*, trans. C. H. Gempf (Tübingen: J. C. B. Mohr [Paul Siebeck], 1989); F. F. Bruce, "The Acts of the Apostles: Historical Record or Theological Reconstruction?," in *Aufstieg und Niedergang der römischen Welt II 25/3*, ed. W. Haase (Berlin: de Gruyter, 1985), 2596–603; W. W. Gasque, "The Historical Value of Acts," *Tyndale Bulletin* 40 (1989): 136–57; William Mitchell Ramsay, *The Bearing of Recent Discovery on the Trustworthiness of the New Testament* (Grand Rapids: Baker, 1979).

the Bible's grand themes guide us. Jesus declared that Scripture's theme is his person and work:

> Everything must be fulfilled that is written about me in the Law of Moses, the Prophets and the Psalms. . . .
> This is what is written: The Christ will suffer and rise from the dead on the third day, and repentance and forgiveness of sins will be preached in his name to all nations, beginning at Jerusalem. (Luke 24:44–47)

The promises give us *hope* of a Redeemer; the law reveals our *need* of a Redeemer. The history of Israel shows that no one is faithful and so teaches us to long for the faithful, Jesus. The leadership structures of Israel also lead us to Christ. He is the Great Prophet, revealing God to the world. He is the Great High Priest, offering the final sacrifice. He is the Great King, protecting his people from their foes.

Third, we read the Bible *personally.* We take the Bible to heart instead of using it to condemn others. How often preachers hear this: "Wonderful message, Pastor; I wish my friend had come to hear it. She really needs it." Yes, the friend probably does need to hear it, but did *you* hear it? Let's apply God's Word to ourselves and remove the plank from our own eye before we remove a speck from our neighbor's.

Finally, we should read the Bible *meditatively.* It's good to listen to teachers and preachers, whether live or through a convenient medium, but at some point, if someone wants to grow as a Christian, he or she must become an active reader, carefully contemplating everything the Word says. We must also read with godly goals. Donald Carson observes:

> We human beings are a strange lot. We hear high moral injunctions and glimpse just a little the genuine beauty of perfect holiness, and then prostitute the vision by dreaming about the way others would hold us in high esteem if we were like that. The demand for genuine perfection loses itself in the lesser goal of external piety; the goal of pleasing the Father is traded for its pygmy cousin, the goal of pleasing men.[11]

So let us read meditatively, to apply Scripture to ourselves, that we might repent and believe and grow in godliness. Let us read for real history, for sound doctrine, and for the person of Jesus Christ, Son of God and Savior.

11. D. A. Carson, *The Sermon on the Mount: An Evangelical Exposition of Matthew 5–7* (Grand Rapids: Baker, 1978), 55.

4

Hope and Holiness

1 Peter 1:13—21

> *For you know that it was not with perishable things such as*
> *silver or gold that you were redeemed from the empty way of*
> *life handed down to you from your forefathers, but with the*
> *precious blood of Christ, a lamb without blemish or defect.*
> (1 Peter 1:18–19)

In 1588, the Spanish Armada, with 130 ships, sailed toward England, bent on depositing over fifty thousand Spanish soldiers on English soil and deposing Queen Elizabeth. But before the troops could go ashore, Spanish ships had to get past the English navy. The Spanish warships were larger and had bigger guns, but the English ships had superior commanders and greater speed and maneuverability. The Spaniards knew all this when they set sail. How, then, could they hope to succeed in battle if their guns could not attain a firing position? The Spaniards believed that God was on their side. Therefore, they *hoped* the English would expose themselves to their heavy guns. They *hoped* the English would foolishly engage them ship to ship in hand-fighting, so that the many soldiers aboard them would win the day. But as we say, "hope is not a plan." The British kept their distance and shot the Spanish ships to pieces. The Spanish paid dearly for a vain hope.

Misplaced hope is worthless, but well-founded hope is potent. First Peter 1:13–21 begins and ends with such hope. Peter first commands his readers to "set your *hope* fully on the grace to be given you when Jesus Christ is revealed" (1:13). As he closes, he tells his people that Christ, the Lamb of God, ransomed them from a futile life. "Through him you believe in God, who raised him from the dead and glorified him, and so your faith and *hope* are in God" (1:21).

HOPE LEADS TO HOLINESS

Between verses 13 and 21, Peter describes what happens when we hope in the grace of Jesus. We no longer conform to evil desires (1 Peter 1:14). We exercise self-control rather than indulging every urge. Further, because "he who called you is holy," we are holy (1:15). That leads to God's central command: "Be holy, because I am holy" (1:16, quoting Lev. 11:44–45; 19:2).

Over the next verses, Peter explains *why* believers should be holy. First, God "judges each man's work impartially" (1 Peter 1:17), so that we will have to render an account for everything we say (Matt. 12:37), everything we do (2 Cor. 5:10), and our use of every gift (Matt. 25:14–30; Luke 12:13–21). Second, the Father redeemed us from our empty life at great cost—by Christ's precious blood (1 Peter 1:18–19). If he ransomed us from a vain life, how can we return to it?

In this call to gospel-driven holiness, Peter harvests his prior themes to enhance his point. For example, Peter addressed his epistle to "God's elect, strangers in the world" (1 Peter 1:1). Now he says that we should live "as strangers" (1:17), since our holiness will set us apart from the practices of this age. Peter also said that we have a sure and "living hope" that we will gain an imperishable inheritance, guaranteed by Jesus' resurrection and "kept in heaven" (1:3–4). We await "praise, glory and honor when Jesus Christ is revealed" (1:7). Because we have salvation by grace (1:9–10), we can and should put our hope in Christ (1:13).

Now Peter recapitulates his first themes. In 1 Peter 1:13–21, he exhorts his people to live out their hope of redemption. In 1:3, Peter says that we have been born again to a living hope; in 1:21, he says that "your faith and hope are in God." But in 1:13, he commands, "Set your hope fully on the grace to be given you when Jesus Christ is revealed." We see the indicative-imperative pattern once more. Because we *have a hope* that relies on God, we should *set our hope* on him.

This section of 1 Peter has two parts. A series of imperatives state the ethical implications of the life of hope in 1:13–17. Then in 1:18–21, Peter returns to his celebration of the work of God that gives us hope.

Peter commands us to "set your hope fully on the grace to be given you when Jesus Christ is revealed" (1 Peter 1:13). Peter surrounds his central message with subordinate commands that develop the meaning of hope. Translated literally, 1 Peter 1:13 reads, "Girding the loins of your mind, being completely self-controlled, hope on . . . Jesus Christ." The NIV sensibly translates "girding the loins of your mind" as "prepare your minds for action." For the whole of biblical history, most people wore loose robes that worked well for ordinary activities, but inhibited strenuous labor, fighting, and running. To gird the loins is to wrap up flowing garments to gain freedom to work hard or run. Our parallel phrase is: "Roll up your sleeves."

God told the Israelites to eat the Passover with loins girded and sandals on their feet, so that they would be ready to flee Egypt at any moment (Ex. 12:11). Jesus alludes to this in Luke 12:35, when he tells his disciples, "Stay dressed for action" (ESV). When Peter states that our *minds* must be ready, he doesn't mean the intellect in a narrow sense. The word translated "mind" (*dianoia*) means the understanding with its dispositions and plans. When Jesus tells us to love the Lord our God with all our heart, soul, and mind, he means that we should love God with the whole person, with all our faculties (Matt. 22:37).

The next command, "be self-controlled" (1 Peter 1:13), develops the concept of preparation. The word (*nephō*) usually means to be sober, balanced, or self-controlled.[1] Peter wants us to be realistic and clear-minded. The opposite of sobriety is drunkenness, folly, and lack of self-discipline, whether due to wine, anger, fear, or greed. Peter wants us to focus our full attention on Jesus, through whom God gives his grace.

His emphasis falls not on the subjective *feeling* of hope, nor on the intensity of our hope, but on the *object and direction* of our hope. Christians

---

1. Frederick W. Danker, ed., *A Greek-English Lexicon of the New Testament and Other Early Christian Literature*, 3rd ed. (Chicago: University of Chicago Press, 2000), 672.

should hope in the grace of Christ to be revealed. *Hope* is the principal verb in 1 Peter 1:13 and the programmatic command for the passage.[2] The subsequent commands, to be holy and to conduct ourselves with fear of God, follow from it.

Specifically, we rest our hope on the grace that God will give "when Jesus Christ is revealed," that is, on the day he returns. Traditionally, we focus on the grace revealed in Jesus' life, death, and resurrection, and rightly so, since Jesus' completion of the plan of redemption brings us peace with God. Nonetheless, Peter here says that the grace to come decisively affects the present. Our hope in the grace to be revealed prepares us for self-discipline and action today.

Consider, for example, a student as she toils to complete her master's thesis in education. If she is a part-time teacher's aide and part-time barista, she might find it difficult to motivate herself to complete the project if she constantly thinks, "What's the point of this? I can't even get a teaching job now. When I finish my degree, it will be even harder to get a job because I'll fall into a higher pay bracket." But if the student has been teaching at a fine school for ten years and knows that she will get a raise and leadership responsibilities as soon as she finishes, she has every reason to pour herself into her studies. Similarly, the promised return of Jesus motivates us to faithfulness now, since we know our labor is not in vain (1 Cor. 15:58).

Most of Peter's spiritual children began life as pagans who bowed to gods who possessed greater power, but not greater virtue, than humans. The popular religions of the day, especially polytheism and emperor worship, demanded loyalty and little more. The leading philosophical or ethical systems, Stoicism and Epicureanism, aimed (respectively) to minimize pain and to realize sustainable pleasures.[3] Therefore, Peter asserts, "As obedient children, do not be conformed to the passions of your former ignorance" (1 Peter 1:14 ESV). This almost sounds insulting, but it's an honest description

2. J. Ramsey Michaels, *1 Peter*, Word Biblical Commentary 49 (Nashville: Thomas Nelson, 1988), 55. Michaels calls this a "programmatic" imperative, and puts it with other aorist imperatives that lay out Peter's program. Grammatically, "being girded," *anazōsamenoi*, and "being sober/attentive," *nēphontes*, are subordinate participles modifying "hope." Translations take them as imperatives, since participles preceding an imperative often function as imperatives.

3. For a sharp summary of Christianity's first ethical competitors, see Ellen T. Charry, *God and the Art of Happiness* (Grand Rapids: Eerdmans, 2010), 3–24. Epicureanism is more subtle than hedonism, whose motto, quoted by Paul in 1 Corinthians 15, dictated, "Eat, drink, and be merry, for tomorrow we die."

of their former life. They were ignorant of God and his standards. According to their myths, their "gods" followed their passions, so the people did the same.

If this sounds judgmental, let's recall that the same Lord who said, "Do not judge, or you too will be judged" (Matt. 7:1), also said, "Do not judge by appearances, but judge with right judgment" (John 7:24 ESV). Clearly, it is no sin to state the facts about the moral bankruptcy of pagan polytheism. It is a sin to condemn the innocent and to judge with haste, or to play the hypocrite by condemning others for committing sins we indulge. But it is good for Peter to speak against the pagan ways that his first readers once followed.

But now Peter's people are "obedient children," so it is their nature—and ours—to obey. It is normal for God's family to obey the Father and to walk in the way marked by his character and law. Therefore, Peter exhorts, "do not be conformed to the passions of your former ignorance" (1:14 ESV). The command "do not be conformed" is a present passive imperative. The present tense suggests that Peter continually and permanently forbids indulgence of ignorant passions. Peter chose the passive voice for the command because he knows that we are, to some extent, passive in the presence of forces that press us to conform to them. Whatever is customary seems normal, and whatever is normal seems right. But we must resist the pressure to conform to the age. We resist evil desires that we once indulged. We turn from sinful acts that are so common in the culture and in the lifestyle of many who grew up outside the covenant.

In some ways, all evil desires are similar. All seek to deify man and all violate God's law. Yet the specific forms of evil vary from one time and place to another. Today, Americans typically live together for a season before marriage. We wear clothing that flaunts our wealth or sexuality, and we indulge the material desires that our income allows us to purchase. Since we behave essentially the way others in our social group behave (and since there is always someone who is worse), we are nearly blind to our errors. It is easy to yield to our desires.

Peter recognizes that a convert will still *feel* passions, but he knows that disciples also resist them, for two reasons. First, he states, "just as he who called you is holy, so be holy in all you do" (1 Peter 1:15). Second, we must resist because "you were ransomed from the futile ways inherited from your forefathers" (1:18 ESV). Consider the summons to holiness and the obstacles to holiness first.

OBSTACLES TO HOLINESS

Peter describes two obstacles to holiness. His people conformed themselves to their passions, and they followed the futile way of life inherited from their ancestors (1 Peter 1:14). As a counter, they must set their hope on Christ and remember their identity as obedient children of the holy God.

Peter teaches that God's children should take on his traits. Jesus teaches that we should be *perfect* as our Father in heaven is perfect (Matt. 5:48). Paul declares, "Be imitators of God, therefore, as dearly loved children" (Eph. 5:1; see also 1 Thess. 1:6). We should "live a life of love, just as Christ loved us and gave himself up for us" (Eph. 5:2). The Bible sometimes exhorts believers to imitate other believers (e.g., 1 Thess. 2:14), but imitation of even the finest people is fraught with the danger that we will adopt their flaws as well as their virtues. Yet we can always imitate God, for he is holy. As Peter says, "Just as he who called you is holy, so be holy in all you do; for it is written: 'Be holy, because I am holy'" (1 Peter 1:15–16). The holiness of God is a fundamental tenet of Scripture. The Pentateuch often repeats, "Be holy, for I am holy" (Lev. 11:44; 19:2; 20:7, 26; cf. Isa. 6:3; 1 Thess. 4:7).

Biblical holiness entails a person's righteousness, justice, and separation from sin. If a man is holy, he is set apart *from* this world, *for* God. Later, Peter will insist that holiness manifest itself in positive actions by masters, servants, husbands, and wives (1 Peter 2:18–3:17). That can lead to social disruption and trouble for the person who is holy (4:1–4). We are strongest when we know how to separate from worldliness while staying engaged with the world.

OBSTACLES TO HOLINESS ILLUSTRATED BY THE CRUSADES

It is easier to stay holy if we withdraw from society, but when we engage the world our hands can get dirty. If we dig into the process of social reform, it is too easy to adopt the culture's perspectives and methods. To explore this, I want to consider the Crusades as a cautionary tale about engagement with the world.

The Crusades had several origins. When they began, North African Muslims had held most of Spain for centuries and threatened southern France. Turkish Muslims had slaughtered their way to the gates of Constantinople, the capital of a Christian realm. They reportedly butchered men, raped women, and defiled sanctuaries as they went, and they threatened central Europe up to Austria. Muslims sometimes persecuted and humiliated Christian pilgrims who traveled to Jerusalem, after having granted them safe passage for centuries. From this perspective, the Crusades *could* be construed, in part, as wars of self-defense or counterattack against an invader who had taken lands. The distinction is that the war was not nationalistic, but aimed at protecting Christian lands and peoples, wherever they lived. (Certain scholars argue that Muslim leaders of the time saw the Crusades as fairly normal wars.[4]) The Crusades had at least one positive trait—Christians' willingness to risk their lives to assist fellow believers. So the Crusades represent an effort to engage the world.

Unfortunately, the Crusades went wrong in almost every way. Historically, we think first of terrible, often indiscriminate, violence done in the name of Christ. There were also theological errors. Christian leaders inspired and supported the Crusades by mixing Christian ideas with errors—meritorious pilgrimages, indulgences, penance, and the notion that self-imposed punishments could satisfy the punishments that God might inflict on sinners in this life or in purgatory.[5] They also drew on completely secular concepts: the centrality of land, the blood-feud. More broadly, the Crusades accepted a militarized perspective on life: "Europe had become . . . an armed camp," and the pope, in his promotion of the Crusades, leveraged that concept rather than questioning it.[6]

Between the collapse of Rome in A.D. 476 and the rise of the high Middle Ages, Europe endured centuries of violence and chaos. Rulers were essentially warlords whose strength legitimated their rule. Warriors felt deep loyalty to their lords as kings, popes, and barons struggled for supremacy. Clan and

4. Efraim Karsh, *Islamic Imperialism: A History* (New Haven, CT: Yale University Press, 2007), 73–87.

5. Jonathan Riley-Smith, *The Crusades: A Short History* (New Haven, CT: Yale University Press, 1987), 9.

6. Thomas F. Madden, *The New Concise History of the Crusades* (Lanham, MD: Rowan & Littlefield, 2006), 6–7.

honor were paramount, and offenses against them had to be avenged. In the eleventh century, a reform movement arose in the church. Some wanted to repristinate the church, others to liberate it from the domination of local lords. In that process, popes sought knights of Christ to defend the church against lords who tried to control it. Knights were professional warriors. Because church reform had spiritual effects, the knightly class become concerned for their souls, as they realized that there was a conflict between the gospel and their profession as warriors who often fought fellow Christians in neighboring areas. They learned to ask whether they could do penance to cover their sins. Might their work condemn them eternally? Pope Urban had an answer, as we will see.[7]

The desire to defend Christian lands, along with a desire to avenge affronts to the honor of Christians, combined explosively with the concerns of Christian knights when, at Clermont in November 1095, Pope Urban II preached a sermon that some call the most influential speech in history. Hundreds of bishops, abbots, noblemen, and warriors heard Urban that day (and he delivered it again in many other settings). He knew his audience well and readily appealed to its faith, outrage, and warrior spirit.

Five summaries of the speech have survived.[8] All agree on its principal themes, although the specific language differs. Each account agrees that Urban called for Christian knights to stop fighting each other. Instead, they should battle infidels who devastated Christian lands with fire and sword. In Robert the Monk's version, Urban called the knights to liberate Christians, especially in Constantinople, and to avenge the pillage, fire, rape, and torture (described in lurid detail) wrought by "an accursed race," and to free Jerusalem, including the most holy relic, the Holy Sepulchre, from their control.[9]

7. This paragraph and the next follow ibid., 1–11; Riley-Smith, *Crusades*, 1–17, 37–40; and Edward Peters, ed., *The First Crusade: The Chronicle of Fulcher of Chartres and Other Source Materials* (Philadelphia: University of Pennsylvania Press, 1971). I am especially indebted to private communication with medieval historian Walker Cosgrove of Dordt College.

8. All were written after the event, and after the first Crusade, the success of which may color the accounts, so that it is impossible to be certain of their accuracy. The five accounts can be found in various places; I have principally drawn on the version of August C. Krey, *The First Crusade: The Accounts of Eye-Witnesses and Participants* (Princeton, NJ: Princeton University Press, 1921), preserved in *The Chronicle of Fulcher of Chartres*.

9. Robert the Monk, in *The Chronicle of Fulcher of Chartres*, 2–3. For Robert the Monk, the translation is from Dana Munro, "The Speech of Pope Urban II at Clermont," *American Historical Review* 11 (1906): 231–42.

In Balderic of Dol's account, Urban appeals to knights of Christ, who should "have compassion" for their "brothers" in the east. "You should shudder . . . at raising a violent hand against Christians; it is less wicked to brandish your sword against Saracens. It is the only warfare that is righteous, for it is charity to risk your life for your brothers."[10]

Urban linked the campaign to liberate Jerusalem to the most popular form of penance, the "holy pilgrimage" in which travelers become holy sacrifices.[11] The knights wanted to do penance, and Urban gave "whoever wishes to save his soul" an opportunity to do so.[12] He told the warriors that "remission of sins will be granted" to all who go to struggle "against the heathens."[13] And they will taste "imperishable glory in the kingdom of heaven."[14] Urban's "Letter of Instruction to the Crusaders, December, 1095," also offers "the remission of all their sins."[15] The knights were, in essence, *armed pilgrims*. For separate reasons, the concept of a soldier as a knight of the church was familiar, although the notion of armed pilgrims *was* new.

Urban also tied the cause to a popular form of spirituality, monasticism. Crusaders took monastic vows so that, in theory, the forces were armed, mobile monasteries. He also appealed to offended honor. Since their Christian brothers suffer and their lands are taken, the knights should, like Christ, be willing to suffer to regain their lands and the church's holy sites. In short, every theme of Urban's speech resonated with his listeners: pilgrimage, honor, vengeance, land, brotherhood, monasticism, knighthood, and remission of sin. Urban's speech had unprecedented effect because it combined familiar themes in a new way—and had an initially successful result.

Urban claimed that warriors were "knights of Christ" who went in the way of the Lord by fighting evil. If the knights loved their souls, they should fight the barbarians who had slain their brothers. And if they perished, they died as martyrs and gained "everlasting glory."[16] Thus, warfare was viewed as a redemptive work.

10. Balderic of Dol, in *The Chronicle of Fulcher of Chartres*, 8–9.
11. Robert the Monk, in ibid., 2–5.
12. The Gesta Version, in ibid., 6.
13. Fulcher of Chartres, in ibid., 30.
14. Robert the Monk, in ibid., 4.
15. Pope Urban II, "Urban's Letter of Instruction to the Crusaders, December, 1095," in ibid., 16.
16. Baldric of Dol, in ibid., 9.

At a distance, the errors are obvious. But Urban drew on noble and almost undisputed themes. The cultural milieu made his appeal plausible. His arguments were so well suited to the perceived needs of the hour that almost every major Christian leader of the age endorsed the Crusades: Bernard of Clairvaux, Thomas Aquinas, St. Francis of Assisi, Catherine of Siena, and more. Why did the great Christians of the day so fervently support the Crusades that they sacrificed wealth, health, even life itself in a cause that they believed to be so just?[17] First, there was a sliver of justice in their cause. It *is* right to defend one's people and to protect the defenseless. After that, we see them legitimating themes from their culture that have no place in God's economy. Three errors are especially prominent: the desire to avenge affronts to honor, the belief that one can advance the cause of Christ through physical warfare, and the belief that one can perform deeds or do penance to gain the remission of sins and eternal life. Historians see that once the Crusades began, Christian warriors almost immediately adopted the worst tactics of their adversaries (as so often happens in war).

The goal here is not to denigrate Christians past. I have tried to frame my account so that we feel the force of Urban's plea, even if we are convinced that he was disastrously wrong. The goal is to beware lest we do the same thing. It is so easy to baptize the standards of our day: First, we accept an idea because almost everyone else in the culture does. Second, we find some link between Scripture and that cultural conviction. Third, we fail to see how valid biblical teaching or doctrine corrects the error.

For the Crusades, first, warfare, honor, vengeance, and meritorious deeds were in the air. Second, there is teaching on justice, love of Christian brothers, and spiritual warfare in Scripture. All three were weaponized, by assimilation to the themes above. Third, the church failed to see that salvation rests on the completed work of Jesus, received by faith alone. The church taught that exceptional deeds either opened the gate to heaven or shortened the time in purgatory. Pilgrimages to places such as Jerusalem were already seen as aids to salvation. That made it easy to justify the Crusades as pilgrimages. It is easy to conform to the age and so to be of the world rather than being in the world but not of it. It is easy to engage the world and capitulate to it instead of separating from it. Peter stresses the need to be holy and separate (1 Peter 1:15–16).

17. Riley-Smith, *Crusades*, 256–57.

THE ACCOUNTABILITY OF THE REDEEMED

Peter states three reasons why believers should be holy. First, we should be holy because the God who called us is holy (1 Peter 1:15–16). God will remake us in his image, in the likeness of the Son (Rom. 8:29; Phil. 3:21; 1 John 3:2). We should therefore be holy because it is both our obligation and our future to conform to God's character. As we see his glory, we become like him (2 Cor. 3:18).

Second, Peter notes that his people should be holy for this reason: "Since you call on a Father who judges each man's work impartially, live your lives as strangers here in reverent fear" (1 Peter 1:17). Peter here combines two concepts that we needlessly separate: God is both Father and Judge. It is a great privilege to call God *Father* (Matt. 6:9; Luke 11:2; Rom. 8:15). But this intimate relation hardly exempts us from obedience. On the contrary, Peter declares (to quote the ESV translation of 1:17), you must "conduct yourselves with fear throughout the time of your exile." That is, while we live as strangers in this world, we both think of God with familial love, as Father, *and* retain an awe of the mighty and holy Lord. C. E. B. Cranfield observes:

> It is of God's infinite condescension that you are allowed to call him "Father." You are not to presume on his goodness, but rather let it make you reverent and humble. He has not ceased to be the impartial Judge of all men. The more truly, the more intimately, we know him, the more of awe and reverence we shall feel.[18]

The fear of the Lord, including fear of his justice, is the beginning of wisdom (Prov. 1:7; Matt. 10:28; Heb. 4:1). Since human fathers also judge their children, this joining of intimacy and justice should not surprise us. Indeed, just as human children both respect and obey the parents who love them, so those who call God *Father* should love and obey him. If we seek his benefits, if we invoke him as Father, we should act like his children and meet his standards for the family.[19]

18. C. E. B. Cranfield, *I & II Peter and Jude* (London: SCM Press, 1960), 53.
19. The NIV and ESV translate the Greek verb *epikaleō* as "call" in the phrase "you call on a Father" (1 Peter 1:17). In the middle voice, used here, it is an intense form of the typical word for *call, kaleō.* We render it "invoke."

This leads to a third reason for holiness. God the Father also "judges each man's work impartially" (1 Peter 1:17). He neither looks at appearances nor plays favorites. He judges our deeds, and nothing is hidden from him. Jesus states that "he will reward each person according to what he has done" (Matt. 16:27). Paul agrees: "For we must all appear before the judgment seat of Christ, that each one may receive what is due him for the things done while in the body, whether good or bad" (2 Cor. 5:10; cf. Jer. 17:10; Matt. 12:37; Rev. 20:12). This in no way nullifies justification by faith. But God will judge and Jesus will be proved right when he says, "You will recognize them by their fruits" (Matt. 7:16, 20 ESV). This is not salvation by works. It reflects the great principle that our works follow our heart commitments so that genuine faith will show itself in words and deeds. In Psalm 62, David says that the LORD is his rock and salvation and that he "will reward each person according to what he has done" (Ps. 62:12). Because David trusts the Lord, he knows his works will reflect that. God will see them and be pleased.

For this reason, Peter says, "conduct yourselves"—create a way of life[20]—marked by reverent fear of God "throughout the time of your exile" (1 Peter 1:17 ESV; the NIV uses "live . . . as strangers"). The term *exile* is *paroikia*. There are two Greek words for the idea of settling in a place. One is *katoikia*, which signifies settling down. The other, which Peter uses here, is *paroikia*. It means "to settle temporarily." Since we are sojourners, resident aliens, in this world, we never fully settle or perfectly fit here. We should neither expect nor attempt to do so.

Two of our children have spent time abroad in college. One lived in France. Her French was good enough that the French did not recognize her as an American, but they still knew she wasn't French. Another knew enough Mandarin to negotiate the streets of provincial Chinese cities, but no one thought she was Chinese. Neither fully belonged. They were resident aliens, and so are we.

Genesis calls Abraham, Isaac, and Jacob "aliens" (Gen. 17:8; 19:9; 28:4). Abraham and his family "admitted that they were aliens and strangers on earth" (Heb. 11:13). They "lived in tents" with no land of their own (Heb. 11:9). The Israelites were also strangers in Egypt. They lived there for centuries, but never fully belonged (Ex. 22:21; 23:9). Indeed, despite his power and wealth, even King David proclaims, "We are aliens and strangers in your sight, as were all our

---

20. The Greek noun, *anastrophē* (a word that Peter favored), is closer to the English word *lifestyle* than *life*.

forefathers. Our days on earth are like a shadow" (1 Chron. 29:15). If even David, the king of Israel, could call himself an alien, every believer must be an outsider in his or her age. Instead of trying to fit our times, we should look "forward to the city with foundations, whose architect and builder is God" (Heb. 11:10).

We should see our life the same way, especially if we fit rather well into our culture. It seems that there is always a crisis in morals, politics, or the economy that can remind us, if we are perceptive, that this world, in its present form, cannot be our final home. Americans and others from the dominant West must recognize this. If we believe we are mighty, let history teach us that mighty nations dwindle away. Alexander the Great led his Greek and Macedonian armies to world domination. Today, Greece and Macedonia are feeble Mediterranean states. The Mongols, once the terror of Asia and Europe, now inhabit a poor and barren land. Every empire falters and falls. If we admire our democracy and dynamism, our energy and invention, let us remember that we are strangers in this fallen world.

In fact, most of us are double-minded, conflicted, when we evaluate our culture. We lionize and demonize, sometimes in the same conversation. If there is much to praise, there is also, in every culture, much to blame. At this moment, late in 2014, orthodox Christians lament the West's steady march toward family chaos, as serial cohabitation, easy divorce, and sexual license stretch, apparently irresistibly, toward same-sex marriage, polygamy, and polyamory. In years past, racism and abortion stirred our passion. Within a few years, a new moral failing will seize our attention. But we have a hard time seeing other cultural problems. We seem almost blind to the materialism and individualism that afflict our culture.

If this world in its present form is not our home, let us keep a loose grip on its benefits and a gimlet eye on its ideologies. Let us live to please our Father and stay ready to engage the times, maintaining a certain distance from our culture.

We have said that there are several reasons for a believer to be holy. First, the God who called us is holy. Second, God the Father is still God the Judge. Third, because we never fully belong in this world, we should live by God's standards. Finally, we should be holy because Jesus came to redeem us from an empty life inherited from our forefathers:

> For you know that it was not with perishable things such as silver or gold that you were redeemed from the empty way of life handed down to you

from your forefathers, but with the precious blood of Christ, a lamb without blemish or defect. (1 Peter 1:18–19)

Today, *redeem* is an essentially religious term, but in Peter's day it was a commercial term for the liberation of a slave or a war-captive by the payment of a price for purchase or ransom. This implies, first, that our sin has reduced us to the status of slaves or captives. Second, we cannot extricate or liberate ourselves from this predicament. A Christian friend who is a professional tennis coach illustrated slavery this way: A self-taught player picks up certain bad habits and flaws in technique. A gifted athlete can make a flawed stroke work, but in the process the flaw becomes an ingrained pattern. As a result, the player is in bondage to his flaw and cannot deliver himself from it. We need someone—Jesus—to intervene in order to secure our release from the power and consequences of sin. The consequences are guilt, condemnation, and physical and eternal death.

With any ransom, a price is paid. This payment is not monetary, "not with . . . silver or gold" (1 Peter 1:18). Rather, Jesus, God's spotless Lamb, gave his "precious blood" as he suffered the death that our sins deserve (1:19). As a result, whatever our circumstances, believers are never spiritual slaves.

According to 1 Peter 1:18–19, Jesus *ransomed* us (Greek *lutroō*). Using a slightly different image, Paul says that Jesus *obtained* or *acquired* us (Acts 20:28; Greek *peripoieō*). Paul also teaches that Jesus *bought* us at a price (1 Cor. 6:20; Greek *agorazō*). We are free and must live accordingly. "You were bought at a price; do not become slaves of men" (1 Cor. 7:23). Therefore, a disciple must especially shun sins that have the capacity to enslave or addict, whether drugs, alcohol, nicotine, pornography, or even anger. Of course, that is easier said than done. For that reason we should be watchful, and seek aid when we feel trapped. Yet as the metaphor suggests, the believer is not absolutely free. We belong to the Lord, who liberated us from a malign master and placed us in his household, where we offer him our service.

THE CALL TO HOPE IN CHRIST

Peter assures his people that their status as redeemed children is neither an accident nor an afterthought. Human rebellion did not surprise God. The prophets foretold Jesus' life, betrayal, and sacrifice. Jesus also predicted it, but even more, he said that it happened according to the plan that predates all history. Jesus said that he *had to be* "delivered into the hands of sinful men, be crucified and on the third day be raised again . . . and then enter his glory" (Luke 24:7, 26). John calls Jesus "the Lamb that was slain from the [foundation] of the world" (Rev. 13:8). Paul explains that this was God's will, plan, and good pleasure, put into effect at the right time (Eph. 1:9–11). Joining that train of biblical theology, Peter states that God foresaw and predestined the redemptive work of Jesus, for Jesus "was chosen [by God] before the creation [or *foundation*] of the world" (1 Peter 1:20a). Then God accomplished his eternal plan, so it "was revealed in these last times for your sake" (1:20b). These are the last times, the times of Christ, when we await one last element of God's plan, the return of Christ. All of this, Peter says, is "for your sake."

We must apply "the precious blood of Christ" to ourselves, which we do when we put our "faith and hope" in God (1 Peter 1:19, 21). Hebrews teaches, "Just as man is destined to die once, and after that to face judgment, so Christ was sacrificed once to take away the sins of many people" (Heb. 9:27–28). Judas presents the clearest case of the man who rejects the One through whom we can face judgment without fear. Because Judas rejected Jesus, he comes to judgment naked and alone, holding his terrible sin in his hands. All who reject Christ will find themselves in Judas's position when they stand before the Judge. But Christians do not come alone, in our sin, for Jesus has redeemed us and ushers us into God's presence with our sins covered by his blood. When we believe in him, we live with him. "Through him you believe in God, who raised him from the dead and glorified him, and so your faith and hope are in God" (1 Peter 1:21). Thus, day by day, the Spirit convicts people of sin and illumines them so that they see the beauty of Jesus' redemption and trust and hope in him.

This returns us to our first theme. Holiness governs 1 Peter 1:14–16, but our passage begins and ends with hope. Through Jesus, Peter says, we believe and have confidence in God. This hope is well founded, not vain, because it rests on Jesus Christ, the Lamb of God (1:20). He has redeemed us from an empty life (1:18), covered our sins (1:19), summoned us to holiness (1:15–16), and given us reason to hope, even if we feel like strangers in our own land.

5

GOSPEL PURIFICATION

1 Peter 1:22—2:3

Now that you have purified yourselves by obeying the truth so that you have sincere love for your brothers, love one another deeply, from the heart. For you have been born again, not of perishable seed, but of imperishable, through the living and enduring word of God. (1 Peter 1:22–23)

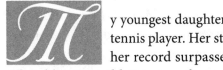y youngest daughter was a reasonably good high school tennis player. Her strokes and movement were solid, but her record surpassed expectations if an observer considered her raw athleticism or the technical purity of her game. She won because she never gave up on a point, never gave up on a match, and almost never played anyone who was tougher, physically or mentally, than she. I counseled her, "In the third set you still have energy, so keep bouncing between points. You *are* in better shape than your opponent, so let it show. You never wear out; make sure the other girl knows it." The longer a match went, the more likely a victory became.

Peter used the same pattern of reasoning, which theologians have given the inelegant label "the indicative and the imperative." The phrase notes the way in which the apostles move from what *is* to what, logically, *ought*

to be. I told my daughter, "You *are* in better shape [indicative], *so act like it* [imperative] and reap the results." In a similar vein, Peter begins, "Now that you have purified yourselves by obeying the truth so that you have sincere love for your brothers [indicative], love one another deeply, from the heart [imperative]" (1 Peter 1:22). The next section begins, "For you have been born again [indicative] . . . . Therefore, rid yourselves of all malice [imperative]" (1:23; 2:1). The final imperative, "crave pure spiritual milk," rests on a final indicative, "you have tasted that the Lord is good" (2:2–3).

The indicative-imperative interplay governs most of 1 Peter 1. Earlier, Peter described the Godward responsibilities that the gospel creates. God's elect should set their hope in God's grace (1 Peter 1:13), be holy (1:16), and live in reverent fear (1:17). In this passage, Peter accents the manward responsibilities of the gospel. We love each other deeply (1:22) and put away all malice (2:1). First Peter 1:22–25 also develops his interest, seen earlier in 1:10–12, in the veracity of God's Word. Peter says that believers are purified by obeying the truth (1:22). They have been born again by the "enduring word of God" (1:23). Further, the Word of the Lord endures forever (1:24–25). Since we are shaped by the Word, believers can rid themselves of sins such as malice and deceit (2:1).

God's Word Is Truth That Brings Life

Peter has just told his readers that God has redeemed them "with the precious blood of Christ, a lamb without blemish or defect" (1 Peter 1:19). Jesus was chosen for this task "before the creation of the world" (1:20). Through him, they "believe in God, who raised him from the dead and glorified him" (1:21). Now, therefore, Peter tells his people, "you have purified yourselves by obeying the truth" (1:22). The phrase "obeying the truth" is important. Peter does not say that we obey a *command*; he says that we obey *"the truth."*

For Peter, "the truth" is neither abstract nor general. In this setting, "the truth" means "the gospel." The closest parallel to 1 Peter 1:22 is Galatians 5:7, where Paul asks the Galatians, "You were running a good race. Who cut in on you and kept you from *obeying the truth*?" In the context of Galatians 5:1–6 and the entire epistle to the Galatians, "the truth" means "the gospel."

First Peter 1:25 also mentions "the word of the Lord . . . that was preached to you." Elsewhere, the New Testament uses the parallel phrase "the word of truth." In Ephesians 1:13, Paul identifies "the word of truth" with "the gospel": "And you also were included in Christ when you heard *the word of truth, the gospel* of your salvation." Again, "the word of truth" is identical to "the gospel" in Colossians 1:5b–6: "Of this you have heard before in *the word of the truth, the gospel*, which has come to you" (ESV). Finally, James 1:18 says that God chose to give his children spiritual life or birth by "the word of truth" (cf. John 14:17; 2 Tim. 2:15).

So when Peter declares that we purify ourselves "by obeying the truth," he means that we purify ourselves when we believe the gospel, which is "the word of truth" par excellence. All Scripture is God's true Word, yet within it we find something that the apostles call "*the* truth" (1 Peter 1:22) and "*the* word" (1:25). If we collapse 1 Peter 1:23–25, it becomes clear: "For you have been born again, not of perishable seed, but of imperishable, through the living and enduring word of God. . . . And this is the word that was preached to you."[1]

Elsewhere in the New Testament, to obey the truth (1 Peter 1:22) is to believe it. This is clearest when Paul cites Isaiah in Romans 10, marveling, " 'How beautiful are the feet of those who preach the good news!' But they have not all *obeyed* the gospel. For Isaiah says, 'Lord, who has *believed* our message?' " (Rom. 10:15b–16 ESV). Notice that Paul equates the two; we obey the gospel when we believe it. To believe is to obey. The expression "obey the gospel" is also found in 2 Thessalonians 1:8 and 1 Peter 4:17. In both texts, the writer warns those who "do not obey the gospel." That is, they do not know God or bear his name or belong to his family. In short, every proclamation of the person and work of the Lord Jesus implies that the listener should trust and follow him. Hence the apostles say that we should "obey the gospel."

We obey the truth when we believe the gospel that Peter declared: Jesus is God's Anointed, the Savior. He suffered, shed his innocent blood, died and rose, and promised to restore all things (1 Peter 1:3–9). We obey the truth when we believe that Jesus died as a sacrifice for sins and that God "raised him from the dead and glorified him" (1:21). We obey the gospel when our "faith and hope" (1:21) rest in Jesus Christ, who "bore our sins in his body on the tree, so that we might die to sins and live for righteousness" (2:24).

---

1. The verb translated "preached" is *euaggelizomai*, which means to "proclaim good news" or "bring a good message."

53

We *can* obey the gospel because the Word is understandable and authoritative. And we *should* believe the gospel because it summons a response—obedience. Some disciples think it is very pious to talk about their faith in passive terms. They say, "I was saved; I surrendered to God." Indeed, there is a passive element to the faith; we *rest* in Christ. But faith is active, too. Joel 2:32 says, "And everyone who calls on the name of the LORD will be saved." The active language of calling on God appears frequently in the New Testament (Acts 2:21; 9:14–21; 22:16; Rom:10:13; 1 Cor. 1:2; 2 Tim. 2:22).

We should *call* on God actively. If we fail to call on the Lord, we disobey the gospel. That has consequences: "Those who do not obey the gospel . . . shall suffer . . . exclusion from the presence of the Lord and from the glory of his might" (2 Thess. 1:8–9 RSV). Here Paul links the gospel to God's glory. He also links the gospel to his *power* in Romans 1:16: The gospel is "the power of God for the salvation of everyone who believes." So, then, the gospel is the *truth* of God that brings the *power* and *glory* of God to all who believe.

The gospel also makes believers holy: "Now that you have purified yourselves by obeying the truth so that you have sincere love for your brothers, love one another deeply, from the heart" (1 Peter 1:22). To restate, Peter says that the gospel empowers moral change, specifically the ability to love our brothers "from the heart." Since the heart is "the most important anthropological term" in the Bible, this is no minor claim.[2]

Solomon warned, "Above all else, guard your heart, for it is the wellspring of life" (Prov. 4:23; cf. 23:19). The heart makes plans (16:1, 9) and controls every member of the body (4:23–27; 6:16–19), even our facial expressions (15:13) and our tongue (12:23). The heart seeks knowledge (15:14) or follows foolish impulses (6:25). It can trust God (3:5), make decisions, and establish a life direction (Ex. 14:5; Num. 32:9; 1 Sam. 13:14; 1 Kings 12:27; 18:37).[3] The heart is evil beyond cure (Jer. 17:9), unless God regenerates it, which he promises to do (Jer. 31:33). As Ezekiel 36:26 puts it, "I will give you a new heart and put a new spirit in you; I will remove from you your heart of stone and give you a heart of flesh." In our passage, Peter states that God uses the gospel to change the heart, so we are pure and "love one another deeply, from the heart" (1 Peter 1:22).

2. Bruce K. Waltke, with Charles Yu, *An Old Testament Theology* (Grand Rapids: Zondervan, 2007), 225–27.

3. The Hebrew term for *heart* (*leb* or *lebab*) appears in each verse above.

Love is both a feeling and a way of life.[4] Peter says that the gospel both purifies the heart and teaches us to love. This challenges a common belief. Many Christians think of the gospel as the *starting point* of Christian life, the first step in the journey, but something we surpass in time. Yet the gospel isn't the first step of many; it is the core of the faith, the hub of the wheel. The gospel is not for outsiders and beginners, something that insiders supersede as we grow in knowledge and obedience. No, the gospel is "the word of his grace, which can build you up" (Acts 20:32; see also 20:24). Grace makes us strong. From it all action radiates.

About twenty years earlier, Peter learned this the hard way. He enjoyed full fellowship with Gentile Christians in Galatia until some Christian legalists passed through. They apparently chided people for eating with Gentiles who didn't follow Jewish food laws. Peter caved to their pressure and stopped eating with his Gentile brothers. Paul called this hypocrisy and a failure to act (literally, *walk*) "in line with the truth of the gospel" (Gal. 2:14). That is, the gospel should have taught Peter not to separate from fellow Christians over matters of food.

This point implies that we can solve many of life's questions by asking, "What action is in line with the truth of the gospel? What decision is consistent with the gospel?" Suppose someone wrongs you. What response is consistent with the gospel? Anger? Self-pity? Revenge? Forgiveness? A conversation?

If your career is uncertain, if you lose your job or lose income, what response is in line with the gospel? Panic? Shame? Despair? Anger? Or is there a better way to walk in line with the gospel and obey it? The gospel says that we are beloved of God, regardless of our achievements. What response follows that?

We should always seek the path that is in line with the gospel. Looking at life through the lens of the gospel is part of "obeying the truth." We "obey the truth" when we know we are *justified* by grace and *sanctified* by grace. We get right and stay right with God the same way: through the gospel, not works.

Both religious and irreligious people can disobey the gospel. Moral people can be just as far from God, just as antagonistic to the faith, as immoral

4. We will consider love in more detail in chapter 10, as we comment on 1 Peter 3:8–12.

people and atheists. Revelation 11:7–8 points out that *Jerusalem*, the city of religion, murders the prophets. *Religious* leaders insisted on Jesus' crucifixion. A secular man wants to be his own lord, but a moral, churchgoing man can be just as far from Jesus. If he hopes to earn God's favor by religious activities and moral goodness, he trusts himself, not Jesus. He might admire Jesus the teacher and holy man, but if he thinks God must reward his piety, he does not obey the truth of the gospel.

Religion says, "If I obey, God will love me." The gospel says, "Because God loves me, I will obey." When Peter says that "you have purified yourselves," he uses a perfect participle, signifying that this purification is an ongoing state. By obeying the truth, the gospel, we are purified in a definitive way, even though we must yet grow into it. As Hebrews 10:14 notes, "by one sacrifice [Jesus] has made perfect forever those who are being made holy." To be made perfect forever is the definitive element; to be made holy is the progressive element. Both are true and essential, and both rest on the gospel.

Peter asserts that this gospel grants life. "You have been born again, not of perishable seed but of imperishable, through the living and enduring word of God" (1 Peter 1:23). Some Christians balk at the phrase "born again" because certain people use it as a shibboleth. The Greek could be translated "born anew" (NRSV), but the concept is clear. By his Spirit, God grants his people a new and second life. The theological term for this is *regeneration*. Paul says that we "were dead in our transgressions and sins," but that God "made us alive with Christ" (Eph. 2:1–5). Because they care nothing for God and his truth, the unregenerate are compared to the deaf and the blind (Ps. 38:13; Prov. 28:9; Isa. 43:8; Rev. 3:17). Humans are not deaf as a rock is deaf. We hear but rebel. Our "being is intact," but our "nature is corrupt."[5] In regeneration, God quickens the mind, opens the eyes, and renews the will. The renewed person comprehends the gospel (1 Cor. 2:14–15) and is attracted to it, so that he comes to Jesus freely and willingly.[6]

Regeneration is God's decision and act (John 3:1–8). It is rooted in Jesus' resurrection (1 Peter 1:3). When a newly regenerate person reads the Word, the gospel, the Spirit grants "intellectual illumination." He liberates the will from its bondage to sin and cleanses the heart. He grants new affections,

---

5. Abraham Kuyper, *The Work of the Holy Spirit*, trans. Henri Devries (New York: Funk & Wagnalls, 1900; repr., Grand Rapids: Eerdmans, 1979), 304.
6. The concept is from Westminster Confession of Faith 10.1, "Of Effectual Calling."

which drive out old desires.[7] In his oft-quoted sermon "The Expulsive Power of a New Affection," Thomas Chalmers says that we do not cease to love the world by a "mere demonstration of this world's insignificance." The heart *will* love something, so that it is impossible to extirpate or expunge love of the world directly. The heart needs "another object more alluring" and "another love . . . more worthy" of our affection. Nothing else creates new life and new energies. No one believes or obeys the gospel apart from this work of God.[8]

Ordinarily, God's Spirit regenerates the human spirit as a man, woman, or child reads or hears the Word. Peter states, "For you have been born again, not of perishable seed, but of imperishable, through the living and enduring word of God" (1 Peter 1:23). Peter's main interest is the gospel, yet he declares that Scripture, which makes the gospel known, is imperishable, living, and enduring, so that it will always have the power to give life.[9]

The gospel is a special case of all Scripture, which, unlike humans, lives and endures forever. To this point, 1 Peter 1:24–25a quotes Isaiah 40:6–8:

> All flesh is like grass
> and all its glory like the flower of grass.
> The grass withers,
> and the flower falls,
> but the word of the Lord remains forever. (ESV)

Because Scripture is God's Word, it shares his attributes—it endures forever. Human life is, at best, like flowering grass, splendid for a season, but short-lived. The brevity of life could lead us to despair. Or it could take us to Woody Allen, who has often declared his trust or hope in "the power of distraction." That is, by attending to things such as the arts and comedy, we can forget that we must die. Or it could hear the grandiloquent atheist

---

7. Sinclair B. Ferguson, *The Holy Spirit* (Downers Grove, IL: InterVarsity Press, 1996), 118–23.

8. Thomas Chalmers, "The Expulsive Power of a New Affection," in *Sermons and Discourses*, 3rd complete Am. ed. (New York: Robert Carter, 1846), 2:271–75.

9. In Greek, the last phrase of 1 Peter 1:23 is *dia logou zōntos kai menontos*. The word-for-word translation runs "through the word of the living God and abiding." We would be inclined to link "living" with "God" because of the well-known phrase "the living God." But that would leave *menontos*— "abiding"—dangling meaninglessly. Since "living" is sometimes linked with "word" (Heb. 4:12) and the sentence reads far better, the consensus is that "living" describes "the word," not "God."

Bertrand Russell, who said, "I believe that when I die I shall rot, and nothing of my ego will survive." Further, he believed that

> man is . . . the outcome of accidental collocations of atoms; that no fire, no heroism, no intensity of thought and feeling, can preserve an individual life beyond the grave; that all the labors of the ages, all the devotion, all the inspiration, all the noonday brightness of human genius, are destined to extinction in the vast death of the solar system. . . .
>
> Brief and powerless is man's life; on him and all his race the slow, sure doom falls pitiless and dark. Blind to good and evil, reckless of destruction, omnipotent matter rolls on its relentless way; for man, condemned today to lose his dearest, tomorrow himself to pass through the gate of darkness, it remains only to cherish, ere yet the blow fall, the lofty thoughts that ennoble his little day.[10]

But the brevity of life does not drive Peter to despair. Although "all flesh is like grass," God and his Word stand forever. "And this," Peter continues, "is the word that was preached to you" (1 Peter 1:25b). Because we believe the gospel Word, because that Word unites us to the risen Lord, an imperishable and unfading inheritance, kept by God, awaits us (1:3–4, 9). God created Russell's chancy atoms, wove them together in their vast numbers, and then chose to subject them to futility and death, for it is better that man know his futility than that he live on and on, oblivious to his doom. Then, if renewed by the Spirit, he can taste life eternal.

New Life Brings Spiritual and Moral Reform

Genuine faith brings change in behavior. Again, Peter says, "Now that you have purified yourselves by obeying the truth so that you have sincere love for your brothers, love one another deeply, from the heart" (1 Peter 1:22). That is, when someone obeys the gospel, it creates "sincere love for your brothers . . . from the heart" (1:22). We will explore the emotional aspect of love later, when we examine 1 Peter 3:8–12. Here we notice that love has both emotional and volitional elements. We both

10. Bertrand Russell, "A Free Man's Worship" (1903), in *Why I Am Not a Christian* (New York: Simon and Schuster, 1957), 107, 115–16.

feel love and *resolve* to love. Love is a result of conversion, since believers become members of God's loving family.

Love

Love is a way of life. It fulfills the law (Matt. 22:34–40). If we love others, we respect them, promote their lives, honor their property, tell them the truth, and seek their good, not their goods.

Peter describes this love in three ways. First, it is sincere and deep, affectionate and heartfelt—earnest, unfeigned, and without pretense. Second, it is brotherly and filial, not calculating. It has no thought of gaining something in return. It is natural, when we help a brother, to be aware that the friend might return the favor in our own time of need. Indeed, James says that believers have a duty to assist their brothers and sisters in the faith whenever any of them needs food or clothing. Yet genuine Christian love does not calculate a return on acts of kindness. Third, love is deep. The term translated "deeply" can mean "earnestly" or "unremittingly." The root is a verb that means "stretch out" and can describe a man or animal running at full speed. Thus, love should be strenuous and enduring.[11]

Ideally, sincere, brotherly, and earnest love come together, and we gladly help each other in the hour of need. We stick with each other when the need lasts for weeks or months. We never begrudge our labor. Love is sincere and earnest when we invite a stranded family to stay with us, and the welcome stays warm even if a dish breaks or a carpet is stained.

The End of Malice, Envy, and Slander

The indicative-imperative structure continues to guide Peter's commands in 1 Peter 2:1–3. In this case, however, the indicative comes last, in 2:3: "now that you have tasted that the Lord is good." Logically, however, our experience of the Lord's goodness comes first. Because we know that God is good, we are good, and it must show in our attitudes and actions.

"Rid yourselves" of sin, Peter exhorts us in 1 Peter 2:1, using a verb (*apotithēmi*) often used when someone takes off or lays aside clothes (cf. Acts 7:58). When Peter says that we "rid" ourselves of (NIV) or "put away" (ESV) these sins, he imagines our taking them off, as if they were soiled garments.

---

11. C. E. B. Cranfield, *I & II Peter and Jude* (London: SCM Press, 1960), 57.

The sins that Peter names are not the "gross vices of paganism" but "community destroying vices" so often tolerated by the church: malice, deceit, and hypocrisy or insincerity.[12] It is worthwhile to define them.

Malice signifies evil or wickedness in the broadest possible sense, ill-will to all, perhaps for its own sake. Or it can signify the bad blood and nursing of grudges that seem to motivate some people. Joseph Stalin embodied all sides of malice. With callous indifference, he issued political and economic decrees that led to the deaths of millions of his own people. He also murdered his underlings, with his own hand, in public, with a laugh, as if he enjoyed it.

Hypocrisy can also be translated "insincerity." While *hypocrisy* signifies deliberate deception in English, the Greek term does not necessarily have that sense. It includes ordinary inconsistency between belief and practice, between one's inner and outer life. It includes self-deception as well as deception of others. The hypocrites of Matthew 23 seem quite sincere—they travel land and sea to make one convert (Matt. 23:15, 27–28). If we reflect a moment, we see that one can be both sincere and hypocritical. If we first deceive ourselves, we will readily deceive others.

Peter links malice with *envy*. Malice easily leads to envy, which is the gnawing sorrow we feel when someone else has something that we think we deserve. Immanuel Kant said that envy is a wretched vice because it hurts everyone. It torments the subject, who envies, and it hopes to destroy the happiness of the one envied.[13] Envy's apologists claim that envy can at least spur achievement, but most observe that envy is that rare state that brings no good to anyone. Vain as it is, almost everyone succumbs to envy at some point. The envious compare themselves to others and, for some perverse reason, always decide that they come up short. To quote Bertrand Russell with favor, "If you desire glory, you may envy Napoleon. But Napoleon envied Caesar, Caesar envied Alexander, and Alexander, I dare say, envied Hercules, who never existed."[14]

In his monograph *Envy*, Joseph Epstein confesses that his childhood was filled with it. He envied "boys who were better looking . . . with wealthier parents, brighter, more popular, and physically more courageous than I." He envied boys who were "more attractive to girls, . . . better athletes, more

12. Peter H. Davids, *The First Epistle of Peter* (Grand Rapids: Eerdmans, 1990), 80.
13. Joseph Epstein, *Envy* (New York: Oxford University Press, 2003), xxi.
14. Bertrand Russell, "Conquest of Happiness," in *Why I Am Not a Christian*, 57.

adept and more at ease in the world." His eyes were quick to detect friends with more freedom, more spending money, and cooler parents, so that he lived in a faint cloud of envy.[15]

Malice and envy readily lead to deceit and slander. The envious want to bring other people down; they will *slander* or malign others to do so. *Deceit*, like malice, is a wide-ranging vice. It includes all dishonesty, whether in words or deeds. Yet deceit and slander are both primarily sins of the tongue. When we deceive, we shade the truth, ordinarily to someone's face. Slander is bald opposition to the truth, ordinarily behind someone's back. The deceiver hides the truth. The gossip sometimes tells the truth, but delivers it to the wrong people. The slanderer boldly lies, pretending to deliver the truth.

Slander can be the child of envy. In the Middle Ages, Europe had one church but many reform movements. When a reformer became too popular or powerful, church officials typically accused the reformer of financial corruption or unchastity in order to undermine the reformer's credibility.

Peter tells his readers to "rid yourselves of . . . deceit . . . and slander" (1 Peter 2:1) because he knows that God's people don't always tell the truth. I still recall a day, decades past, when I hid the truth to avoid a perceived danger. I didn't lie, but I skirted the truth in order to evade the consequences of truthfulness. A simple domestic scene suggests how we are tempted to deceive.

Suppose a wife asks her husband the dreaded "Did you remember?" question. Did you remember to walk the dog? To take out the trash? To take the cake out of the oven? No, he forgot, but wait, he remembered three seconds ago, when she asked, so he can possibly say, "Yes, I remembered." But there is a follow-up question, "So you took the cake out?"

Now the guilty husband drops the phone, grabs hot pads, and yanks the cake from the oven. He picks up the phone again and says, "Sorry, honey, I dropped the phone. . . . Yes, the cake is out of the oven." She asks one more question: "So is it cool?" The husband faces one more choice. Will he finally tell the plain truth, "No, it's not cool"? Or will he evade one more time: "It's not quite cool, but it's getting cooler"?

Deceit is tempting in private conversation, when we hear embarrassing questions, such as "What are you thinking?" or "Did you remember?" But

15. Epstein, *Envy*, 89–91.

deceit has public dimensions, too. Political operators deceive when they distort the record of an opponent. Business reports deceive when they hide problems or overstate assets and opportunities.

Since the church is full of sinners, it is also full of deceivers, hypocrites, and slanderers. People say one thing, then the opposite, and act baffled if someone points this out. For some people, words are tools they deploy to fulfill their goals or desires. For them, *the truth* is any statement that gets them what they want, and a lie is any statement that keeps them from getting what they want.

As we believers put off deceit, hypocrisy, and slander, we tell the truth more and more consistently. But we don't simply tell the truth; we speak the truth in love, we edify, and we strive to give grace to all who hear (Eph. 4:15, 29). If we must tell painful truths, we do so gently. If we must bring bad news, we take care not to wound or degrade anyone. If we tell a cheering truth, we shun boasting and flattery.

GROWTH IN GOD'S SALVATION

Peter connects the sins and the cures for sin. Among the sins that Peter mentions, malice leads the way. If we try to hide our malice, we deceive and play the hypocrite. We show malice toward *rivals* by slandering them. We show malice toward *the strong* by envying them.

The gospel liberates us from these sins. God pours his love into our hearts, displacing our malice, so that we can love others sincerely, from the heart (1 Peter 1:22). The gospel teaches us to confess our sins, and that drives out hypocrisy and deceit. Faith in the Lord liberates us from envy, since we know that he gives good gifts to his children (Luke 11:13). Envy is the opposite of grace, for it wants to grasp rather than to give. It is also the opposite of love, for the envious see nothing but their anguished desires. No wonder Paul calls envy one of the "works of the flesh" (ESV), a partner of discord, jealousy, and selfish ambition (Gal. 5:19–21).

But the gospel breaks this cycle of sin so that we can put away sin. We put off sin and crave spiritual milk because we "have tasted that the Lord is good" (1 Peter 2:3). Although it is the last line in our passage, tasting God's goodness is the indicative that *logically* precedes all the imperatives. Because we have tasted—personally experienced—his goodness, we can rid ourselves of malice and envy, for example. God loves us and pours his love into our hearts; surely that should expel all malice toward others. And why should we envy others? "The Lord is good," and he will give us what we need, what is best for us.

Peter knows that we cannot break with all these sins at once or by a mere act of the will. Since sins become familiar habits, our progress may be slow and our actual behavior discouraging. Still, we must strive to purify ourselves (1 Peter 1:22). Peter commands, "Like newborn babies, crave pure spiritual milk, so that by it you may grow up in your salvation" (2:2).

Grammatically speaking, "crave pure spiritual milk" is the lone imperative in 1 Peter 2:1–3. In the New Testament era, *milk* could be a metaphor for basic principles, foundational truths, taught to new converts (1 Cor. 3:1–2; Heb. 5:13), or for any spiritual nourishment. It has everything that a new Christian needs, that we may "grow up in [our] salvation" (1 Peter 2:2).

Notice that Peter doesn't counter his list of vices—malice, deceit, and the rest—with a list of virtues for which we strive. Instead, he commands that we *desire* something, God's pure spiritual milk. That milk is pure (literally, *undeceiving*). It has no corrupting errors or extraneous additions. Therefore, disciples desire God's truth as an infant longs for her mother's milk.

Humans must take nourishment in order to grow. We crave God's milk and spiritual growth because we "have tasted that the Lord is good" (1 Peter 2:3). We don't crave "religion" and its fantasy that we can earn God's favor if we keep the rules. Religion breeds pride and self-righteousness if we keep the rules, and self-loathing and despair if we cannot. But we crave God's truth and grace.

Peter names a series of sins and sinful attitudes in 1 Peter 2:1, but he surrounds his call to reform with a call first to the gospel and second to life in God's family. In Peter's language, if we *obey* the truth by believing the gospel, we will *tell* the truth, by putting off deceit and slander. We have tasted that the Lord is good and know that we belong to his family. God feeds us and grants us sincere, heartfelt love for each other so that we put away sin and grow up in our salvation.

6

CHRISTIAN IDENTITY

1 Peter 2:4–10

In Scripture it says: "See, I lay a stone in Zion, a chosen and precious cornerstone, and the one who trusts in him will never be put to shame." Now to you who believe, this stone is precious. But to those who do not believe, "The stone the builders rejected has become the capstone." (1 Peter 2:6–7)

Someone once said that we should be careful how we finish sentences that start with "I am." We should never say, "I am a loser," because we should not define ourselves by our weaknesses. Nor should we say, "I am a powerful executive," because we should not establish our identity through our achievements. Someone will ask, "If I can't define myself by my strengths and weaknesses, what's left?" If we pause, we see that we should not define ourselves by our skills and powers because they readily change. Still the question remains: how should we define ourselves?

IDENTITY AND COMMUNITY

In the West, self-definition typically begins with *I*-statements. But in some cultures, it starts with *we*-statements that establish a person's town, family, and guild. We notice that Israelites defined Jesus as "Joseph's son" and "the carpenter's son" in Luke 4:22 and Matthew 13:55. First Peter 2:4–10 moves from the character of Christ to the identity of the believer. For Peter, identity begins with such questions as: "Who is my God? Whom do I trust? What is my community?" The question "Whose am I?" has more weight than "Who am I?" First Peter 2:4–10 says that our faith defines us. Because Jesus is God's foundation stone, we are living stones. Because he chose us, we are a chosen race.

Since 1 Peter 2:4–10 is a pivotal passage in the epistle, we need to place it in context. God's elect are "strangers in the world" (1:1). God the Father chose us (1:1–2), Jesus redeemed us from our "empty way of life" (1:18–19), and the Spirit sanctified us (1:2). Therefore, we have an inheritance in heaven, safeguarded by God himself. By faith we receive God's salvation, and our holy Father summons us to stop conforming to "the evil desires" we followed when we were pagans (1:12–16). Instead, we should be holy as God is holy (1:16) and live "in reverent fear" (1:17–19). Holiness entails a new way of life, especially for Gentiles, once so far from God and now his people (2:4–10).

The first section of 1 Peter, from 1:1 to 2:12, both opens and closes by describing the identity of believers. We are "God's elect," his chosen ones. As a result, we are "strangers in the world" (1:1), no longer at home in our culture (2:10–11). Because we follow Jesus and have withdrawn from our former way of life, we are reviled as evildoers (2:12), so that the label *Christian* is almost a curse (4:16).

First Peter 1:1–21 establishes the theological foundation for the entire epistle. It says that God is holy and has made his elect holy *judicially* by covering their sins with the blood of Christ (1:2, 15–19). He also makes the church holy *morally* by "the sanctifying work of the Spirit" (1:2). When Peter describes the shape of holiness, Christian community is prominent. Once we have purified ourselves by "obeying the truth"—the gospel—we have a "sincere love for [our] brothers" and therefore "love one other deeply, from the heart (1:22).[1]

Peter then warns us to shun a series of vices. Like many other New Testament vice lists, his looks random at first, but careful reading reveals that each vice destroys community. "Therefore, rid yourselves of all malice and

---

1. Scot McKnight, *1 Peter*, NIV Application Commentary (Grand Rapids: Zondervan, 1996), 84–85.

all deceit, hypocrisy, envy, and slander of every kind" (1 Peter 2:1). Later, Peter extols community-building virtues such as compassion, tenderness, humility, and hospitality (3:8; 4:9). Our passage, 2:4–10, describes the basis for Christian community.

A LIVING STONE

In 1 Peter 2:4–10, the apostle calls his churches a "chosen people, . . . the people of God," and imputes to them the status of a new Israel. Throughout, *Peter assumes that to come to Christ is to come into this community*: "As you come to him, the living Stone—rejected by men but chosen by God and precious to him—you also, like living stones, are being built into a spiritual house to be a holy priesthood, offering spiritual sacrifices acceptable to God through Jesus Christ" (2:4–5). According to Peter, all that we are rests on all that Jesus is.

- If we come to Christ, the living stone, we become living stones (2:4–5).
- Jesus is the cornerstone (2:6), and God builds us into "a spiritual house" that rests on him (2:5).
- Because Jesus is the Chosen One (2:4), we are God's chosen ones (2:9).[2]

Some theologians speak of the elect as individuals, but Scripture typically calls Israel "the elect" or "chosen" of God.[3] Isaiah says that the Servant of the Lord, the Messiah, is *the* Chosen One, in whom and by whom all others are chosen (Isa. 42:1; 49:7). At the transfiguration, the climactic revelation of Jesus' glory, the Father declares, "This is my Son, my Chosen One" (Luke 9:35 ESV), a truth that Israel's rulers mocked at the crucifixion (23:35).

In 1 Peter 2, the descriptions of Jesus are singular and the descriptions of his people are plural. From this we learn that following Christ entails joining his community, the church. "To accept the Redeemer means also accepting the people whom he has redeemed."[4] The freelance Christian, who follows Jesus but is too good, too busy, or too self-sufficient for the

---

2. The Greek is *eklektos*, meaning "elect" or "chosen," in 1 Peter 1:1; 2:4; 2:9.
3. The Old Testament occasionally regards individuals such as David and Solomon as God's elect, but that is the exception, not the rule.
4. C. E. B. Cranfield, *I & II Peter and Jude* (London: SCM Press, 1960), 62–63.

church, is a walking contradiction. In the old covenant, God set his people apart *from* the nations. In the new covenant, he sets us apart as we live *among* the nations. But all of Scripture testifies that believers cannot be godly or fruitful without joining God's family and realizing some form of separation from the world.

Above all, the church is *Christ's* community. Peter begins: "you come to *him*" (1 Peter 2:4). Apart from Jesus, there are religious and moral communities, but the church is the one community centered on Jesus rather than morality or spirituality. In both Psalm 118 and Isaiah 28, God declares that he will lay down a foundation stone and build on it (1 Peter 2:6–7 quotes verses from both texts).

Jesus claimed to be this foundation stone in his climactic conflict with the chief priests, elders, and Pharisees. Jesus compared them to tenants who take a well-prepared vineyard, but refuse to deliver the owner's share of the crop to him. They expand their rebellion when they mistreat the master's servants and then kill his only son, hoping to seize the inheritance (Matt. 21:12–46). As Jesus explains the parable, he quotes Psalm 118:22–23: "The stone the builders rejected has become the capstone; the Lord has done this, and it is marvelous in our eyes" (Matt. 21:42).

The imagery evokes a specific scene. Before erecting a building, stone-masons search piles of rocks for boulders with the size and shape to become foundation stones, cornerstones, and capstones. Jesus depicts them as discarding one after another. They finally see the perfect stone, which represents the Messiah. But when they examine it, they reject it, too. So Israel's putative leaders searched for their Messiah, but when they found him, they judged him a false prophet (or worse) and killed him. Peter heard Jesus' teaching; he remembered and found additional "stone" sayings.[5] In Isaiah 28:16, quoted in 1 Peter 2:6, God declares, "See, I lay a stone in Zion, a chosen and precious cornerstone."

Peter twice refers to Jesus as being chosen and precious, highly valued, or honored ("precious" was a sound translation, until it began to imply weakness).[6] When we come to this living stone, we become living stones, incorporated into God's "spiritual house."

---

5. See Acts 1:15–20 for an early instance of Peter's searching Scripture to good effect.

6. The Greek adjective *entimos* is traditionally translated "precious," that is, "of great price or value." But "highly valued," "honorable," or "distinguished" is a better translation, since "precious"

Peter's teaching also has roots in the Gospels, where Peter confesses to Jesus, "You are the Christ, the Son of the living God" (Matt. 16:16). Jesus replies, "I tell you that you are *Peter*, and on this *rock* I will build my church." This line contains a play on words (16:18). The name *Peter* means "rock" or "rocky" in Greek. Jesus makes subtle use of this, for when he continues, he uses a slightly different word when he says that "on this rock I will build my church." The Greek (transliterated) reads, "You are Peter [*petros*], and on this rock [*petra*] I will build my church" (*petros* and *petra* have nearly the same sense, roughly like *rock* and *stone*).

We wonder what Jesus means by this small shift. In a sense, Peter is the rock of the church, and yet not quite. Observe that Jesus did not tell Peter, "*On you* I will build my church," but "*on this rock* I will build . . . ." If Jesus had wanted to refer to Peter, who is standing right there, there would have been a less convoluted way to do it.[7] We conclude, therefore, that Peter is not, *in himself*, the rock of the church. Instead, Scripture says that *Jesus* is the church's cornerstone and foundation. Thus, when Peter confesses Jesus, he continues to build a foundation that has Jesus himself as the chief cornerstone (Eph. 2:19–20; Matt. 21:42; cf. Matt. 18:18). Peter himself is not the rock, because he is too unstable. Indeed, a few minutes later, Peter rebuked Jesus and told him that he must never go to the cross. Later, he denied Jesus three times. Later still, his bout of legalism, mixed with fear, caused a crisis in the Galatian church (Gal. 2). A church built on Peter would be shaky indeed. But Peter did have a pivotal role as the spokesman for the apostles. He testified to Jesus in Matthew 16, then at Pentecost, and then in other moments in the life of the church.

So Peter's status depends on what he says. When he forbids Jesus to go to the cross, he is a stumbling stone, but when Peter, eyewitness and apostle, proclaims that Jesus is Christ the Savior and Son of God, he is a rock. His confession is foundational for the church. When pastors proclaim the apostolic message, they build on Jesus, the prophets, and the apostles. If anyone hears this testimony and believes, he or she becomes a living stone, part of a living temple. Yet we are more than

---

often means "cute," pejoratively, in recent use. For uses of the Greek, see Luke 7:2; 14:8; Phil. 2:29.

7. Alan McNeile, *The Gospel according to St. Matthew* (London: Macmillan, 1915; repr., Grand Rapids: Baker, 1980), 151.

a temple; we are also "a holy priesthood, offering spiritual sacrifices" (1 Peter 2:5).

In the Old Testament, the break between priests and people was sharp. God had set apart the priests to offer sacrifices and forgiveness, to pray for the people, and to instruct them in his truth (Jer. 37:3; Mal. 2:7; Heb. 5:1–5). But now we are all priests (cf. Rev. 5:10). We all pray and ask forgiveness. We have access to God, without intermediaries or permission slips (Rom. 5:2). We can understand God's Word because we know God and he leads us into all truth (Jer. 31:33–34; 1 John 2:27).

As priests, we offer "spiritual sacrifices" that are "acceptable to God through Jesus Christ" (1 Peter 2:5) As we know, God accepts perfect sacrifices, and ours are flawed; therefore, we offer them through Christ, who forgives and perfects them.

Still, Scripture suggests how our sacrifices can approach his standard. Peter has already defined holiness as a way of life, not a series of singular events (1 Peter 1:15–16). Long ago, Asaph and David called prayer, thanksgiving, and a repentant heart a sacrifice (Ps. 50:14, 23; 51:17). Paul calls the dedication of mind and body a "living sacrifice" (Rom. 12:1). In Peter, spiritual sacrifices are first "something offered up to God as worship . . . and, second, a pattern of social conduct." The worship always precedes conduct.[8] So Peter's sacrifices are the daily devotion of obedience and praise to God, as well as "practical ministry to the needs of men (Heb. 13:15–16)."[9]

A MESSAGE THAT DIVIDES

As Peter said, Jesus is God's chosen stone, set in Zion, so that "the one who trusts in him will never be put to shame" (1 Peter 2:6b). This is an eschatological promise. Because of our union with Jesus, believers can recapitulate his life pattern. We may, like Jesus, endure rejection and shame, although God won't let that last. God proclaims, "Those who honor me I will honor, but those who despise me will be disdained" (1 Sam. 2:30). Peter applies this to Jesus. He identifies Jesus as God's chosen and honorable cornerstone, and states that we must respond to him correctly:

8. J. Ramsey Michaels, *1 Peter*, Word Biblical Commentary 49 (Nashville: Thomas Nelson, 1988), 101.

9. Alan M. Stibbs, *The First Epistle General of Peter* (London: Tyndale, 1959), 100.

Now to you who believe, this stone is precious. But to those who do not believe,

"The stone the builders rejected
    has become the capstone,"

and,

"A stone that causes men to stumble
    and a rock that makes them fall." (1 Peter 2:7–8)

Jesus is the cornerstone of God's work on earth, but humans may either trust or reject him. If we trust him, we will share in his honor and never bear lasting shame. In Jesus' day, many rejected him. Today, both the religious and the godless do the same because he fails to meet their criteria: he is too harsh, too demanding, too supernatural. But those who reject him will fall (1 Peter 2:8). Jesus says that when they stumble over him, he falls on them and crushes them (Matt. 21:44).

Of course, all believers stumble momentarily. John the Baptist and the Twelve faltered when Jesus' life took unexpected turns (e.g., Matt. 11:2–3; 26:56). But we do not stumble *so as to fall*. The Lord steadies us (Ps. 37:24). Indeed, Peter warns his people of impending trouble, so that they will not be surprised and falter. In democratic lands and in nations with a Christian heritage, tolerance and pluralism are widespread, so it is safe to be a Christian. But cultures change, and subcultures (e.g., research universities) can have their own spirit. We should be prepared to suffer rejection and shame with Christ if the day demands it.

If we are unprepared, we may falter, as the disciples did at Jesus' arrest. But those who permanently reject the gospel fall permanently, "which is also what they were destined for," Peter concludes (1 Peter 2:8b). Jesus states that people reject his kingdom for several reasons, such as satanic activity, distraction, self-righteousness, and blindness. The decision is theirs, yet God's sovereign hand stands behind all (Matt. 13:1–16; 23:13–28).

Some say that the idea that some were "destined" to fall gives us an unjust God. Paul addresses this charge in Romans 9. Drawing on Genesis and Exodus, he relates that God told Moses, "I will have mercy on whom I have mercy, and I will have compassion on whom I have compassion"

(Rom. 9:14–15). Mercy is God's gift. He does extend his favor to one (Jacob) over another (Esau). But the accusation of injustice rests on a false definition.

God always gives everyone *what he or she deserves* in the sense that he never punishes the innocent. He is perfectly fair in his *retributive justice.* It is true that he does not treat everyone the same way by giving identical gifts to all. Some are born strong, intelligent, or beautiful; others are not. Some have loving parents; others do not. Still, the Lord *never gives anyone less* than he or she deserves.

Suppose a teacher gives a fair but difficult test in mathematics. Out of fifty students, none pass the test. The teacher *could* give everyone the grade that he or she earns. Or he could give everyone a low but passing grade. Again, he could give a high grade to *some* students as he wished, perhaps favoring the poor or the hardworking. If he let the other students keep the grades they earned, there is no injustice. Everyone received what he or she earned; some received more. The term for that concept is *mercy,* not *injustice.*

In election, God does something like the math teacher. Humanity stands before God like a class of failing students. Not one is righteous. Not one seeks God. But God sends his Spirit to the elect, regenerates them, convicts them of sin, and leads them to Jesus. Westminster Confession of Faith 3.5 explains that God, according to his eternal purpose and good pleasure, predestines some to life. He does this by his free grace, not even because he foresees our faith or good works.

When God sees sinners such as Jacob and Esau, neither deserves his favor. Neither seeks God. If God lets one (Esau) go his way and pursues the other for salvation (Jacob), he has shown mercy to the latter, but has done no injustice to the former. God is never unjust. Indeed, his person defines justice. If we say, "I want justice," we ask for condemnation. His mercy is our sole hope. Further, anyone who knows enough to debate the question of God's justice in salvation has heard the gospel promise and should call on Christ, for "everyone who calls on the name of the Lord will be saved" (Rom. 10:13), and no one who trusts in him will be put to shame (10:11; cf. 1 Peter 2:6).

A PEOPLE FOR GOD

We have seen that 1 Peter 2:4–10 shows how the identity of Christ estab- lishes the identity of believers. But two of Peter's statements press deeper into the Christian's identity. Because Jesus chose us, Peter informs us, "You are a chosen people, a royal priesthood, a holy nation, a people belonging to God" (2:9a).

These honorary titles come from Exodus 19, when God constituted Israel as a nation, and Isaiah 43, when God promised to reestablish Israel after the exile. These are foundational statements about Israel. By applying them to his church, Peter tells Gentiles that the privileges of Israel are now theirs. They may be aliens and exiles, cast out and rejected by their former people, but God has taken them in. They are "a chosen people" (1 Peter 2:9). The phrase "a chosen people," derived from Isaiah 43:20, also takes us to 1 Peter 2:4 and 2:6. As God chose Jesus, now he has chosen us. All of God's people, whether Jew or Gentile, are one community by faith.

The phrase "a royal priesthood" may well be translated as "the king's priesthood." We are priests (1 Peter 2:5) who belong to the King and therefore share in Jesus' sovereign rule. We stand before God in strength as we serve and represent him.

God called Israel his "holy nation" in Exodus 19:6, since he had consecrated Israel for a life with him. He ordered *physical* distinctives in food, clothing, and circumcision. These indicated and promoted Israel's *spiritual* distinctives. Israelite culture was not totally different, but it was appreciably different, and that helped to set the "holy nation" apart from "the nations," that is, the pagan world.[10]

Peter also called the church "a people belonging to God" (1 Peter 2:9). The Greek is literally "a people for possession." The phrase is from Isaiah 43:21, where God calls Israel "my chosen people, the people whom I formed for myself" (ESV). *People* is almost a technical term for Israel in its dedication to God. This "possession" is more than mere ownership. God possesses his people because he redeemed them. He exhorts them, "Fear not, for I have redeemed you; I have called you by name; you are mine" (Isa. 43:1).

The privileged *state* of God's people leads to privileged *action*. Because God has redeemed us and we are his, we are heralds who "declare the praises of him who called [us] out of darkness into his wonderful light" (1 Peter 2:9b).

It is striking that Peter calls Gentile converts a "people" and a "holy nation." These were labels that had *distinguished Israel from* the Gentiles.

---

10. See Christopher J. H. Wright, *Old Testament Ethics for the People of God* (Downers Grove, IL: InterVarsity Press, 2004).

Now Peter applies the same labels *to* the Gentiles. They had practiced a pagan polytheism that Peter calls "the empty way of life handed down to you from your forefathers." For them, debauchery, carousing, and idolatry were so common that it seemed strange when anyone departed from them (1 Peter 1:18; 4:3–4). But things have changed: "Once you were not a people, but now you are the people of God; once you had not received mercy, but now you have received mercy" (2:10). Let the contrasts resonate: once darkness, now light; once alone, now in God's family; once awaiting judgment, now receiving mercy.

We see that 1 Peter 2:4–10 is filled with quotations and allusions to the Old Testament. This shows that Peter assumes that his people, former polytheists and largely illiterate, will know key Old Testament terms and promises. It is now *their* book, their story and rule. Since no ordinary person in that day could dream of owning a copy of Scripture, this knowledge came in one way: by coming to church and listening as leaders read the Law and the Prophets. If Peter expected his new converts to gain this knowledge of Scripture, how much more should we lay hold of it. Many of us grew up in the faith, and many of us swim in a sea of Bibles and aids to its understanding. Let us therefore read, use the resources that enhance understanding, and apply what we learn to ourselves.

The Question of Identity

In other times and cultures, questions of identity did not have the urgency, the need for regular review, that many experience today. At one time, a man or woman belonged to a certain city and family, a certain social group and guild. Today, most of us live far from our hometowns and families. At one time, roles and livelihoods were set from birth or adolescence. Today, we have multiple jobs, even multiple careers. All of this erodes confidence in our identity.

In Western nations, the educated live in a meritocracy, so that our identity and our achievements are confused with one another. We define others—and let others define us—by our strengths, weaknesses, and accomplishments. So we live with the pressure to perform. We are measured and measure ourselves by this, even though so much rests on forces far outside our control. Immigration patterns raise or lower wages. The careless acts of distant financiers and governments create environments where profits come easily one year and disappear the next. What happens then, if our earnings and titles define us?

In Peter's day, identity came from externals: town, occupation, lineage, and gender. That is more stable, but not necessarily better, than our way. It was especially painful for Gentile converts who were reviled for leaving old customs and associations; they lost much of their identity.[11] Further, in following Jesus, the Gentiles chose a leader of dubious paternity from an impoverished city. He was a landless artisan and untrained itinerant preacher who died by public execution.

But the Father reversed all that and crowned Jesus with honor by raising him from death. Now, Peter says, those who follow Jesus receive his honor.[12]

The traits of Jesus (1 Peter 2:4, 6)	The traits of Jesus' followers (1 Peter 2:5–12)
A living stone	Living stones (2:5)
Rejected by humans	Exiles, aliens (2:11)
In God's eyes, chosen and elect	In God's eyes, chosen and elect (2:9)
In God's eyes, valued, honored	In God's eyes, royal, beloved (2:9, 11)

Table 6.1 Traits of Jesus and his followers

I write during a season of economic turmoil, when so many individuals have lost their jobs and seen the value of homes and investments plummet. It is tempting to feel rejected, ashamed, even worthless. Some Christians even say things such as "I've lost half my net worth." Nonsense! Financial reversals cannot deprive us of a scintilla of our worth. Our financial assets fluctuate, but our real worth never changes. If we build on Christ, our worth cannot change, since it rests on his unchanging honor, imputed to us.

It is foolish to find our identity in uncertain things such as wealth. Rather, as Paul directs, "If we have food and clothing, we will be content with that" (1 Tim. 6:8). If we get away from the city, from the advertisements and the crowds, and walk in the wilderness for a day, it's easy to see. Warm, dry clothes, water, a sandwich, and an apple are enough.

11. Joel B. Green, *1 Peter* (Grand Rapids: Eerdmans, 2007), 56–58.
12. Adapted from ibid., 59–60.

I once received a promotion to a position that some Christians consider prestigious. A fine Christian man thrust his hand into mine and said, "Congratulations; now you are an important person." I understood his motive and sentiment, but he was wrong. Because we belong to Jesus, we are important whether we have a title or not.

John Calvin wisely observed that we are most teachable when most miserable, for "our ruin compels us to look upward" to God. Further, "our very poverty better discloses the infinite benefits of reposing in God." We know ourselves and our worth when we look into God's face.[13] A disciple's identity begins with Jesus. God has chosen Christ, valued and loved him eternally for his person and his work. Faith unites us to him, so God treasures and loves us as his restored people.

It is Peter's style to move constantly from indicatives to imperatives, from God's actions to our response. If we review the commands of 1 Peter 1–2, we see that they address our attitudes more than our behavior:

- Because we are redeemed, we should "hope fully on the grace to be given you when Jesus Christ is revealed" (1 Peter 1:13).
- Because God judges everyone impartially and redeemed us with Jesus' blood, we should live "in reverent fear" of displeasing him (1:17–19).
- Because we have been born again by God's Word, we "crave pure spiritual milk," God's truth, which stands forever (1:24–2:2).

Our passage adds that Jesus is the cornerstone, rejected by men, but honored by God. When we trust him, we share his honor and join his family. That is where we must find our identity. Let us define ourselves as God does. It is more true and secure, and it liberates us from self-inflicted shame. Let us remember, finally, that each calling and privilege comes from faith in Christ. We are God's chosen ones, living temples, royal priests because he is all these things first. He is God's elect, the Priest "who combines in His person royalty and priesthood."[14] All his privileges become ours as our faith unites us to him.

13. John Calvin, *Institutes of the Christian Religion*, trans. Ford Lewis Battles (Philadelphia: Westminster, 1960), 1.1–2.
14. Stibbs, *First Epistle General of Peter*, 105.

75

7

PILGRIMS AND CITIZENS

1 Peter 2:11–17

*Dear friends, I urge you, as aliens and strangers in the
world, to abstain from sinful desires, which war against
your soul. Live such good lives among the pagans that,
though they accuse you of doing wrong, they may see
your good deeds and glorify God on the day he visits us.*
(1 Peter 2:11–12)

Since humans are social beings, we long to "fit" our surroundings in ways great and small. Consider parties: no one wants to come dressed formally to a casual event or casually to a formal event. Even if we are dressed correctly, some of us worry about the theme of the evening. A sports enthusiast might hesitate to attend a poetry-and-lute-themed soiree. Academics will avoid a party hosted by a celebrity-gossip monger. And almost everyone quails at the thought of an event held at the home of a theologian. The social man hates to be out of place, yet everyone has walked through a door and felt, like a punch to the belly, "These are not my people, and I don't belong here." In our passage, Peter tells us that the "I don't belong here" sensation is endemic to the experience of Christians in this world.

The Life of a Pilgrim

In the first sentence of this letter, Peter told his churches that they are "strangers" (NIV) or "exiles" (ESV) in this world. First Peter 2 repeats the principle that God's people do not fully belong in this world. We are "aliens and strangers" (NIV) or "sojourners and exiles" (ESV) because Jesus redeemed us from a futile life and gave us a new one. By repentance and faith, we became God's people, his prized possession. By the same act, we necessarily became—and ought to remain—partially estranged from this age.

First Peter 2:11–17 occupies a pivotal place in Peter's epistle. The author tells his readers in 1 Peter 1 that they have been purified by the Word of truth, that is, the gospel. He then presents a theology of the Word of God, which concludes with the central exhortation to "crave pure spiritual milk" (2:2). After presenting a concise theology of the Word, Peter turns to a theology of the Christian's identity in 2:4–10. We are living stones in God's spiritual house. Further, we are a holy and royal priesthood, a chosen people, a holy nation (2:5, 9).

First Peter 2:11–17 does not present the gospel, but assumes and builds on the message that we are "redeemed from the empty way of life handed down to you from your forefathers . . . with the precious blood of Christ" (1:18–19). Because we belong to Jesus, because he is our Judge and King, Redeemer and Lawgiver, we have become "aliens and strangers in the world" (2:11). We belong to a Ruler who transcends this world's rulers and follow him, so we inevitably experience a partial alienation from this age. Because Jesus is Lord (1:3), all earthly lords take second place.

Nonetheless, we must live beautiful lives "among the pagans" (1 Peter 2:11–12). To fashion a beautiful life, we must know how to live as free men operating in a hierarchical world (2:13–17). Thus, 1 Peter 2:11–17 reviews the *status* of believers (2:11–12) and then moves to their right *conduct* in this world—a way of life that is consistent with our identity and follows our convictions (2:13–17).

Never Fully at Home

Given his status as apostle and elder, Peter could have commanded his readers to behave a certain way. Instead, he appeals to them as "dear friends," saying, "I urge you, as aliens and strangers in the world, to abstain from sinful desires, which war against your soul" (1 Peter 2:11). The "alien" is a long-term resident, someone not born where he now lives, yet someone who has lived in the new land for a long season. The "stranger," by contrast, is a temporary resident, the traveler whose stay is shorter.[1] But both terms suggest that believers belong *elsewhere*. When Peter calls disciples "aliens and strangers," he means that we are never fully at home in this world. Strangers have no permanent residence. Aliens rarely hold positions of power and privilege. Indeed, there is no sign that Peter's people ever held special rank.

Peter's point challenges a certain conception of the relationship between Christians and their cultures. Decades ago, Richard Niebuhr categorized the dispositions that Christians can take toward their surrounding society and declared, with some justification, that the Calvinist's posture is "Christ transforms culture."[2] That is, we neither flee nor avoid "the world." We believe we should critique the culture, engage the culture, and even "make culture."[3] Calvinists take some pride in affirming their confidence, to use Richard Niebuhr's phrase, that "Christ transforms culture." Those who believe that Christians can transform culture will not boycott "the world." We balk at talk of alienation and powerlessness. We detect and reject whiffs of world-negating thought. We aim to engage and change the culture by maintaining a faithful presence in it.[4]

But Peter's statement that we are aliens and exiles summons us to trace the Bible's view of culture and to assess our confident approach to the culture. In the beginning, Adam was perfectly at ease in this world, since the Lord shaped the world to be humanity's perfect home. And the day will come when heaven and earth will be one in "the life *after* the life after death."[5] But between creation and the fall, harmony disappears. Whether the lost *feel* alienated or not, they *are* alienated from God's world. The redeemed, Paul explains, put off the "former way of life" (Eph. 4:22). As

---

1. Peter H. Davids, *The First Epistle of Peter* (Grand Rapids: Eerdmans, 1990), 95.

2. H. Richard Niebuhr, *Christ and Culture* (1951; repr., New York: Harper & Row, 1975).

3. Andy Crouch, *Culture Making: Recovering Our Creative Calling* (Downers Grove, IL: InterVarsity Press, 2008).

4. James Davison Hunter, *To Change the World: The Irony, Tragedy, and Possibility of Christianity in the Late Modern World* (New York, Oxford University Press, 2010), 243–52.

5. N. T. Wright, *Surprised by Joy: Rethinking Heaven, the Resurrection, and the Mission of the Church* (New York: HarperOne, 2008), 148–52.

a result, according to Peter, we will inevitably be at odds with family and neighbors who remain committed to idolatry, sensuality, and drunkenness (1 Peter 4:1–5).

Believers therefore experience at least a *partial* alienation from *their* age, whatever that age may be. Abraham said that he was "an alien and a stranger" in Canaan (Gen. 23:4). Likewise, Peter's people are "aliens" because they live (literally) "among the nations" (1 Peter 2:12). This is a striking statement. We wonder how Peter's people can be aliens *among* the Gentiles, given that they *are* Gentiles and had been fully immersed in the Gentile life until they came to faith. Yet when they trusted in Jesus, they belonged to a new nation, one without borders, one determined by neither race nor nationality. Believers are no longer part of "the nations"; we are God's people, God's nation (2:9).

Because we are aliens, we often feel ill at ease in our own culture. We walk into a conversation, read a piece on a new trend, and find ourselves amazed at what we hear or read. We watch a popular movie that, to our surprise, suddenly turns sordid or debauched and wonder, "Who thought people would enjoy this? How can it be that they were right, that masses of people would come to this and approve it?" We hear a degrading joke and marvel, "What kind of person could find this funny?" We sometimes ask, "Is this really my land, my culture?"

Notice, however, that Peter advocates neither despair nor flight. After a disappointing election result, Americans utter empty threats about moving to Canada or Tahiti. But no, we are not moving to Canada, because Canada is no better than the United States. And we're certainly not going to Fiji, Tahiti, or any other island in French Polynesia. The islands are too far away, the climate is too hot, and (most importantly) even if the pollutions there are *different*, they are no *lighter*.

Peter proposes two responses to the challenge of life in a world that first tempts to seduce us and then mocks those who resist its lures: first, we *fight*; second, we *live beautifully*.

Ready for a Battle

First, then, Peter urges us, as aliens and strangers, "to abstain from the passions of the flesh, which wage war against your soul" (1 Peter 2:11 ESV). As aliens, we strive to abstain from the sinful paths that our culture presents. Indeed, each society panders to certain "sinful desires," presenting certain sins as plausible and easily indulged. The disciple both abstains from them and fights them, because they battle against us.

In his autobiography, Benjamin Franklin writes that he was a vegetarian, refusing all animal flesh, for a while in his youth. Then one day he was on a boat. The wind died away. With nothing else to do, the sailors decided to cast for fish and caught a number of cod. Soon the fish were frying, and the delicious smell, coupled with his rising hunger, tempted Franklin. Franklin's vegetarian principles and physical desires briefly battled for control of his will. Then he noticed that as the fishermen prepared the fish, they found smaller fish in the bellies of some of the cod. Therefore, he reasoned this way: If fish eat one another, why can't people eat fish? Satisfied with his logic, Franklin ate some fish, adding, "So convenient a thing is it to be a reasonable creature, since it enables one to find or make a reason for everything one has a mind to do."[6] Franklin lived by this principle in his private life, deftly finding a reason or excuse for anything he wanted to do. Sadly, this kind of rationalization is common to mankind, not just Franklin.

But disciples aim neither to rationalize self-indulgence nor to readily acquiesce to temptation. We wage war against the flesh because it wages war against us.

It behooves us to define what both Peter and Paul call the "passions of the flesh" (1 Peter 2:11 ESV). Paul, using the same language, lists fifteen "desires" or "works of the flesh" in Galatians 5. He starts with sexual immorality and debauchery and ends with drunkenness and orgies, yet the bulk of the list looks more like sins of mind, will, and emotions: idolatry, hatred, discord, dissension, jealousy, rage, and selfish ambition (Gal. 5:19–21). Thus, we commit sins of the flesh with all our faculties, physical or mental. Therefore, while we resist physical lusts, we also wage war against idolatry, discord, rage, selfish ambition, and even sins such as despair. Peter knew his culture was corrupt, but *he never let his people blame the culture for their problems.* There are evil desires in us (James 4:1–3). Therefore, we must "abstain from sinful desires," whether they be physical or spiritual (1 Peter 2:11). Sins that begin in the mind and the body are equally evil, equally troublesome. The apostles suggest this by labeling both classes of sin the same way: "passions

6. Benjamin Franklin, *Autobiography* (New York: Henry Holt, 1916), 68.

of the flesh." And we wage war against all of them because all wound our spirit and grieve God's Spirit.

Since Peter says that the Christian life is like war, we should be prepared for battle. We should be ready to fight our misdirected physical appetites and to combat bad moods, evil ambitions, and unruly emotions. As they sit in the counselor's chair, pastors see too many people who are surprised by desires that entice them to forsake wedding vows and duties to children, friends, and relatives. We must endure in the contest with our unruly desires, lest we grow weary of battling sin and surrender to it.

For centuries, Christian leaders, including the Reformers and the Puritans, maintained that it is not beneficial for men and women to get whatever they want too readily. If we are always warm, comfortable, and well fed, we come to expect it. If we always have comfortable clothes and good food at regular intervals, it adds to our happiness in certain ways, but after a while we expect comfort and complain, perhaps bitterly, when it is missing.[7] Custodians and administrators expect complaints if the temperature in their buildings falls to 67° (freezing!) or rises to 73° (boiling!). How absurd. In days past, kings could not conceive such comforts; today, woe to all who let the temperature escape our notion of the comfort range. Too much ease makes us soft and selfish. In his album of that name, David Byrne (of Talking Heads) said that we need some "sand in the Vaseline." It might make us tougher and more prepared for battle, even with sin.

Leading a Beautiful Life

A good, holy life is desirable *intrinsically*, for its own sake. We should also be holy because God is holy (1 Peter 1:16). But Peter also thinks of the good life *instrumentally*: "Keep your conduct among the Gentiles honorable so that whenever [or *in case*] they speak against you as evildoers, they may see your good deeds and glorify God on the day of visitation" (2:12 ESV).[8]

7. Joel Kupperman, *Six Myths about the Good Life: Thinking about What Has Value* (Indianapolis: Hackett, 2006), 16–19.

8. This is the ESV, except for the term *whenever*. The phrase *hina en hō katalalousin humōn* can be rendered several ways. If we read it temporally, then "*when* they slander"; if concessively, then "*although* they slander"; if conditionally, then "*if* they slander." But if in the phrase *hina en hō* we give the relative pronoun its weight, the translation must be "in a case in which" or "whenever." See J. Ramsey Michaels, *1 Peter*, Word Biblical Commentary 49 (Nashville: Thomas Nelson, 1988), 117; J. N. D. Kelly, *A Commentary on the Epistles of Peter and Jude* (New York: Harper & Row, 1969), 105;

When we lead a beautiful life among secular people, we can anticipate a positive result, at least occasionally. In chapter 3, Peter teaches that pagan men "may be won over without talk by the behavior of their wives" (3:1, 4–5).

But Peter, knowing that slander "is always a favored weapon of persecutors," expects that pagans will commonly (not constantly) vilify Christians.[9] Whenever pagans do resort to slander, the believer counters with good deeds, a life so attractive that the pagans will at least glorify God for it one day—on the day of visitation. This is a dense statement, and several subpoints merit notice.

First, Peter expects us to stay in this world, living "among the pagans" (1 Peter 2:12a). We may be strangers in this world, but we don't flee from it.

Second, Peter says that "the pagans . . . accuse you of doing wrong" (1 Peter 2:12), rightly assuming that Christians would often be slandered. Tacitus and Suetonius were leading Roman historians who wrote around A.D. 100. Tacitus said that Christians were "loathed for their vices." Nero blamed Christians for the great fire of Rome because they were "hated for their abominations" and adhered to a "pernicious superstition." After the fire, Christians were arrested and slain "not so much on the count of arson as for hatred of the human race."[10] Suetonius stated that Nero punished Christians as a sect professing a new and impious "superstition."[11] Their crimes? Some accused them of cannibalism, in a pernicious, possibly willful misconstrual of the Lord's Supper. The charge of "hatred of the human race" grew from their refusal to join in worshiping the emperor or local patron deities. We would simply say that they refused to compromise their faith. But if refusal to worship false gods is hatred of humanity, then false charges are inevitable.

Third, however, the believer must live so well that the pagan can make no valid accusations. An excellent life shines as an alternative to pagan ways. The antidote is (literally) a *beautiful* way of life. The Greek behind the phrase "live such good lives" in 1 Peter 2:12 is literally "having a beau-

---

Max Zerwick, *Grammatical Analysis of the Greek New Testament*, 3rd ed. (Rome: Editrice Pontificio Istituto Biblico, 1988), 707.

9. C. E. B. Cranfield, *I & II Peter and Jude* (London: SCM Press, 1960), 73.

10. Tacitus, *The Annals*, trans. John Jackson (Cambridge, MA: Harvard University Press, 1962), 4:283–85 (bk. 15, para. 44).

11. Suetonius, "Nero," in *The Twelve Caesars*, trans. Robert Graves (Baltimore: Penguin, 1962), 217 (para. 16).

tiful lifestyle." Peter's term for *good* (*kalos*) typically means "beautiful" or "attractive," rather than "morally good" (for moral goodness, the New Testament typically uses *agathos*). And his word for *life* is not the common *bios* or *zōe* but *anastrophē*, which denotes a way of life.[12] The Christian life entails more than law-keeping. It is a way of life, a style that slowly attracts people to its beauty.

Christians should have a beautiful life. Such a lifestyle might include a good supply of social graces, since kindness and politeness can be tokens of genuine love, not mere social conventions. But the beautiful life transcends law, personality, and manners. Secular friends might notice that we have a good time and laugh hard without needing alcohol. At a restaurant, our server hears us talking about our faith; she also notices that we treat her with dignity and leave a generous tip. There is a beauty in the way in which some godly women always seem to have a friendly meal for the hungry and a soft bed for the weary. There is a beauty in the life-affirming response that so many Christians have when they learn that their unborn child has Down syndrome. Medical personnel often offer such parents a genetic counselor who presents "options." At such times, we are glad to be aliens. We belong to another homeland, one that has another code, a code that extends love to every unborn child. All these things are beautiful, although we might not recognize it, since our style is often more visible to others than it is to us.

At best, we perform acts of kindness and grace automatically, just as we automatically make the turns on the familiar road heading home. These habits seem to be a factor in the happy surprises that await us on the day of the Lord. Then Jesus will bless his people, saying, "Come, . . . take your inheritance, the kingdom prepared for you . . . . For I was hungry and you gave me something to eat, I was thirsty and you gave me something to drink." God's people will wonder, "When did we do these things?" We will not remember because they became our way of life. We fed the hungry as a matter of course (Matt. 25:34–39).

Jesus points out that this lifestyle is the result of our union with him. The life he gives becomes "a spring of water welling up to eternal life" (John 4:14; cf. John 15). Paul says that these changes are also the fruit of the Spirit.

---

12. The word *anastrophē* is a Petrine favorite. Eight of its thirteen uses in the New Testament are in 1–2 Peter.

According to Peter, a beautiful life is also the result of our battle against sin (1 Peter 2:11).

A noble life can inspire others by giving them a model of righteousness that incarnates God's wisdom (James 3:13). Peter promises that our good life will be recognized, even if not in this life. The pagans may glorify God for us "on the day he visits us" (or, literally, "the day of inspection"), that is, judgment day (1 Peter 2:12). Then the Lord will review mankind and reveal all that we have done and all that it means. The pagans *might* glorify God for the beautiful lives of Jesus' disciples before then, but at least it *will* happen on the last day.

A SOBER VIEW OF CULTURE

Since we are "aliens and strangers in the world" (1 Peter 2:11), we cannot fully approve the triumphalistic-sounding motto "Christ transforms culture" without caveats. Calvinists do rightly stress the lordship of Christ over all of life. Fallen as our culture is, we prefer to critique it rather than condemn it. We prefer to engage it and to transform it if we can, rather than flee from it or accommodate ourselves to it. In *Culture Making*, Andy Crouch persuasively argues that cultural engagement is more than criticism of secular worldviews. Worldviews must be embodied in things as hard to pin down as language and high art, and in concrete things such as houses.[13] Historically, the Reformed view of culture is optimistic.

But Peter's comments, in 1 Peter 2:11–12 and later in 4:4–6, should adjust our view. He warns against too much optimism and too much familiarity with the world. This world can be an implacable foe, steadfastly opposed to the influence of Christ. We will never fit perfectly in this age. We cannot laugh at some jokes, cannot enjoy some parties, cannot take some books seriously. We may never fully agree about what is funny, what constitutes a good topic of conversation, and what counts as a good argument. Peter, writing during a time of persecution, may see this better than we do. We want our light to shine, but we must accept that some do not want to see it. So, then, our goal is to live a good life *whether any human recognizes it or not*. The great English architect Christopher Wren operated on this prin-

---

13. Crouch, *Culture Making*, 53–64. On possible approaches to culture, see 78–98.

ciple. He had his workmen polish the back of the heads of the sculptures that ornamented a great cathedral. Someone asked him, "Why all this work for something that no one will ever see?" Wren answered, "God will see it."

THE LIFE OF A RESIDENT[14]

Because the Christian is a pilgrim, he will never be fully at home in this world. Yet we do reside here, and what we do matters. Therefore, Peter tells disciples how to conduct ourselves in public: "Submit yourselves for the Lord's sake to every authority instituted among men: whether to the king, as the supreme authority, or to governors, who are sent by him to punish those who do wrong and to commend those who do right" (1 Peter 2:13–14).

A Resident's First Duty: Submission to His Governors

We submit to authority for God's sake. He ordains this world's authorities, so we should submit to the *human authorities* that he created. We submit to *all* authorities: first to the king or emperor, for he is the supreme authority, from whom (theoretically) all authority flows (cf. Matt. 8:8–9).[15] After the king, we submit to governors, that is, to the array of local authorities, procurators, proconsuls, and lesser magistrates. Every nation has its supreme and lesser governors, and we must submit to them, even to local commissioners who rule roads, commerce, the military, markets, even (today) parking and sewers. The authorities that rule us most directly are local. These are the authorities at work, in schools, in the family, even in the church.

In democracies, it is tempting to balk at this, especially if our candidate lost the vote. But everyone can submit "for the Lord's sake" (1 Peter 2:13). At a minimum, we respect the office and pray for the governor. When Peter wrote this, Nero was emperor. Few had *less* merit than he. Beyond his cruelties, he ruled poorly for most of his reign and, more than most other emperors, claimed deity. If Peter could command the church to submit to Nero, we can certainly submit if our governor takes a stand that we consider erroneous.

14. It is tempting to use the word *citizen*, for it is a nobler term than the pedestrian *resident*. But the term *citizen* implies a level of privilege and a sense of belonging that defies Peter's intent. We are outsiders, not insiders.

15. The Greek is *basileus*, "king," but it meant "the emperor" in Peter's setting.

Submit is an ugly word for many of us. In our parlance, we submit when we have been dominated, even humiliated. In certain forms of combative athletics, a wrestler or fighter submits when someone has him in a hold that would allow the winner to injure him.

But *submit* did not have sharply negative connotations in biblical times and languages. *Submit* (*hupotassō*) does convey the idea that someone in authority can give orders that others ought to follow, but there are differences. *Submit* can be a milder term than *obey*. To *submit* means to arrange one's life under the authority or guidance of another. That is, a person who submits still has some freedom because he or she decides how to follow the leader.[16]

In Scripture, the believer's submission to human authorities is always partial and proximate; blind obedience is never required. Early Christians practiced civil disobedience "when the demands of society" threatened to override "the demands of the Lord."[17] The Christian is always, in principle, ready to rebel, ready to say No in the face of a wicked command, for "we must obey God rather than men" (Acts 5:29).[18] Wolfgang Schrage summarized our position, saying that Christians "are free with respect to the authorities, and normally this freedom manifests itself in . . . submission and honor" (cf. 1 Cor. 7:17–24).[19]

A Governor's Duty to His People

Governors have a twofold task: "to punish those who do evil and to praise those who do good" (1 Peter 2:14 ESV). It is universally accepted that the government must maintain public order by punishing crime. Even profoundly flawed governors promote order and "preserve some semblance of conformity to pagan standards of good, and that is better than chaos."[20] We might disagree with their methods, but governments do some good. There is criminal law in

16. Leonhard Goppelt, *A Commentary on 1 Peter*, trans. John E. Alsup (Grand Rapids: Eerdmans, 1993), 174–76; Scot McKnight, *1 Peter*, NIV Application Commentary (Grand Rapids: Zondervan, 1996), 143–45.

17. McKnight, *1 Peter*, 144.

18. For this reason, perceptive rulers always view Christians with concern, if not suspicion. They know that a Christian has an allegiance to something higher than the state and is, in principle, willing to suffer for that allegiance. See Conrad Russell, *The Causes of the English Civil War* (Oxford: Clarendon Press, 1990).

19. Wolfgang Schrage, *The Ethics of the New Testament*, trans. David Green (Philadelphia: Fortress, 1988), 278.

20. Davids, *1 Peter*, 100.

the Old Testament,[21] and Peter joins Paul in affirming that pagan governors have both a right and an obligation to punish misconduct (Rom. 13:1–4).

Although we pay little attention to it, authorities often do single out certain people for praise for special community service. Bruce Winter notes that epigraphic and literary evidence demonstrate that "not only did rulers praise and honour those who undertook good works which benefited the city, . . . they promised likewise to publicly honour others who would undertake similar benefactions in the future."[22] Peter says that it is right for authorities to praise what is good. Therefore, whether we have political, economic, scholastic, or familial authority, we should use it to commend proper behavior.

Other Scriptures mention the additional tasks of governors. They must defend their people from attack by hostile powers. They should abide by the laws of the land, for they should consider themselves one of the people (Deut. 17:14–20; contra 1 Kings 21).

Justice is "God's primary demand on human authorities."[23] They must judge fairly, shunning bribes, so that they may be impartial in their judgments. They must protect the rights and property of all, but especially of the poor, the needy, and the weak (Deut. 16:18–20; Ps. 72:1–4; Jer. 22:2–5).

Rulers must not become too fond of the privileges of their office, lest they betray their calling. Isaiah chastises judges who are better at mixing drinks than providing justice (Isa. 5:22–23). Jeremiah denounces King Shallum, son of Josiah, for building great houses and pursuing dishonest gain rather than administering justice (Jer. 22:13–17). Ezekiel flogs rapacious "shepherds" who attend the flock only to plunder it, while ignoring their wounds and hunger. Proverbs warns rulers of the somewhat milder problem of distraction:

It is not for kings . . . to drink wine,
 not for rulers to crave beer,
lest they drink and forget what the law decrees,
 and deprive all the oppressed of their rights. . . .

21. Christopher J. H. Wright, *Old Testament Ethics for the People of God* (Downers Grove, IL: InterVarsity Press, 2004), 289–92.

22. Bruce W. Winter, "The Public Honouring of Christian Benefactors, Romans 13:3–4 and 1 Peter 2:14–15," *Journal for the Study of the New Testament* 34 (1988): 87ff.; W. C. van Unnik, "A Classical Parallel to 1 Peter 2:14 and 20," *New Testament Studies* 2, 3 (1955–56): 198–202.

23. Wright, *Old Testament Ethics*, 269–75; the next two paragraphs follow Wright.

> Speak up for those who cannot speak for themselves,
>> for the rights of all who are destitute.
> Speak up and judge fairly;
>> defend the rights of the poor and needy. (Prov. 31:4–5, 8–9)

Failures notwithstanding, even flawed governors do much that is good. The threat of punishment of evil prevents anarchy. Governors defend a nation's borders, build roads, and promote public order. Even if we disapprove of a governor's goals or methods, even if a government is corrupt, we should respect it (1 Peter 2:17). In a democracy, political activity is a duty as well as a privilege. At a minimum, we vote in elections, carefully considering the candidates and the issues, comparing all to God's will.

The next verse, 1 Peter 2:15, summarizes the result of obedience to the previous commands: "For it is God's will that by doing good you should silence the ignorant talk of foolish men." Peter is well aware that believers might suffer because of persecution and false condemnation. Still, we do good as much as we can. This includes obedience to civil law (unless it requires sin), but there is more. We should "do good" in ways small and large, from picking up trash to volunteering in homeless shelters. Peter knows that accusations will never finally disappear, but hopes that good deeds may silence the most ignorant and foolish slanders. If we live well enough, people simply refuse to believe the lies.

USING FREEDOM CORRECTLY

Peter anticipated that some of his readers would object that the demand of submission to human rulers vitiates the principle of the freedom that believers have in Christ. They might say, "But I am a free man, liberated by Jesus. How can I submit to human rule?" To this Peter replies, "Live as free men, but do not use your freedom as a cover-up for evil; live as servants of God" (1 Peter 2:16). We are free from sin, from the law, and from death, but that is no excuse for insubordination. The Christian is free from sin, but is the slave of God: "For he who was a slave when he was called by the Lord is the Lord's freedman; similarly, he who was a free man when he was called is Christ's slave" (1 Cor. 7:22; cf. Rom. 6:22). As Martin Luther observed, "A Christian is a perfectly free lord of all, subject to none. A Christian is a perfectly dutiful servant of all, subject to all."[24]

There are many ways to abuse freedom. In Peter's day, some wanted to rebel against Rome, an idea that was doomed to fail and lacks biblical warrant. Others simply wanted to follow their own ideas or desires. Some Corinthians adopted the slogan "All things are lawful for me" (1 Cor. 6:12a ESV). They considered themselves liberated from all laws and plunged into an array of sexual sins (1 Cor. 5–6). Paul retorted that even if, in some unusual sense, "all things are lawful," it is also true that "not everything is beneficial" (6:12b). Some "freedoms" hurt others. Some freedoms enslave the one who exercises that freedom (6:12c). We must use our freedom correctly: to love neighbors and to serve God. He brought us out of slavery for something more than self-indulgence.

THE DUTY OF HONOR: LOVE THE BROTHERS, FEAR GOD, HONOR THE KING

Finally, Peter says, "Show proper respect to everyone: Love the brotherhood of believers, fear God, honor the king" (1 Peter 2:17). Thus he reiterates the summons to honor the emperor and governors, but rearranges it as four commands that govern many relationships. Structurally, honor comes first and last, while love and respect (literally, *fear*) stand in the middle. (Thus the commands have the simplest chiastic structure: ABBA. The first and last commands are cooler, commanding honor. The interior imperatives are warmer, requiring love and fear.) First, we "honor all men," treat everyone with a respect they deserve, if only because they bear God's image. Second, we love the brothers, showing affection and offering aid to all within the family of faith. Third, we fear God. This is affectionate fear, not cringing or servile terror, that we owe to a person we respect. We revere the Almighty. Fourth, we honor the king—or the emperor, president, or prime minister.

The particular way we apply the political commands will vary from nation to nation. If we live in an autocratic nation, the duties of submission and honor are clear enough. Today, many Christians live in democracies where submission and honor take gentler forms because of the nature of our form

24. Martin Luther, *Martin Luther's Basic Theological Writings*, ed. Timothy Lull and William Russell (Minneapolis: Augsburg Fortress, 2005), 393.

of government. If the constitution and the authorities tell us that we have a right and duty to choose our leaders by examining the qualities of the candidates and the content of their policies, then it is right for us to choose. If our critical analysis leads us to reject a governor's policies, we should vote him (or her) out of office. But we must still honor that authority, even while we protest or vote against it.

In a democracy, governors themselves say that we need not adopt every policy or yield to every government plan. We can resist. Civil disobedience is even an option, although we must bear the consequences of rebellion. Indeed, our governments often invite us to get involved, individually and collectively. This is a right that Peter's poor and powerless people never enjoyed, a right that should increase our desire to honor our governors. Sadly, in democracies, too many people (even Christians) take pleasure in the harshest criticism of the authorities.

Our political order allows, even recommends, candid disagreements, especially when great issues of the economy and justice, war and peace, life and death, are debated. But we must disagree honorably, respectfully. We may think of Martin Luther King's protests against racism and segregation. His people ignored some laws, including laws about who sits where on a bus. Rallies swelled to vast numbers, but the protests were nonviolent and respected the authorities even as they opposed those same authorities. We, too, can speak and work to reform the ills of our society, remaining peaceful, loving our foes through accurate critique and respectful talk.

Meanwhile, we should remember that the greatest forces are not political and economic but personal, mental, and spiritual. For that reason, the church of Christ is a force in this world, even if we never fully belong here. Better yet, we are a force precisely because we have a dual citizenship. So let us give honor, respect, justice to all, always submitting to the Lord Jesus first, and to every human authority as we then can. In this way we silence slanderers, live as servants of God, and honor the King of kings, even Jesus.

8

A Life Shaped by the Crucified Christ

1 Peter 2:18—25

Slaves, submit yourselves to your masters with all respect,
not only to those who are good and considerate, but also to
those who are harsh. For it is commendable if a man bears up
under the pain of unjust suffering because he is conscious of
God. . . . To this you were called, because Christ suffered for
you, leaving you an example, that you should follow in his steps.
(1 Peter 2:18–19, 21)

rom 1 Peter 2:11 to 4:11, the apostle Peter constantly instructs the faithful in their social obligations. Peter insists on giving this sustained attention for both *pragmatic* and *intrinsic* reasons. Pragmatically, his people were a tiny and nearly defenseless minority, a group of aliens and exiles in their own culture (2:11–12). Further, a pagan convert to the faith found that his contemporaries were surprised at his departure from their way of life and maligned him for it (4:1–6). So Peter foresaw that believers would be increasingly exposed to persecution in coming days and wanted to help them to minimize their exposure to trouble (3:10–17; 4:12–16). Perhaps that is part of the reason why Peter tells his people to submit to some authority five times in just thirty-five verses (2:13, 18; 3:1, 5, 22). But the call to submit is more than a survival strategy. God has woven authority structures all through society, indeed through all creation, and we needlessly harm ourselves and miss the blessing of walking in his ways if we ignore those structures. Social ethics are essential both to Christian living and to the cause of Christ. If a fleet is about to sail, the sailors need to know how to avoid bumping into each other.[1] Peter's social instruction enhances both the public reputation and the inner peace of the church.

Peter's social teaching emphasizes submission to masters and governors. Because Peter's people were aliens in their own culture and because they refused to worship the emperor, it was imperative that they submit to governing authorities wherever they were. Thus, they could "silence the ignorant talk" of their accusers (1 Peter 2:11–17). Still, apart from the social benefits, it is intrinsically good to yield to the authority that God establishes, "for he is God's servant to do you good" (Rom. 13:1, 4).

THE DUTY OF A CHRISTIAN SERVANT

After describing the social obligations of all disciples in 1 Peter 2:11–17, Peter commands, "Slaves, submit yourselves to your masters with all respect, not only to those who are good and considerate, but also to those who are harsh" (2:18). This is necessary "because Christ suffered for you, leaving you an example, that you should follow in his steps" (2:21).

In order to apply Peter's message, we need to know the status of slaves in the empire. Their life differed both from that of ordinary laborers today and from that of the slaves in the Americas in prior days. Roman slavery was not race-based. Slaves did not look, talk, or dress in a distinct way. Most slaves were poor, but almost everyone was poor.

The term translated "slaves" in 1 Peter 2:18 denotes *household* slaves.[2] There were several kinds of slaves in the empire. People became slaves through war, poverty, or birth to enslaved parents. Slaves could be well educated. A slave might be a doctor, teacher, shipbuilder, or even city trea-

---

1. Peter Kreeft, *Three Philosophies of Life* (San Francisco: Ignatius Press, 1989), 17.
2. First Peter 2:18 uses *oiketēs*, the term for household slaves, not *doulos*, the generic term for slaves.

surer.[3] But nobler tasks were exceptional. Most were household slaves, and their lot varied with the status and character of their masters and mistresses. Field slaves worked hard, and house slaves lacked freedom.

American slavery was worse than Roman slavery in most ways. Roman slaves could own property and follow their traditions. Although a slave's life expectancy was short, many slaves gained their freedom eventually.[4] American slavery was race-based, had limited paths to freedom, and rested on kidnapping, which is a sin—and a capital crime in Moses' law (Ex. 21:16; Deut. 24:7). While the Mosaic law tolerated slavery, it regulated potential abuses. For example, if a master so struck a slave as to cause major injury, the slave went free (Ex. 21:26). The law also had several paths to manumission. For example, all slaves normally went free every seventh calendar year (Deut. 15:12–18). Roman slaves also had several paths to freedom.

Still, the life of a slave was difficult. Aristotle opined that slaves were inferior by nature. Since they were unable to govern themselves, Aristotle claimed, they were better off under a master, just as domestic cattle were better off than wild cattle. Further, he said, it was impossible to mistreat a slave, because slaves were mere property.[5] This was the consensus, although Seneca observed that men "of distinguished birth" sometimes became slaves through war. Social rank, he said, "is only a robe that clothes us." So someone could have slave status while "his soul . . . may be that of a free man."[6] But Seneca was the exception.

Legally speaking, slaves were not persons. They had virtually no rights. A slave was the *property* of his or her master. Therefore, a master could sell a slave at will, separating him or her from family and home. People said that "a slave is a living possession," a "talking tool," and "property with a soul."[7]

---

3. In Matthew 25:14–15, a master entrusts one to five talents to his slaves. One talent equaled twenty years' wages.

4. S. Scott Bartchy, *Mallon Chrēsai: First-Century Slavery and the Interpretation of 1 Corinthians 7:21* (Missoula, MT: Society of Biblical Literature for the Seminar on Paul, 1973), 66.

5. Aristotle, *Politics*, in *The Basic Works of Aristotle* (New York: 1941), 1131–35 (bk. 1, chaps. 4–6).

6. Seneca, "Epistle 47, On Master and Slave," in *Moral Epistles* (*Epistulae Morales*), trans. Richard Gummere (Cambridge, MA: Harvard University Press, 1967), 1:307, 311.

7. Richard Horsley, "Slavery in the Greco-Roman World," *Semeia* 84 (2001): 41–55; M. I. Finley, *Ancient Slavery and Modern Ideology* (New York: Viking Press, 1980), 93–122; P. R. C. Weaver, *Familia Caesaris: A Social Study of the Emperor's Freedmen and Slaves* (Cambridge: Cambridge University Press, 1972), 205.

A household slave could hope for economic security, decent treatment, and a position as a leading slave in a great house.[8] But a slave's body belonged to his master. Demosthenes reported that slaves were "answerable in their body for all offences while freemen . . . can protect their persons." That is, slaves were liable to a beating for all offenses.[9] A master or mistress could take any slave, male or female, to gratify the owner's sexual desires. How often this happened, we don't know.[10] We do know that some slaves endured terrible privation to buy their freedom.[11]

Given that slaves were barely regarded as human, we see that Peter elevates slaves simply by addressing them. Although some slaves were literate, most Greco-Roman writers thought it pointless to address them, since they didn't see them as responsible moral agents.

Clearly, the status of contemporary employees is not the same as that of Roman slaves. Today's workers can feel trapped by social and economic forces. While we should not minimize the resulting distress, our rights and freedoms keep us far from slavery. Nonetheless, millions are still enslaved throughout the world today. Most live in lawless countries, but they are scattered across the continents. Further, some people live in situations akin to slavery, even in the West. Children who suffer hidden abuse at the hands of violent parents and immigrants with no knowledge of their rights are like slaves if they are defenseless, powerless, and trapped.

Peter's first word to slaves is: "Slaves, submit yourselves to your masters with all respect" (1 Peter 2:18). Peter is not endorsing or blessing slavery. Rather, he tells believing slaves how to live within a pervasive, entrenched institution. Peter commands slaves to submit "with . . . respect"—literally,

8. Finley, *Ancient Slavery*, 101–7; Dale B. Martin, *Slavery as Salvation: The Metaphor of Slavery in Pauline Christianity* (New Haven, CT: Yale University Press, 1990); Bruce Winter, "St. Paul as a Critic of Roman Slavery in 1 Corinthians 7:21–23," *Pauleia* 4 (1998): 1–20. A curious indicator of this appears in the name *Secundus* in a list of men who accompanied Paul in Acts 20:4. *Secundus* was a popular slave name that essentially meant "second-ranking slave." The assumption is that it was an honored position in a large household.
9. Demosthenes, "Against Androtion," trans. J. H. Vince, in *Demosthenes III*, Loeb Classical Library (Cambridge, MA: Harvard University Press, 1935), 22.55; Horsley, "Slavery," 41–44.
10. Bruce W. Winter, *After Paul Left Corinth: The Influence of Secular Ethics and Social Change* (Grand Rapids: Eerdmans, 2001), 110–13, 122–23; Albert A. Bell, *A Guide to the New Testament World* (Scottsdale, PA: Herald Press, 1994), 234–37; Horsley, "Slavery," 44–45. Winter notes two limits on sexual activity with slaves: (1) social disapproval of excess and (2) a consensus that a free man must not be passive in homosexual acts with a slave.
11. Horsley, "Slavery," 48–52. Winter paints a less bitter portrait of slavery in "St. Paul as a Critic."

"with fear" or awe. Ultimately, the believer fears God, not man, Peter notes (3:14–15). But God appoints all human authorities, so we obey them for God's sake. Our respect for masters is ultimately respect for God, who ordains and commissions all authorities (Rom. 13:1–4).

Even if there is no precise analogy between slaves and free workers today, Peter's instructions do apply to all who serve harsh or perverse leaders. Evil authorities are not slave masters, but they can give harmful orders and can punish all who violate them. We should think this way: If God can command a harder thing, that slaves respectfully submit to harsh masters, surely we can submit to harsh superiors, since their power is more modest.

Nonetheless, we find the command daunting, possibly without fully realizing why. If we have an angry or unjust supervisor and feel trapped by him, we are tempted to return anger for anger, disrespect for disrespect. Yet Peter commands believers to submit, with respect, to difficult leaders at home and at work. We can extend the principle to schools, churches, and governments. We obey if we can. If we must disobey, we do so humbly and respectfully, and we bear the consequences (Acts 5:17–33).

Most citizens of Western countries resist Peter's teaching. We treasure our independence, criticize our authorities, and honor our rebels. We don't like to submit to leaders unless we think they are worthy.

In college I worked at a resort hotel as an assistant to "George," who supervised all food operations. George was a hardworking, shrewd, witty, but flawed man. He could be loud and critical, he was faintly awkward, his clothes were out of style, and he played favorites. He divided the world into two camps: his friends and his enemies, whom he regarded with constant suspicion. The chief baker was an enemy. Nothing she did pleased him. One day she made apple cinnamon pancakes. George sent me to requisition a taste of the batter. He took a spoonful. "Not sweet enough," he thundered. "Send it back." I hustled the batter to the baker, then brought a taste of the sweetened concoction to him. "Too sweet," he fumed. "Send it back." The third time, the baker got an idea. She noisily shook empty containers over the batter, waved her spoon around, and returned the batter unchanged. The boss sampled it again. "Perfect," he beamed. "That woman wouldn't do anything right if I didn't keep my eye on her."

George was competent and he treated most people fairly. His misdeeds were minor indignities and irritations, not grievous wounds. But the students judged him uncool and the pros judged him bombastic. Because of these petty flaws, people bristled at the thought of giving him respect. They seemed to think, "If I had his job, I'd treat people better and everyone would like work better."

The root of discontent with people like George is a concept of work that is grounded in our culture, not Scripture. We believe work should offer more than tasks and income. We think work should be a place where we grow, find fulfillment, and find and develop our gifts, so that we flourish as individuals. In his monograph, *Vocation*, Douglas Schuurman writes that college students view work as "a realm for self-fulfillment" and "optimal self-actualization." By working hard and consulting career experts, students think they should find fulfilling careers.[12] As a result, they think they will never work for someone like George.

Schuurman calls this a myth that applies, at best, to people who already have the advantages of native intelligence, a network of supportive adults, and access to an elite education (by world standards). The middle and lower classes rarely have such opportunities, even in the West. In recent years (at this writing), the most common occupations in America are cashier and retail sales assistant. Neither post offers especially fulfilling work. Even upper-class adults are prone to exaggerate their options. Clearly, we should reconsider our concept of vocation.

THE GIFTS AND CALLING OF A CHRISTIAN WORKER

All this does not mean that work should be miserable. God gives gifts to his people, and when we serve others out of the capacities that he has given us, we can expect to take pleasure in using our skills. Romans 12:6–8 tells us to exercise our gifts freely and cheerfully, which seems to imply joy in our work.

But Peter and Paul, along with Martin Luther and John Calvin, see our work, as well as our family relationships, "as domains not freely chosen, but providentially assigned to each person." Sociologists call this *ascriptivism*. That is, a person's significant social relations are not primarily matters of "individual choice, but are assigned based largely on class, parentage, and

12. Douglas J. Schuurman, *Vocation: Discerning Our Callings in Life* (Grand Rapids: Eerdmans, 2004), 117–21.

gender. *One does not so much choose one's callings as discover oneself within their network."* Vocation is not so much about choosing the right spouse, work, friends, and residence as it is seeing the web of our relationships "as divinely assigned places to serve God and neighbor."[13]

Of course, God still grants us freedom to escape oppression, if we can. Paul told slaves, "If you can gain your freedom, do so" (1 Cor. 7:21). Jesus told his disciples, "When you are persecuted in one place, flee to another" (Matt. 10:23). But sometimes we can't move. Then, Peter says, "submit yourselves to your masters with all respect" (1 Peter 2:18). Each word is instructive.

First, everyone must *submit*. The concept of submission assumes that this world has God-given structures and authorities. We must organize our lives within those structures. Even if we suspect that our leaders are wrong, we should subordinate ourselves to legitimate commands. We should yield to the authority and defer to it.

The NIV, like some other translations, uses a verb and reflexive pronoun to translate a one-word Greek participle in the phrase "submit yourselves" in 1 Peter 2:18. The participle (*hupotassomenoi*) has the middle voice, which can be reflexive. The middle voice makes perfect sense in this case. It suggests that we act on ourselves: we tell ourselves to submit.[14] Regardless, our submission should be voluntary. We should *yield* to leaders, rather than making them force their will on us. We yield to people, laws, and institutions that have authority because the Lord placed them over us. He ordains the leaders, teachers, and parents who govern the world under him.

We submit *with respect*. When people feel trapped at work, they obey the boss because they need to keep their jobs. But respect is more than obedience. We should respect leaders *even when we disagree* with their decisions. We should respect and pray for political leaders even if we voted against them, disagree with their policies, and doubt that they can govern well.

The early English Puritans lived in a hierarchical society, under often-hostile bishops and kings. They reflected deeply on the duties of subordinates to flawed superiors. All agreed that leaders gain their authority through their God-given positions, not superior character or achievements.

---

13. Ibid., 117.
14. Nigel Turner, *Grammar of New Testament Greek* (Edinburgh: T. & T. Clark, 1963), 53–57. Yet some scholars see "submit yourselves" as overtranslation, since the middle voice generally lacked the full reflexive sense in New Testament usage.

William Perkins observed that master and servant may be equal in Christ, in the inner man, yet in the "civil order," masters rule and servants "must be subject."[15] Speaking of marriage, William Gouge said that the principle holds even if the husband was "a beggar" before marriage and is, after marriage, "a drunkard, a glutton, and a profane swaggerer." Even if the wife is sober, wealthy, and religious, she must respect her husband because of "the civil honor which God hath given unto him."[16] Further, her outward submission must be matched by an inward reverence. The mantle of authority for husbands, ministers, parents, and masters is bestowed by God, not earned, although a wise leader will strive to enhance his authority by using it wisely.[17]

The term *submit* (*hypotassō*) requires definition. *Submit* ordinarily means "to subject, subordinate, or bring under control" (Acts 19:35; Phil. 3:21; Heb. 2:5, 8). Yet to *submit* is not precisely to *obey*. To obey is to do what is commanded, willingly or not. Submission can also be willing or unwilling, but the concept can be more nuanced. In Paul's teaching, children obey their parents, and slaves obey their masters, but wives *submit* to their husbands (Eph. 5:22; 6:1, 5; Col. 3:18–22). To submit, in that setting, entails more freedom or latitude than obedience. Submission can include freedom to arrange affairs under general directions or principles, not necessarily under precise commands. So wives have freedom to consider *how* to follow their husbands, especially since marriage is a close relationship that is essentially parity-based. A worker, similarly, may have freedom in the way he gets things done, even while fulfilling tasks given by the authority.

The word *submit* implicitly refers to authority structures. The Romans believed that authority structures stretch up and down in a chain. In the chain, lower authorities had to yield to higher ones, ending with the emperor and the gods above him; a Roman centurion expresses this concept in Matthew 8:8–9.

Scripture says that all authorities are answerable to God, and must therefore be disobeyed if their commands contradict his. Because no human authority is absolute, no summons to submit to it is absolute. If an authority

15. William Perkins, *Works* (Cambridge, 1616–18), 3:698.
16. William Gouge, *Of Domesticall Duties* (London, 1622), 272–77, 355, passim. See also Thomas Gataker, *Certaine Sermons* (London, 1635), 2:190.
17. Gouge, *Duties*, 273.

gives a wicked command, it must be refused. Peter himself made this point during a crisis in the first days of the church: "We must obey God rather than men!" (Acts 5:29). The call to submit always has this caveat: We obey the authorities unless they contradict God.

Nonetheless, rulers have real authority. Peter tells slaves to submit to masters. Elsewhere, Scripture commands all believers to submit to authorities. If the term *authority* (*exousia*) refers to humans, it typically has the nuance of *legitimate* rule (Rom. 13:1–3).[18] If we yield to authorities, we yield to rulers ordained by God. By contrast, we do not have to submit to every *power*, for a power can have brute strength—a gun, for example—and no legitimacy (Heb. 2:14). There is no moral obligation to bow to brute force.

Some people quickly ask, "So when is it time to rebel?" The question is common in nations born in rebellion against colonial powers and in nations that currently suffer oppression. People ask, "Did God really appoint *all* authorities?" Authorities and powers take their place by many means. Emperors claim power through conquest, intrigue, murder, and inheritance. A master might gain his place by inheritance, bribery, or merit. If an authority was hired or appointed, we can ask whether the decision was based on skill and training or favoritism.

But in the final analysis, the Lord appoints all authorities. He even has purposes for evil leaders. Consider the words of Daniel, who long served a flawed monarch: "The Most High is sovereign over the kingdoms of men and gives them to anyone he wishes and sets over them the lowliest of men" (Dan. 4:17). Paul stated, "He who rebels against the authority is rebelling against what God has instituted, and those who do so will bring judgment on themselves" (Rom. 13:2).

Calvin said that there is a magistrate who is "a father of his country, . . . [a] shepherd of his people, guardian of peace, protector of righteousness, and avenger of innocence—he who does not approve of such government must rightly be regarded as insane."[19] We must submit to deserving authorities. We should resist the inclination to second-guess everyone and everything. It is easy to criticize and hard to remember how readily we err.

18. The Greek term most often translated "authority" (*exousia*) refers to human authorities relatively rarely. It often refers to spiritual powers and authorities or to legal rights.

19. John Calvin, *Institutes of the Christian Religion*, trans. Ford Lewis Battles (Philadelphia: Westminster, 1960), 4.20.24.

Some authorities are careless, self-indulgent, and corrupt wastrels. These, too, are ordained by God. Speaking through the prophet Daniel, God told ruthless, egotistical Nebuchadnezzar, "The God of heaven has given you dominion and power and might and glory; in your hands he has placed mankind and the beasts of the field . . . . Wherever they live, he has made you ruler over them all" (Dan. 2:37–38; cf. 5:18–19).

Other Scriptures teach that there *is* a time to resist evil authorities. If possible, the Reformers knew, the righteous will not simply rebel, but ally themselves with other authorities, with "lesser magistrates," whether civil or ecclesiastical. If we must stand against "the fierce licentiousness of kings," we should do so not as private individuals, but through the authority of "magistrates of the people [who were] appointed to restrain the willfulness of kings."[20] Thus, the Christians who attempted to assassinate Hitler did so in allegiance with faithful German military leaders.[21] So there is a place for godly rebellion, but too many people are quick to doubt authorities and to declare that they have a right to rebel.

Peter declares, "It is commendable if a man bears up under the pain of unjust suffering because he is conscious of God" (1 Peter 2:19). The phrase "it is commendable" literally reads "this is grace." *Grace* here does not mean "unmerited favor," but "that which counts with God" and with which he is pleased. (Jesus said something similar in Luke 6:32–34. There the Greek word *grace* is usually translated "credit" [NIV, RSV, NASB].)[22]

No one likes to suffer unjustly. Still, the Lord *is* pleased when we endure unjust suffering, for it is a form of imitation of Christ. But there is no glory or praise if a slave endures punishment for doing evil: "How is it to your credit if you receive a beating for doing wrong and endure it?" (1 Peter 2:20a). Peter does not say that anyone *deserves* a beating. (Scripture tells masters that they should not threaten. If it is evil to *threaten* violence, surely actual blows are a greater evil [Eph. 6:9].) Peter is simply stating the obvious: We have no right to complain if we are punished for misdeeds. God is not

20. Ibid., 4.20.31.

21. Eric Metaxas, *Bonhoeffer: Pastor, Prophet, Martyr, Spy* (Nashville: Thomas Nelson, 2010), 380–500, passim.

22. J. Ramsey Michaels, *1 Peter*, Word Biblical Commentary 49 (Nashville: Thomas Nelson, 1988), 139; Frederick W. Danker, ed., *A Greek-English Lexicon of the New Testament and Other Early Christian Literature*, 3rd ed. (Chicago: University of Chicago Press, 2000), 1079, states in a note under the definition of *charis* that it can mean "that which brings someone (God's) favor."

impressed when we endure well-deserved punishment. It *is* praiseworthy if we, like Jesus, quietly endure injustice.

The Model of Christlike Service

The exceptional case of justified rebellion is not Peter's main concern. The Romans were already suspicious of Christians for refusing to worship the emperor. If Christians commonly rebelled, it would exacerbate the suspicion that all Christians were seditious. Beyond that, rebellion misses a vital lesson from Jesus' life.

According to Peter, slaves please God when they endure "unjust suffering" (1 Peter 2:19). Why? The believing slave did not live on naive hopes that his master would reform. Slaves follow the life and teaching of Jesus.

Slaves are to endure mistreatment: "To this you were called, because Christ suffered for you, leaving you an example, that you should follow in his steps. 'He committed no sin, and no deceit was found in his mouth'" (1 Peter 2:21–22). There are two lessons here. First, almost unbearably, Peter tells those who suffer abuse to follow Jesus' "example" or pattern, and to "follow in his steps."[23] We should walk in his very steps, as he silently bore unspeakable hatred and violence.

Second, Jesus is our example because he "committed no sin" (1 Peter 2:22). Peter lived with Jesus all day for three years. If Jesus had grabbed tasty morsels of fish for himself or exploded in frustration at his thickheaded disciples, Peter would have known. But Peter never saw Jesus stray in deed or word. He never got upset unjustly, never made a bad decision, never got a laugh at another person's expense. His proper self-interest was never tainted by selfishness. Echoing Psalm 34:13 and Isaiah 53:9, Peter says that no "deceit was found in his mouth" (1 Peter 2:22). So Jesus is holy even in that realm where holiness is most elusive for humans: in our speech (James 3:8).

Peter focuses on Jesus' exemplary suffering. Blind, vindictive authorities killed Jesus. Passersby joined in as they mocked and reviled him even as he suffered the most wretched death. Yet "when they hurled their insults at him, he did not retaliate; when he suffered, he made no threats. Instead, he entrusted himself to him who judges justly" (1 Peter 2:23). Jesus' patience

---

23. The word for "example," *hupogrammos*, refers to the properly formed letters that children trace as they learn to write. The word for "steps," *ichnos*, refers to footprints.

and calm in suffering is our model. There is no glory in calmly receiving *deserved* punishment, but there is glory in bearing insults silently and committing ourselves to the Father to judge and vindicate us. That is precisely what Jesus did and what we should aspire to do.

The Pharisees accused Jesus of serving the devil (Matt. 12:22–26). On the cross, Jesus suffered taunts: "He saved others, . . . but he can't save himself! . . . Let him come down now from the cross, and we will believe in him" (27:42). Yet he endured in silence, and entrusted himself to the Father to exonerate him.

The Greek verb translated "he entrusted himself" is *paradidōmi*. It most commonly means "hand over," and it is often used of Jesus. Strikingly, Jesus was handed over for ill again and again, but he handed himself over to the Father, for good:

- Judas handed Jesus over to the priests out of greed (Matt. 26:14–49).
- The priests handed Jesus over to Pilate out of envy and self-righteousness (Mark 15:10).
- Pilate handed him over to the soldiers out of cowardice (Matt. 27:26).
- On the cross, Jesus handed himself over to God for vindication as he endured the mockers' taunts (1 Peter 2:23) and anticipated his final vindication in the resurrection (Rom. 1:4).

For disciples, Jesus is the supreme example of the man who suffered patiently because of confidence in God. Like David, we receive thoughtless praise; like the Lord, we receive groundless scorn. Church leaders are criticized for sound decisions that we cannot fully defend, lest we reveal confidential matters. People condemn us for telling hard truths that people need, but do not wish, to hear. They blame us for failing to salvage a collapsing marriage. One pastor has said, "I spend half my time apologizing for words I never said and for actions I never took." There is a time to defend our reputation ("A good name is more desirable than great riches," Prov. 22:1). Yet we must also be willing to trust God the Judge for our vindication.

Let us notice that the imitation of Christ is a common New Testament theme. Some Protestants are wary of this. They fear that an emphasis on imitating Jesus' life might lead to neglect of his atoning death.[24] But Jesus repeatedly presented himself as an example, especially in his endurance of unjust suffering: "Remember the words I spoke to you: 'No servant is greater than his master.' If they persecuted me, they will persecute you also" (John 15:20; cf. Matt. 10:24–25; Luke 6:40). Paul tells us that we should love as Jesus loved (Eph. 5:2), forgive as he forgave (Eph. 4:32), and put others first as he did (Phil. 2:3–8). Peter instructs elders to be "examples to the flock" (1 Peter 5:3).

Yet Jesus is more than an example. Because we neither heed God's commands nor follow Jesus' example, we stand guilty before God. But, Peter says, Jesus "suffered for you" (1 Peter 2:21). More than that, "He himself bore our sins in his body on the tree, so that we might die to sins and live for righteousness; by his wounds you have been healed" (2:24).

Jesus' suffering is unique, for his death, and his death alone, is an atoning sacrifice, a penal substitution for sin. First Peter 2:24 quotes (and slightly rephrases) Isaiah 53, taking readers to the Old Testament prophecy that so clearly foretells Jesus' substitutionary sacrifice:

> But he was pierced for our transgressions,
>   he was crushed for our iniquities;
> the punishment that brought us peace was upon him,
>   and by his wounds we are healed.
> We all, like sheep, have gone astray,
>   each of us has turned to his own way;
> and the LORD has laid on him
>   the iniquity of us all. (Isa. 53:5–6)

Perhaps Jesus himself pointed the apostles to this passage after his resurrection, when he "opened their minds to understand the Scriptures" that foretold his suffering and resurrection (Luke 24:44–46 ESV). The Westminster Confession of Faith 11.3 summarizes: "Christ, by his obedience and death, did fully discharge the debt of all those that are thus justified, and did make a proper, real, and full satisfaction to his Father's justice in their behalf."

24. Daniel M. Doriani, *Putting the Truth to Work: The Theory and Practice of Biblical Application* (Phillipsburg, NJ: P&R Publishing, 2001), 201–6.

The concept of penal substitution is under attack today from liberals and even from so-called evangelicals. They claim that it is barbaric for God to punish sin by death. Worse, it is "cosmic child abuse" for God to kill his Son for the sins of others. These criticisms pervert both the problem of and the cure for sin. Sin leads to death intrinsically, not arbitrarily, because it separates us from God, the Author of life. Further, the principle of substitution is not strange or cruel; it is a common element of human life. Lawyers speak on behalf of others. Family members offer to pay each other's debts. And Jesus offered to pay our debt to God. God's justice requires that sin be punished, and Jesus chose—as an abused child cannot—to pay for our sins, as 1 Peter 2:24 makes clear.

Above all, Jesus is not an arbitrary substitute. There is a real relationship between us. If a member of my immediate family fails another person, it is sensible, not arbitrary, for me to pay what my spouse or child owes. Similarly, it is sensible, not arbitrary, for the traits of one family to be ascribed to another. For example, people regard me as a warm person, even if I might convey a touch of professorial detachment, because my wife is so warm. Similarly, people assume that she can answer almost any question about the Bible because she is united to me. By faith, the Christian is united to Jesus. Because of our relationship, it is sensible to ascribe his traits to us.

First Peter 2:21–24 is one highly structured, quasi-poetic sentence.[25] A series of dependent clauses explore the master concept: "Christ suffered for you" (2:21). Peter says that he "committed no sin . . . . When he was reviled, he did not revile in return . . . [but] bore our sins in his body" (2:22–24 ESV).

See how the passage interweaves truths about the *person* and the *work* of Christ. In his *person*, he is sinless and morally perfect. In his *work*, he atoned for sin. His work brings us salvation. Jesus is our trailblazer; he opened the path to life. By the same work, Jesus redeems us and sets us an example.

Everyone needs Jesus the Redeemer. Slaves—and all others who feel trapped by toxic masters—need Jesus' example. Whenever anyone in power makes life difficult, Jesus shows the way. He never returned insult for insult. He trusted God to vindicate him. There *is* a place for justice, and everyone

---

25. Structurally, verses 22–24 form three dependent clauses. The first word in each clause and in each verse is *hos*—roughly, "the one who." To paraphrase, Christ suffered for us, leaving an example, and "he is the one who committed no sin, and the one who, when reviled, did not revile in return, and the one who bore our sins."

deserves dignity and protection. But it can be futile to seek our rights. (If a public figure decided to defend himself from all false accusations, he might finally do nothing else.) Jesus' example teaches us that it can be best to absorb a blow. Imagine the result if we laid down our rights. Marriage disputes would fade. How can two people quarrel if both give up their rights and live a cruciform life? Church life would improve if people refused to become angry when they (or their child) did not get their way. Peace would flourish if we refused to take offense.

The lessons are clear. First, let us submit to all God-given authorities. Almost everyone has spent time under someone who seemed to lack the qualities essential to good leadership. It seems natural to balk at the prospect of submitting to the unworthy. Besides, humans are prone to rebel, even against noble authorities. Notice, then, that Peter does not say, "Submit to good leaders." If we follow leaders only if we concur with their directions, the descriptive term is *agree*, not *submit*.

Peter exhorts us to submit "with all respect" (1 Peter 2:18). Authorities deserve respect for the sake of God, who placed them in their role, if not for their merit. Sadly, it is typical, in Western cultures, to criticize a leader even as we obey, and to disobey if we can. Even if we labor under a flawed authority, Peter says that we should be governed by our obligations, not the putative qualities of the leader. Remember, Jesus submitted to his parents despite their limitations. When we honor flawed leaders, we follow Jesus. The Father notices when we yield to masters who seem neither wise nor good.

In 1 Corinthians 7, Paul encourages us that we can be content wherever we are, without changing marital status, ethnic status, or economic status. We can remain in our place if we remain with God, since he provides for us there (7:1–24).[26] This principle neither denies that some authorities are evil nor excuses their misdeeds. God's capacity to override evil cannot remove their culpability. On the contrary, because the Lord cares for the poor, lesser lords should, too. All who exercise authority should recall that they have an authority and a Judge over them.

26. Gordon D. Fee, *The First Epistle to the Corinthians* (Grand Rapids: Eerdmans, 1987), 29, 306–13; C. K. Barrett, *A Commentary on the First Epistle to the Corinthians* (New York: Harper & Row, 1968), 167–71; Gregory Dawes, " 'But If You Can Gain Your Freedom' (1 Corinthians 7:17–24)," *Catholic Biblical Quarterly* 52 (1990): 691n32. See also Gustaf Wikgren, *The Christian's Calling*, trans. Carl Rasmussen (Edinburgh: Oliver and Boyd, 1958), 1–7. Against these, S. Scott Bartchy argues that "calling" refers to salvation, not a life situation. See *Mallon Chrēsai*, 129–57.

It is possible to live well under a bad master. Besides, everyone belongs to someone, and everyone is enslaved to something. Seneca observed that one man "is a slave to lust, another to greed, another to ambition, and all men are slaves to fear."[27] Believers, whom God "bought at a price" (1 Cor. 7:23), now belong to Jesus, and that is liberating. So our first thought is not to change masters or jobs but to remain faithful, whatever our bonds may be.

Jesus carries us through suffering under unjust masters. He set an example and, through his sacrifice, offers forgiveness when we fail. By his wounds we are healed, so we may live for righteousness, under the care of the Lord, the Good Shepherd and Overseer of our souls.

27. Seneca, "On Master and Slave," 311.

9

BEAUTIFUL WIVES, CONSIDERATE HUSBANDS

1 Peter 3:1—7

Wives, in the same way be submissive to your husbands so that,
if any of them do not believe the word, they may be won over
without words by the behavior of their wives, when they see the
purity and reverence of your lives. (1 Peter 3:1–2)

VIGNETTES OF MARRIAGE TODAY

Not long ago, I officiated at four weddings in the span of a month. Every bride and groom was a dedicated Christian. None had cohabited, all were young, and four of them had just completed college. With one exception, the eight sets of parents were happily married and supportive. We might call these weddings "normal," and they are, in the sense that they adhere to God's norms. But in Western society, the norm has become rare.

While the four brides prepared to marry, a popular television show detailed the spectacular wedding of a celebrated model/actress and a handsome professional athlete. The program followed the newlyweds until they divorced after just ten weeks. They cited irreconcilable differences, but the program showed nothing worse than petty selfishness and insensitivity.

Why did millions watch? The typical fascination with beauty and wealth played a role, but many viewers were glad to see that however faulty *their* relationships might be, at least one couple looked worse.

Sadly, it's hard to know whether my four weddings or the "reality" show is more typical today. At present, over 40 percent of all American babies are born outside marriage, with the percentage rising in every ethnic and social group. Despite a slight drop in recent years, over 40 percent of all marriages still end in divorce. While 72 percent of all adults (defined as anyone over eighteen years of age) were married in 1960, barely half are married today. That is, nearly 50 percent of adults are never married or formerly married (whether through divorce or the death of a spouse). The number of adults who never marry keeps rising, as does the number of women who never become mothers. Most couples now cohabit before they marry (a recent survey said that 70 percent cohabit before marriage), and many cohabit but never wed. Those who cohabit indefinitely want some kind of relationship, but nothing as strong as marriage. Many shun marriage because they fear divorce. People want to protect themselves, and marriage seems risky. Perhaps the great trauma of their childhood came the day that their parents announced, "We're getting a divorce." In their pain, they vowed, "I will never put my children through that."[1] Some stay married, no matter what happens, for the sake of the children. But some decide that the surest way to avoid divorce is to refuse marriage altogether.[2] I pray that these sad statistics have reversed themselves and that my concerns are outdated by the time anyone reads my words. But whether Western society is recovering or plunging toward greater chaos, the woes of this century have something in common with the social setting of Peter.

The Contexts of 1 Peter 3

The message of 1 Peter 3:1–7, with its double call to submission (3:1, 5), might strike the casual reader as chauvinistic or degrading. The passage lacks symmetry, since it has six parts instruction for women to one part

1. Susan Gregory Thomas, "Divorce Generation," *Wall Street Journal*, July 9, 2011.
2. For analysis of trends and statistics, see Andrew J. Cherlin, *The Marriage Go-Round: The State of Marriage and the Family in America Today* (New York: Knopf, 2009).

for men. First Peter 3 says that wives should submit to their husbands, beautify themselves with good deeds rather than fine garments, and imitate godly women like Sarah, who called her husband "lord." What shall we make of this?

Above all, we can't dismiss Peter's message as a temporary command, a concession, or an adaptation to the times that the church would outgrow. The message of Scripture always transcends its occasion. Furthermore, the text has no hint that it is temporary counsel. Still, a firm grasp of this passage's occasion—its historical, cultural, literary, and canonical contexts—is vital. First, *historically*, while Peter's message applies to all, he addresses Christian women who are married to unbelieving men. He teaches these wives how to conduct themselves, that they might win their husbands to the faith (1 Peter 3:1).

Second, *culturally*, Peter draws on norms admired by Greco-Roman moralists as he counsels wives in winsome behavior. Ethicists often urged women to be chaste and respectful, to shun gaudy clothes and hair, and to show a meek and quiet spirit.[3] Wherever biblical and Greco-Roman norms agree, Peter urges Christian women to behave in ways that both God and their pagan husbands would approve.[4] Furthermore, that age assumed that wives would adopt the religion(s) of their husbands. A Christian woman, upon conversion to the faith, could no longer participate in pagan worship rituals. Since the Greco-Roman wife was expected to share her husband's faith, that refusal would seem subversive. Thus, Peter tells godly wives to conduct themselves in ways that demonstrate respect for their husbands and so to mitigate the potential tension caused by their faith.

Third, from a *literary* perspective, we recall that 1 Peter taught Christian converts how to be faithful disciples in a pagan world. Peter opens by calling his people "strangers in the world" (1 Peter 1:1). In the long section on social behavior, he adds that they are "aliens and strangers" in the world and therefore must "abstain from sinful desires, which war against your soul" (2:11). But, he continues, Christian virtue has an apologetic function: "Live such good lives among the pagans that, though they accuse you of doing

---

3. None but the elite could afford the elaborate headdress and gold that Peter mentions, but others imitated as they could. See Craig S. Keener, *The IVP Bible Background Commentary: New Testament* (Downers Grove, IL: InterVarsity Press, 1993), 715–16.

4. In the same spirit, when Paul commends hospitality and self-control to church elders in 1 Timothy 3, he names traits that Greco-Roman moralists admired.

wrong, they may see your good deeds and glorify God on the day he visits us" (2:12). So the good conduct of the believer is missional or pre-evangelistic. A good life silences accusers.

Yet Peter also knows that Christian conduct will seem disruptive, since, at least in principle, it undermines the hierarchical relationships that structure society. The thinking person knows that every Christian is a potential rebel or subversive. When the Christian calls Jesus *Lord*, he or she denies that title (in its fullest sense) to all others—whether kings, husbands, fathers, or masters. The Christian seems to disrespect the emperor by refusing to worship him. The Christian wife appears to dishonor her husband because she refuses to join the worship of his deities, whether the emperor or the local gods that allegedly sustained the social fabric.

Because Christian conviction can always foster dissident behavior, Peter stresses the need for respect. He has already told his churches to submit to every human authority, including the emperor, whom they also honor (1 Peter 2:13, 17).[5] The believing slave or servant also submits (same verb) to the master "with all respect [or *fear*]," whether the master deserves it or not (2:18).[6] The word to wives begins the same way, with a call to submit with respect or fear (3:1-2).[7] In each case, Peter commands the social subordinate to show honor, respect, and obedience to the social superior. That is how they silence accusers, as Peter said they should (2:11-12).

It might seem that Peter's instructions burden women and excuse men. But it is more accurate to say that Peter aimed to guide Christian women who were married to pagan men. Further, simply by addressing them, Peter honored the women of his churches. The literature of the day normally ignored the subordinate partner in a relationship. Authors addressed governors, masters, husbands, and fathers and overlooked ordinary men, plus slaves, wives, and children, who were judged unworthy or incapable of receiving instruction. By guiding wives, children, and slaves, Peter (like Paul in Ephesians 5:21-6:9) has already elevated them.

Fourth, we locate Peter's message in *canonical* context when we examine how he applies general biblical principles for marriage to the union of Chris-

---

5. The verbs are *hypotassō*, which Peter repeats in 1 Peter 3:1, 5, and *timaō*, the principal verb for "honor."

6. The verbs here are *hypotassō*, "submit," and *phobeō*, literally, "fear."

7. The verb is *hypotassō* again. *Fear* is now a noun, but the root is the same as in 1 Peter 2:17.

tian women and pagan men. Peter assumes that the wife will aim to preserve the marriage, because even a mixed marriage is good (cf. 1 Cor. 7:1–16). Marriage is a creation mandate, ordained for mankind in our innocence, to provide companionship and partnership as we bear children and govern God's creation for him (Gen. 1–2). Divorce was well known in Israel and in the empire, but because marriage is a *covenant*, the law, prophets, and apostles oppose divorce (Deut. 24:1–4; Mal. 2:14–16; Matt. 19:3–12; 1 Cor. 7:10–13).

Since marriage is a covenant, husband and wife commit to each other. By contrast, Solomon says that the unfaithful woman "forsakes the companion of her youth and forgets the covenant of her God" (Prov. 2:16–17 ESV). And Malachi condemns the man who arbitrarily divorces his wife, since "she is your partner, the wife of your marriage covenant" (Mal. 2:14).

Both Peter and Paul understood the problem for the wife who converts to Christianity when her husband does not. Neither said that a lack of faith is the basis for divorce. Paul stressed that marriage is permanent and the bonds hold, unless the unbelieving husband or wife abandons the marriage (1 Cor. 7:10–16). Peter focused on wives, since they implicitly challenged cultural norms by adopting a faith that kept them from joining their husbands' religious practices.

To summarize, 1 Peter 3 applies enduring biblical principles to an urgent contemporary issue. The apostles often did this. Today's church leaders should follow that strategy by applying teaching to the challenges of our day. In that spirit, a preacher might tell young, unmarried Christians to resist cohabitation and to embrace marriage and childbearing as essential elements of God's plan. He might exhort them to commit, without fear, to intentional relationships that could lead to early marriage and parenthood. But now we turn to Peter's message for his day and strive to lay aside our preconceptions so that we may hear his message.

A COUNTERCULTURAL WIFE

Peter's command "Wives, . . . be submissive" (1 Peter 3:1) will divide, even offend, contemporary readers. When Peter tells wives to obey their husbands and call them "lord" (3:6 ESV), skeptics groan. Sadly, men have fueled the critics by abusing their God-given authority and physical strength. If husbands loved their wives as they should, this passage would not be controversial. It *is* controversial, yet we will not read Peter accurately if we let contemporary gender debates become our lens for interpretation. It is better to acknowledge our preferences and let Scripture test them (1 Thess. 5:21), since God's Word is infallible and we are not. The prevailing mind-set of our age *does* influence us. Therefore, if our Bible-reading never challenges us, we probably aren't reading well. A faith that never upsets us is a designer faith, with the self as designer.

So, then, hear Peter as he begins and (nearly) ends with an exhortation to submit (1 Peter 3:1, 5). He begins, "Likewise, wives, be subject to your own husbands, so that even if some do not obey the word, they may be won without a word by the conduct of their wives, when they see your respectful and pure conduct" (3:1–2 ESV). While the command has a purpose—the winning of unbelieving husbands—it has no restriction. Peter commands all wives to "be subject to your own husbands," not men in general. Thus, *all* wives submit, and *some* have a distinct circumstance and goal—to win an unbelieving husband.

The idea of submission, as we saw in chapter 7, did not have the negative connotation that it has today. Submission does entail the concept that authorities give orders that subordinates follow, but *submit* is milder than *obey* for two reasons. First, a wife who submits to her husband's guidance may still decide *how* to follow his direction. Second, a believer's submission to human authorities is always qualified, never blind. If a husband commands his wife to do evil, she is to heed the Lord, not the man.

Peter addresses all wives, but especially Christian women whose husbands "do not obey the word" (in this case, to "obey the word" means to believe the gospel, 1 Peter 3:1 ESV). As we have seen, since wives were expected to adopt their husbands' religion, Christian women could seem rebellious if they abandoned familiar gods. Because that culture assumed that adults could subscribe to multiple religions, wives could adopt new religions *in addition to* the faith of their husbands. And some women, attracted to the ethic of Judaism, adopted it as a second religion. But when the gospel came to the synagogue and wives believed, dual allegiance became impossible. It was vital, therefore, that believing wives submit whenever possible, since they seemed rebellious in religious affairs. (If a man converted, he had a greater chance of carrying his pagan wife with him, and if not, he at least did not disrupt the social order when he practiced his chosen religion.)

Again, Peter commands wives to submit to *their own* husbands, not to all men. Submissiveness manifests itself in several ways: in reverent and pure conduct (1 Peter 3:2), in modest clothing and inner beauty (3:3–5), and in respectful speech (3:6).

Unbelieving husbands will be won by observing their Christian wives' respectful, pure conduct (1 Peter 3:2).[8] Wives should conform to social conventions and fulfill expected duties in order to win their pagan husbands "without words" (3:1). One can be relatively silent yet not mute; there are clear cases of this in Scripture.[9] So Peter doesn't mean that the wife never speaks. Nor does he mean that speech is pointless. She does not speak because Peter did not expect *her* words to be helpful in that context. He knew that others might be more persuasive. Even today, a believing wife often finds it best to be (relatively) quiet and let others engage a skeptical husband. The same often holds for Christian children who want to convert unbelieving parents. They need to hear the gospel, but perhaps from someone outside the family. As a believing woman longs for her husband's conversion, Peter tells her how best to proceed. C. E. B. Cranfield notes: "Of course, she must be ready to speak about Christ. But to persist in talking to someone who does not want to listen only hardens." The gentle and quiet way may be more effective than what seems like nagging. And "those whose hearts are proof against preaching may at least be softened by . . . behavior."[10] Whether this results in a conversion or not, godly wives can please the Lord (1 Peter 3:3–4) and follow the footsteps of godly Sarah (3:5–6).

Spiritual Beauty

Peter urges women to pursue the highest beauty: "Your beauty should not come from outward adornment, such as braided hair and the wearing of gold jewelry and fine clothes. Instead, it should be that of your inner self,

8. The word translated "see" in most translations is *ekopteuō*, a rare verb that typically means "to be a spectator."

9. For example, 1 Corinthians 14:34 says that "women should remain silent in the churches," even though 1 Corinthians 11:5 expects women to pray and prophesy. Clearly, the silence of 14:34 is partial and situationally appropriate. In context, the Greek verb, *sigaō*, usually means to keep something to oneself or to fall silent after speaking (Luke 9:36; Acts 15:13; 1 Cor. 14:34). See Daniel M. Doriani, *Women and Ministry: What the Bible Teaches* (Wheaton, IL: Crossway, 2003), 81–84.

10. C. E. B. Cranfield, *I & II Peter and Jude* (London: SCM Press, 1960), 89.

the unfading beauty of a gentle and quiet spirit, which is of great worth in God's sight. For this is the way the holy women of the past who put their hope in God used to make themselves beautiful" (1 Peter 3:3–5a). Paul gives similar counsel in 1 Timothy 2:9–10: "I . . . want women to dress modestly . . . , not with braided hair or gold or pearls or expensive clothes, but with good deeds." For both Greeks and Jews, extravagant dress could signify promiscuity or disregard of a husband's authority.[11] "Rejection of external adornment was part of a woman's submission to her husband."[12] Modesty is the principle. The problem does not lie with braided hair or gold per se. A gold wedding band is a simple symbol of commitment. But elaborate hair took hours to prepare and so became a conspicuous display of wealth and rank. Inner beauty is what counts. "Virtue is the one garment any woman can wear with pride."[13] Peter singles out a gentle and quiet spirit. He blesses amiable friendliness, calm peace, a refusal to quarrel or show bad temper.

As a test of Peter's principle, we may ask ourselves how much time we spend on our physical looks and how much time we spend on our mental and spiritual strength each day. If we give more attention to hair and clothes than to mind and heart, something might be wrong. We justifiably pay close attention to physical appearances when we first meet someone. Face, hair, posture, height, weight, proportions, clothes, and voice tell us whether this new person is male or female, young or old, confident or awkward, friendly or closed. But the longer we know someone, the less appearances matter. And in God's eyes, "a gentle and quiet spirit" is true beauty.

Surviving statues, relief carvings, and references to hair in Greco-Roman literature are consistent.[14] In portraits (stone carvings, feasible only for the wealthy), adult women (typically wives) wore their hair curled or braided

---

11. After a long complaint about the luxuries of women, Juvenal adds, "Meantime she pays no attention to her husband." See Juvenal, "Satire 6," in *Juvenal and Persius*, trans. C. G. Ramsey (Cambridge, MA: Harvard University Press, 1965), 121–25.

12. David Scholer, "Women's Adornment: Some Historical and Hermeneutical Observations on the New Testament Passages," *Daughters of Sarah* 6, 1 (1980): 5.

13. Peter H. Davids, *The First Epistle of Peter* (Grand Rapids: Eerdmans, 1990), 118.

14. Cynthia Thompson, "Hairstyles, Head-coverings, and St. Paul: Portraits from Roman Corinth," *Biblical Archaeologist* 51 (1988): 99–115; David Gill, "The Importance of Roman Portraiture for Head Coverings in 1 Corinthians 11:2–16," *Tyndale Bulletin* 41, 2 (1990): 244–60; James B. Hurley, *Man and Woman in Biblical Perspective* (Grand Rapids: Zondervan, 1981), 66–68, 168–71, 254–71; Craig S. Keener, *Paul, Women and Wives: Marriage and Women's Ministry in the Letters of Paul* (Peabody, MA: Hendrickson, 1992), 22–30; Ben Witherington III, *Women in the Earliest Churches* (Cambridge: Cambridge University Press, 1988), 81–83; Jerome Murphy O'Connor, "Sex and Logic in 1 Corinthians

and up on their heads.[15] When husbands and wives are shown together, the women's heads are usually covered by cloth shawls on top of the head (not face veils).[16] Girls, maidens, and immoral women went bareheaded.[17] For an adult, any deviation from the norm might have significance. Short hair might signify prostitution or lesbianism. Shorn or unbound hair could signify mourning. Long, loose hair could also indicate rejection of the husband's authority or sexual promiscuity.[18]

Peter singles out hair, gold, jewelry, and fine clothes because people displayed wealth in them. Today, people display their wealth through houses, cars, and vacations more than clothing. Another set tends face and hair or hones a fabulous body from neck to knees, but the point remains. Paul says, "Train yourself to be godly. For physical training is of some value, but godliness has value for all things, holding promise for both the present life and the life to come" (1 Tim. 4:7b–8). And Peter encourages disciples to seek "the imperishable *quality* of a humble and quiet spirit."[19]

If spiritual virtue is imperishable and all bodily strengths perish, let us therefore spend less time on our bodies and more time caring for mind and spirit, pursuing love, justice, and truth. Of course, we should be good stewards of our God-given bodies, but what would a tally of our hours spent say about what matters most to us? Alan Stibbs says that a Christian wife should seek to please God by her conduct, not her clothes, especially by cultivating a gentle spirit. "This will reveal that her behavior is governed by a new standard of value," by "characteristics highly esteemed" by God rather than men.[20]

11:2–16," *Catholic Biblical Quarterly* 42 (1980): 482–500; Jerome Murphy O'Connor, "1 Corinthians 11:2–16 Once Again," *Catholic Biblical Quarterly* 50 (1988): 265–74.

15. See photographs in Thompson, "Hairstyles, Head-coverings," 101–11; Bruce W. Winter, *After Paul Left Corinth: The Influence of Secular Ethics and Social Change* (Grand Rapids: Eerdmans, 2001), xviii–xx.

16. Gill, "Importance of Roman Portraiture," 252–54.

17. Witherington, *Women in the Earliest Churches*, 82.

18. Keener, *Paul, Women and Wives*, 30; Winter, *After Paul Left Corinth*, 123–26.

19. So translates J. Ramsey Michaels, *1 Peter*, Word Biblical Commentary 49 (Nashville: Thomas Nelson, 1988), 161. "Quality" seems a better translation than "beauty" (per NIV, ESV), since the word *beauty* is not present in the Greek. Rather, Peter has the neuter adjective *aphtharton* (also used in 1:4, 18, 23), with the definite article, so the whole functions as a substantive, which suggests the quality of incorruptibility. See Friedrich Blass and Albert Debrunner, *A Greek Grammar of the New Testament and Other Early Christian Literature*, trans. and rev. Robert Funk (Chicago: University of Chicago Press, 1961), 138 (sec. 263.2).

20. Alan M. Stibbs, *The First Epistle General of Peter* (London: Tyndale, 1959), 124.

Ordinary human wisdom suggests that we should work on our character, if only because a beautiful spirit lasts a lifetime and a beautiful body lasts a few decades. Even if the rate of decline varies, the body does fail and finally die, but the spirit need not. Time inexorably weakens and slows the body. Entropy dulls, then erases, the differences between strong and weak, swift and laggard, vibrant and torpid, beautiful and plain, but time spent with God's Spirit increases the capacity to love, to show mercy. Even a self-interested person should therefore tend the spirit.

A believer is especially pleased to learn that a beautiful spirit "is of great worth in God's sight" (1 Peter 3:4). We should long to please God more than to gain applause or admiring glances. We should pursue God's favor more than human favor, since his appraisal is more accurate, generous, and gracious.

As Peter exhorts women to cultivate inner beauty, he assures them that this is the proven path for godly women: "For this is how the holy women who hoped in God used to adorn themselves, by submitting to their own husbands, as Sarah obeyed Abraham, calling him lord. And you are her children, if you do good and do not fear anything that is frightening" (1 Peter 3:5–6 esv). With this statement, Peter *repeats* that godly women should pursue spiritual beauty and submit to their husbands. But he *adds* that while they might be exiled from their culture of origin, they now belong to a new family. They hope in God, like holy women past. They are Sarah's daughters, beautiful women all, for they, like Sarah, adorn themselves with righteousness and good deeds. Yet they (literally) do not fear terrors, that is, the things that terrify others, for they trust God (cf. 2:23; 3:14–15). Some women are afraid of submitting to their husbands.

While this sense of belonging surely cheered the godly woman of Peter's day, the verse troubles the secular and perhaps even godly woman today. Perhaps her husband, or another man, has acted sinfully or foolishly, so that she hesitates to trust him. Or perhaps she simply wants the freedom that is so highly valued in this age. Yet Peter not only commends submissiveness, but also notes, "Sarah obeyed Abraham, calling him lord" (1 Peter 3:6 esv). If wives balk at submission, how will they react to Sarah's authoritative example? Calling a husband "lord" seems heavy-handed. But *lord* is not *Lord*. In that culture, viewing her husband as "lord" meant that a wife must acknowledge him "with due deference, as her husband and master."

That is how Sarah used the term in Genesis 18:12.[21] More importantly, this recognition of Abraham's leadership did not keep Sarah from speaking her mind to Abraham. And with God's approval, he complied (Gen. 21:8–13).

Obviously, Sarah was submissive to a believing husband, so that her duty was lighter. But Peter argued by analogy: if Sarah, a forceful woman (Gen. 18:12), obeyed Abraham and called him "lord," all women should respect their husbands.

HUSBANDS

Peter began to name the social duties of believers in chapter 2 by directing, "Be subject for the Lord's sake to every human institution" (1 Peter 2:13 ESV). As he worked through social relationships, he repeated the call to subjection or submission. Residents submit to governors (2:13–17), servants to masters (2:18–25), and wives to husbands (3:1–7). Later, Peter says that young men must submit to church elders (5:5).

His commands to husbands, and later to elders, round out the discussion. Peter commands leaders to serve others, but not in reciprocal language. He does not instruct husbands to submit to wives, or elders to submit to the church. Rather, they must be tender and respectful. Peter tells elders that they should lead from beside, not from above, "not domineering . . . , but being examples to the flock" (1 Peter 5:3 ESV). Peter models his own point by calling himself a "fellow elder," even though he is an apostle and could claim superiority. Husbands should be even more tender: "Likewise, husbands, live with your wives in an understanding way, showing honor to the woman as the weaker vessel, since they are heirs with you of the grace of life, so that your prayers may not be hindered" (3:7 ESV). Four vital points emerge from this statement.

First, husbands "live with" their wives. Peter expects husband and wife to live in the same house. It also means that they should sleep in the same bed, since the verb "live with" (*sunoikeō*) was used for sexual relations in the Septuagint (Deut. 22:13; 24:1). Peter assumes that physical intimacy is an element of married life. Sadly, it is necessary for pastors to spell out the implications: Husbands love their wives by living in one house, sharing one

---

21. Ibid., 126. If we review Genesis 18, we see that Sarah's demeanor was hardly submissive, but she did call Abraham "lord" or "master" (Hebrew *adon*), which is Peter's sole point.

bed, in physical intimacy. It tears the fabric of a marriage when husband and wife deprive each other of physical love. We are accustomed to the principle that sexual union seals the love and covenantal commitment that leads to marriage. But we must also know that husband and wife can drift apart, and when they do, sexual love can rekindle our emotional attachment and commitment. Sexual union both seals and strengthens a marriage. Separation weakens affection.

Second, husbands live, literally, "according to knowledge." Peter expects husbands to *know* their wives. Men occasionally excuse careless leadership by pleading ignorance: "I don't understand women." But a man doesn't need to understand *women*; he needs to understand *his wife*. Husbands are scientists with a narrow field of inquiry. A man should know the preferences, moods, needs of his beloved, so that he can love and care for her.

This is important because, third, "the woman is the weaker vessel." The Greek word translated "vessel" (*skeuos*) is used for sundry material objects, especially jars and vessels, but sometimes for the human body.[22] Peter simply means that women are, generally, physically weaker than men.[23] There are many exceptions, but taken as a whole, men are larger and stronger than women. Some say that women are more vulnerable emotionally, although that is disputed, and in most societies women are economically dependent on their husbands. In Peter's age, Jews and Greeks commonly also viewed women as being weaker morally and mentally. But Scripture never says that, and no part of Christian tradition promotes it.

On the contrary, a Christian husband must honor women, and especially his wife. Physically, she is probably weaker, but spiritually she is a joint heir of grace. At a minimum, husbands must never bully, threaten, or strike their wives, nor should they demean their wives for being weak or slow-footed. Marriage is a union of two weak and sinful people, even if we are weak and sinful in different ways.

Fourth, married believers are joint heirs of the life-giving grace of Jesus (1 Peter 3:7b). *Grace* is the first and last word of 1 Peter (1:2; 5:12). The

22. Readers can survey a Greek concordance for a sense of the term. It is debated, but most dictionaries and lexicons say that *skeuos* can be a euphemism for the human body in its sexuality (e.g., 1 Thess. 4:4). See Frederick W. Danker, ed., *A Greek-English Lexicon of the New Testament and Other Early Christian Literature*, 3rd ed. (Chicago: University of Chicago Press, 2000), 927–28.

23. Peter does not here use the most common word for an adult female, *gunē*, which normally means "wife." He uses *gunaikeos*, which is an adjective that means "feminine" or "the feminine [one]."

prophets predicted a gracious salvation (1:10), and the Lord Jesus fulfilled the promise when he suffered for us: "He himself bore our sins in his body on the tree, so that we might die to sins and live for righteousness; by his wounds you have been healed" (2:24). The cross of Christ is the great equalizer. How sweet it is for both husband and wife to know that their comfort in life and hope in death is the sacrifice and resurrection of Jesus. Respect makes prayer easier, but how can a harsh husband pray well, except in repentance? When husband and wife both know Jesus, prayers flow freely. Each is humble over his or her sin, each gives thanks for God's grace. Both present requests confidently, for if the Father "did not spare his own Son, but gave him up for us all—how will he not also, along with him, graciously give us all things?" (Rom. 8:32).

The challenge of marriage and the challenges to marriage are numerous enough that we should take the opportunity to label Peter's abiding lessons.

PETER'S PRINCIPLES FOR MARRIAGE

First, the believer should hope to convert an unbelieving spouse if he or she has one, not by lecturing fervently, but by living well. There is a time to talk, but pushing and harping hardens people. Peter knows that an unbeliever can have misgivings about his or her spouse's faith. Peter says, in essence, "Live so well that he is glad that you follow Jesus." Submission, a fairly prominent theme in Peter, is one part of living well. Submission to authority is one way in which we do good and so "silence the ignorant talk of foolish men" (1 Peter 2:13–15). When we submit to proper authorities, freely, actively, and willingly, it is harder for them to slander the faith.

Second, we must comment on submission. Sadly, the command to submit has been abused by men who attempt to justify selfish demands. But "doing whatever I'm told" is not the biblical concept of submission. To submit does mean that one person ordinarily yields to the will of one in a position of authority. A submissive wife accepts her husband's leadership in general. She listens. She expects him to lead and does not chafe under the burden of following. She understands that submission does not undermine her dignity but expresses it. This is her unique opportunity to model Jesus, who submitted to the Father in the plan of redemption, even though Jesus is coequal and coeternal with the Father. We could mention again the need for husbands to lead with Christlike love and sacrifice. Instead, let's consider how the contemporary zeal to prevent abuses of authority can cause a different problem.

Today, our culture constantly laments the absence of strong, marriageable men. But men need to be stronger within marriages, too. For every home that is crippled by male abuse of authority, several suffer from husbands and fathers who refuse to lead. For every man who dominates, several abdicate. They come home, flop down, plug in, and ignore everyone. The sins of domination are more catastrophic, especially if they include violence, but sins of passivity are more common. Pastors know: more wives lament an absentee husband than a domineering husband.

Of course, there are limits to submission. It is reasonable, and no sign of disrespect, to question our leaders. Moreover, we don't obey wicked commands or endure boundless oppression. Paul told slaves, "If you can gain your freedom, do so" (1 Cor. 7:21). Yet in general, it's right to follow leaders and obey authorities. Loving leadership is a common path to blessing. Happy the nation with just governors, blessed the home with a Christlike husband, peaceful the worker who trusts a fair supervisor.

Third, we must locate Peter's counsel within the biblical understanding of marriage as a covenant. He doesn't urge wives with pagan husbands to *escape* them but to *win* them. This, of course, is contrary to contemporary Western culture, in which too many people think of divorce if their dreams are not realized.

Sound theology serves us well here. Marriage is difficult and disappointing because it unites two sinners. As Stanley Hauerwas notes, we imagine that there is someone "just right" for us to marry. We dream that "if we look closely enough we will find the right person. . . . [But] we always marry the wrong person." If we pause, we know that *we* are the wrong person, too. Furthermore, "We never know whom we marry; we just think we do. Or even if we first marry the right person, just give it a while and he or she will change." If nothing else, *marriage itself will change us.* In short, *no two people are compatible.* Flaws that once seemed tiny, even endearing, loom large. The crucible of an intimate relationship, where everything matters, reveals the fault lines of character. Hauerwas concludes, "The primary problem . . . is learning how to love and care for the stranger to whom you find yourself married."[24]

24. Stanley Hauerwas, "Sex and Politics: Bertrand Russell and 'Human Sexuality,'" *Christian Century* (April 19, 1978): 417–22; Timothy Keller, with Kathy Keller, *The Meaning of Marriage: Facing*

What happens when married strangers dash each other's expectations and make each other unhappy? Many think divorce will restore their happiness. But the sociological study "Does Divorce Make People Happy? Findings from a Study of Unhappy Marriages" concludes that "divorce . . . appeared to reduce adult happiness and increase adult depression in the majority of cases."[25] On the other hand, the study found that "most unhappy spouses who avoided divorce ended up happily married." Specifically, 64 percent were "happily married five years later." Surprisingly, the success rate was higher (78 percent) if a marriage had been rated *very* unhappy. The study found that the essential element was what it called endurance, which Christians might call covenantal commitment:

> Many currently happily married spouses have had extended periods of marital unhappiness, often for quite serious reasons, including alcoholism, infidelity, verbal abuse, emotional neglect, depression, illness. . . . Why did these marriages survive where other marriages did not? A marital endurance ethic plays a big role. Spouses said that their marriages got happier, not because they resolved problems but because they stubbornly outlasted them. With time . . . many sources of conflict and distress eased.[26]

To be clear, the goal is not *mere* endurance, but the restoration of a real marriage. Peter does not advocate a contractual arrangement in which each party contributes to a functional but impersonal relationship. We want more than a compatible roommate and parenting partner. We want more than happy children, a nice house, and an escort for parties and vacations. We want abiding love.

In *The Meaning of Marriage*, Tim Keller observes that biblical covenants blend law and love, the legal and the personal.[27] Covenants are both personal and legal. They rest on loving affection, but they are also binding and unconditional. By telling wives to strive to win their husbands, Peter

the Complexities of Commitment with the Wisdom of God (New York: Dutton, 2011), 37–43.

25. Linda J. Waite et al., *Does Divorce Make People Happy? Findings from a Study of Unhappy Marriages* (New York: Institute for American Values, 2002), 12–14. We note that David Blankenhorn, founder and president of the Institute, supports gay marriage and has presented arguments for polygamy, discounting the likelihood of conservative bias. See the document at www.americanvalues.org/UnhappyMarriages.pdf.

26. Ibid., 6, 30–31. The study notes that marital violence changes the situation.

27. Keller, *The Meaning of Marriage*, 80–87.

reaffirms the covenantal view of marriage. He balances the personal and the legal aspects of marriage. Traditional marriages tend to be legal and contractual. In a traditional marriage, the family arranges a match that seems advantageous for the family as much as for the prospective spouse. Parents seek a spouse from a respectable family to gain connections that promise to strengthen the clan. The ideal for a traditional marriage is that the union of a strong man and woman also unites two strong families, to the benefit of all. By contrast, the romantic marriage seeks the perfect partner, the soul mate who animates our passions and ennobles our spirit. (There is no need to explain the well-known romantic model.) Sadly, there is no perfect romance, and the contractual marriage can be dully materialistic. The romantic model tempts husbands and wives to quit via divorce if—or when—the romance cools. If a traditional marriage falters, the bonds of social expectations might keep the couple together legally, but they can live separate lives, even under the same roof.

But if marriage is a covenant, we don't aim for the perfect romance or for the contractual arrangement. A covenant is a personal bond of love in a lifelong relationship, sealed with vows, taken with God as witness. Indeed, to take public vows is an act of love in itself. If someone says, "I love you, but I don't want to marry you," the person probably means: "You're not quite what I had in mind, and I don't love you enough to end my search with you." Some people claim that wedding vows and covenantal commitments contaminate romance and passion by mixing it with duty. Love flourishes, they state, only when it is free, when it is unconstrained by promises. But without the pledge of fidelity, what happens when feelings change? Or when the ravages of time, illness, and unequal maturation make one partner look weaker?

Someone noticed that when two people are in love, they don't simply declare their affection. They say, "I will *always* love you." They talk about growing old together. True love wants to endure. As Solomon said, "love is as strong as death . . . . Many waters cannot quench love, neither can floods drown it" (Song 8:6–7 ESV). God's covenant faithfulness is our measure and norm. Jesus does not love the church *because* it is pure and spotless; he purifies the church in order to *make* it spotless. Similarly, husbands should love their wives as Christ loved the church—*despite* their blemishes, not *until they get* blemishes (Eph. 5:25–27).

We see, therefore, that Peter applied the great principles of biblical marriage to a pressing question for his churches: How shall a Christian woman live faithfully within the bonds of marriage to an unbelieving husband? He answers that she must live a beautiful life, winning him by faithful deeds rather than faithful words. Peter emphasizes submissiveness for a reason: the very act of choosing to follow Jesus puts the wife's loyalty to her husband in doubt. The ground of Peter's counsel is the biblical view of God and covenant. The Lord has pledged himself to us in a covenant relationship. He is faithful to that covenant, even when we are not. If we trust the Lord, and his life shapes ours, then we, too, must be faithful to our spouses, even unbelievers. That is how we show that the faithful, enduring love of the Lord has redeemed us and transformed us.

10

The Good Life, the Peaceable Kingdom

1 Peter 3:8—12

Whoever would love life and see good days must keep his tongue from evil and his lips from deceitful speech. He must turn from evil and do good; he must seek peace and pursue it.
(1 Peter 3:10–11)

irst Peter 3:8–12 begins with a phrase that sounds as though the author were wrapping something up: "Finally, all of you, have unity of mind, sympathy, brotherly love, a tender heart, and a humble mind" (1 Peter 3:8 ESV). Indeed, Peter is concluding something—not his entire epistle, but his survey of the principal duties of Christians, which he began in 1 Peter 1:13. Peter has moved from general duties to specific obligations and back to general duties. Because God is holy, we are to be holy (1:16). Because Jesus ransomed us from a vain life and because we tasted his goodness, we put away specific sins, such as malice and deceit (1:18–2:3). Because of God's redemptive work, we are his chosen people, a holy nation that abstains from the passions of the flesh and maintains good conduct (2:4–12). Holiness also manifests itself in life's several social structures.

Every believer submits to governing authorities, whether local or global (2:13–17). Servants submit to masters, whether they merit respect or not, for Jesus submitted in the same way (2:18–25). Finally, husbands and wives live together in grace and mutual honor (3:1–7).

ATTRACTIVE CHRISTIAN TRAITS

If we act in these ways, Peter says that we can ordinarily expect to live well and enjoy God's favor. He asks, "Who is going to harm you if you are eager to do good?" (1 Peter 3:13). The next section admits that it *is* possible to suffer harm for doing good (3:14–17). If we live by God's standards, we will never quite fit into any human culture. This was true in the empire, where the Christians' allegiance to Jesus as Lord and refusal to worship the emperor could be taken as a sign of dissent. Today, there is always a moral cause, often involving sexual ethics, in which evangelical Christians take the minority view. To the secularist, the Christian position might sound judgmental, intolerant, or bigoted, so we court disfavor.

Nonetheless, 1 Peter 3:8–13 states the norm. A good life allows peace. Whatever we may say about life in an alien culture, under hostile authorities, the greater part of the Christian life concerns the character and disciplines that shape daily actions and our universal responsibilities. So Peter describes the virtues that bless everyone: harmony, sympathy, love, compassion, and humility. Later he mentions forgiveness, hospitality, and generosity (4:8–10). Earlier Peter said that holy women used to adorn themselves with the "unfading beauty of a gentle and quiet spirit" (3:4–5). Now he mentions the traits that make everyone attractive.

Peace

We pay great attention to appearances when we first meet someone. With a glance, we assess gender, age, height, weight, and facial characteristics. We judge whether the person is confident or reticent, friendly or hostile, open or closed. We assess social status and strength by glancing at clothing, hair, and posture. Visual cues are vital at first. Yet as we discover the person's skills and character, appearances matter less and less. Much more, the Lord looks at the heart and assesses our character. Peter says, "Finally, all of you,

125

have unity of mind, sympathy, brotherly love, a tender heart, and a humble mind" (1 Peter 3:8 ESV).

At first glance, Peter seems to list five random virtues. On closer inspection, a pattern emerges. The first and last are mental or intellectual, the second and fourth are emotional, and brotherly love stands at the center. Further, all these traits have a social dimension. Together, they keep relationships healthy.

Unity

Strong relationships begin with "unity of mind" (*homophrones*). To have one mind is not to have identical opinions about politics, philosophy, ethics, business, food, music, and leisure. Rather, unity means that we are "agreeable and sensitive to each other's concerns."[1] Unity comes not from a creed or a law laid upon us, nor from a pretense that we agree when we actually disagree, but from relationships, respectful dialogue, and common causes.

Love

First Peter 3:8 mentions three forms of love—sympathy, brotherly love, compassion. Sympathy and compassion are emotional virtues. Sympathy is the ability to feel what another feels, whether in joy or in sorrow. We must "rejoice with those who rejoice [and] mourn with those who mourn" (Rom. 12:15). If one suffers, all suffer. If one is honored, all rejoice (1 Cor. 12:26). To sympathize is to enter the experience of others and, if possible, to act on what we feel. Jesus sympathizes with us in our weakness. He "has been tempted in every way, just as we are, yet was without sin," so he knows our struggles (Heb. 4:15). Among humans, sympathy largely rests on shared pains, but Jesus is both strong and empathetic! He doesn't merely sympathize with us in our battle against evil; he defeats Satan and the powers of evil. He feels *with* us and acts *for* us.

The term translated "brotherly love" (*philadelphos*) could be rendered "brotherly affection." The command to love one another is foundational (John 13:34–35; cf. 1 Thess. 4:9). Jesus set a high standard when he said, "As I have loved you, so you must love one another" (John 13:34). In his kindness, his insight into our souls, and his sacrifice for our sins, Jesus embodies love.

1. J. Ramsey Michaels, *1 Peter*, Word Biblical Commentary 49 (Nashville: Thomas Nelson, 1988), 176.

Jesus identifies "Love your neighbor as yourself" as the second great command (Matt. 22:39). Paul agrees: "Be devoted to one another in brotherly love" (Rom. 12:10).

A slight misconception of love has grown up in some Christian circles. Many are aware that Greek has four principal terms for *love* and that three of them appear in the New Testament.[2] Among these, we ordinarily give pride of place to *agapē*, which we call divine love. We commonly say that *agapē* is the greatest or purest form of love, since God has this love even for his enemies. But the contrast between the various words for *love* isn't sharp; the terms overlap and can be used interchangeably. Indeed, the verb *phileō*, from the same family as *philia* (typically, affectionate love), often appears in John's gospel, where it describes the Father's love for the Son (John 5:20), the Father's love for us (16:27), and Jesus' love for his disciples (11:36; 20:2).[3] Further, the Septuagint uses *agapaō* for Amnon's sexual passion for Tamar; we would expect a form of the word *eros*.

Since *agapē* goes to enemies, it is based neither on feelings for the loved one nor on beauty or virtue that we see in that person. Indeed, we can make the case that *agapē* is greater than human or brotherly affection (*philia*), since *agapē* is indiscriminate and inclusive, going to every neighbor or stranger who crosses our path. Further, God himself is the source and model of *agapē*. By contrast, the love of human affection (which *philia* often, but not always, signifies) is exclusive and discriminating. It goes to friends, to the attractive, the skillful, the few. It would seem that such love rises from natural admiration, so that there is no need to require it. Nonetheless, Romans 12:10; 1 Thessalonians 4:9; Hebrews 13:1; and 1 Peter 3:8 all bless and command brotherly, affectionate love. The apostles blessed tender affection between friends and family members.

When Christians say that *agapē* is the highest form of love because it is Godlike and dispassionate, they probably mean that love for enemies is noble and amazing, which it is. And *agapē is* often the term for God's love for unattractive sinners. But God wants, even *expects*, us to *feel affection* for each other. And we can show affection in a warm embrace and in acts of kindness. In short, love is not essentially dispassionate. It *can be* dispassionate—and

---

2. The four are *agapē, philia, storgē, eros.*

3. The emotional component may be weaker in some of these cases, but there is no reason to believe it has disappeared.

it must be if we are to love someone who is misbehaving. But God created us with emotions, so we love emotionally.

The final aspect of love in 1 Peter 3:8 is compassion. Compassion is the emotion or feeling of love, tenderness, generosity, and warmth. Compassion and sympathy come naturally to some. Others have to work to open themselves to it. Some of us are drawn to babies, lonely old people, and sad emotional stories. Others want to run away from all three. Few of us gladly listen to sorrowful friends. Eventually, we want to say, "Don't be a baby. Toughen up. Your problems are nothing. You brought this on yourself. Fight through it and you'll be stronger."[4] In short, whether by nature or nurture, many of us lack sympathy and compassion. In that case, we should question our inclinations, for God is compassionate (Ex. 34:6). Jesus is kind and tender, and he expects us to grow toward conformity to him (Eph. 4:32; Rom. 8:29).

Humility

The final blessed trait of 1 Peter 3:8 is humility. It is easy to see that humility, listed last, corresponds to unity, listed first. To be humble is to suppress the desire to be important and to put our interests first. Since most quarrels come from a desire to have our way, we see that humility fosters unity. Jesus is the supreme model of humility. "Your attitude should be the same as that of Christ Jesus: 'Who, being in very nature God, did not consider equality with God something to be grasped, but made himself nothing, taking the very nature of a servant'" (Phil. 2:5–7).

In book 7 of his *Republic*, Plato commented that the best governors are reluctant to hold power, not eager for it, so that the man who hungers to rule the republic is ipso facto unfit to rule it. George Washington exemplified this in 1788. He hoped to retire from public life and tend his farms, but when America needed a leader, all eyes turned to him and he agreed to serve again. The person who hungers for rule is unfit for rule.

Humility must not be confused with a poor self-concept. It's "a willingness to take the lower place, to perform the less exalted service," and to put the interests of others ahead of our own.[5] As John Calvin said, self-denial is a

4. See Dan B. Allender, *The Healing Path: How the Hurts in Your Past Can Lead You to a More Abundant Life* (Colorado Springs: WaterBrook, 1999), 3–16.

5. Peter H. Davids, *The First Epistle of Peter* (Grand Rapids: Eerdmans, 1990), 125.

good summary of the Christian life.[6] This has nothing to do with personal style. One can be humble *and* assertive. The problem is not assertion; it is *self-assertion*. When I was a young pastor, the CEO of a local company and former navy commander came to my small church. I was not yet thirty years old, and when we spoke I braced myself, even physically, standing with my feet wide apart, shoulders square, leaning toward him, so that his sheer will didn't blow me against the nearest wall. He was very assertive, but because he didn't assert himself, he was a humble man.

Nonretaliation

First Peter 3:9 urges, "Do not pay evil with evil or insult with insult, but with blessing, because to this you were called so that you may inherit a blessing." First Peter 3:8 and 9 present contrasting commands. The opposite of love (3:8) is mean-spirited justice, the cycle of insult and counterinsult, blows and counterblows, retaliations and retaliation for prior retaliation (3:9). That describes life between many hostile groups that border on each other—Serbs and Bosnians, Israelis and Palestinians, Shiites and Sunnis, and many more.

Instead of cursing, we should bless. There is a time for silence, as Jesus showed during his trial (Matt. 26:63). But ordinarily we should be ready to bless those who curse or persecute us (Rom. 12:14; 1 Cor. 4:12). In Scripture, this blessing could be a general word of kindness or *the* word of blessing, the gospel. Jesus commanded us to love our enemies, to pray for them, and so to bless them (Matt. 5:44). He practiced what he preached, speaking words of blessing from the cross. We can do the same in politics and work, in families and friendships.

As Peter knows, it is human nature to do the opposite, repaying injury for injury. Some people even seem to delight in taking offense, feeling wounded, and claiming victim status, even if there is no real harm. A few years ago, I planned to go to Brazil to speak at a conference. Alas, I failed to realize that standards had shifted, so that my visa, which still had life on it from a prior conference, was invalid. I was turned away as I tried to board my plane, and the nearest Brazilian consulate could not set things

---

6. John Calvin, *Institutes of the Christian Religion*, trans. Ford Lewis Battles (Philadelphia: Westminster, 1960), 3.7.1–10.

right in time. Behind this shift in visa policy, I later learned, lay a diplomatic squabble. American officials had allegedly refused to admit some well-qualified Brazilians. The Brazilians took umbrage and retaliated by refusing entry to Americans.

Who starts these skirmishes? Who ends them? Who gets hurt, without reason, in the interim? Peter declares, "Do not repay evil with evil," but bless "that you may inherit a blessing" (1 Peter 3:9). In the Old Testament, the blessing was the Promised Land. In 1:4–7, Peter says that the blessing is now eternal life, which begins when Jesus returns. The principle of returning good for evil follows Jesus' word: "Forgive, and you will be forgiven. Give, and it will be given to you. . . . With the measure you use, it will be measured to you" (Luke 6:37–38). More than that, the prime example of nonretaliation is our conversion, for God called us when we were still his enemies. May we therefore seek ways to bless friend and foe, even if they fail us.

LIVING IN PEACE

First Peter 3:10–12 is essentially a long quotation from Psalm 34. David wrote it as praise: "I will extol the LORD . . . . Glorify the LORD with me" (Ps. 34:1–3). Yet the psalm moves from the blessing of God to the fear of God, and the fear of the Lord plays itself out in daily life. David's God-fearing counsel for life nicely fits Peter's interest in discipleship in difficult times. Peter knows that persecution causes troubles, but there are ways to minimize trouble; Peter quotes some from Psalm 34:

> Whoever would love life
>   and see good days
> must keep his tongue from evil
>   and his lips from deceitful speech.
> He must turn from evil and do good;
>   he must seek peace and pursue it. (1 Peter 3:10–11, quoting Ps. 34:12–14)

"Life" in 1 Peter 3:10 refers to life on earth. The prospect of "good days" shows that Peter momentarily put aside the specter of persecution. He considers how disciples might live when life is fair, when skies are blue, when justice and peace prevail. How might we keep the peace in ordinary times? Peter answers with a short blast of wisdom literature. If you love life and want good days, do things that facilitate peace.

What Peter calls "good days" is roughly what we call happiness. Social scientists have studied happiness for years and have reached consistent conclusions. The poor are generally less happy, but once someone escapes poverty, his or her wealth, career success, and individual liberty add little to happiness. Arduous and constructive challenges are important, but "the daily activities most associated with happiness are all social" things such as a strong marriage and time spent with friends.[7]

First, then, to enjoy "good days"—and good relationships—we must control our tongues. Previously, 1 Peter mentioned verbal sins such as accusing, denouncing, blaspheming, and ridiculing. Here Peter mentions deceit and "evil" speech, which, judging by all Scripture, would include gossip, slander, boasting, bragging, lying, making false promises or vows, rudeness, and abuse of God's name. The opposite is to speak the truth in love, to praise God, and to bless humanity.

Second, we must "turn from evil and do good" (1 Peter 3:11). Peter talks about the right behavior of a disciple in two ways. First Peter 1 says that we must be holy because God is holy. Holiness signifies consecration to God and separation from sin (1:15–16; 2:5–9; 3:5). The statement "Be holy in all your *conduct*," or way of life (1:15 ESV), provides a bridge to the other aspect of right behavior, which is *doing good* to others. The language of "doing good" appears just twelve times in the New Testament, and six of them are in Peter.[8]

Doing good is the active, outward-facing aspect of Christian conduct. Holiness signifies *separation*, even withdrawal, from the evils of this world. By contrast, when we do good we engage the world, seek to reverse evil. We put up buildings, create constructive institutions, perform music, and generally do whatever our skill and experience allows. To *do* good is to *bring* good to all. By doing good, Peter says, believers silence the accusations of foolish men (1 Peter 2:14–15). Three times Peter urges readers to

---

7. David Brooks, *The Social Animal: The Hidden Sources of Love, Character, and Achievement* (New York: Random House, 2011), 195–97.

8. The family of terms is *agathopoieō, agathopoiia, agathopoios*. They appear in 1 Peter 2:15, 20; 3:1, 6, 17; 4:19.

continue doing good in the face of suffering (2:20; 3:17; 4:19). He also tells wives to follow Sarah and do good, whether their husbands share their faith or not (3:6). By doing good, we can frustrate the hostility of some and win others (2:15; 3:1).

The good we enjoy follows the good we do. If we want a good life, we should "turn from evil and do good." This is not a call to naiveté. When Jesus sent his disciples into a hostile society, he told them to be as wise as serpents. We should not needlessly expose ourselves to harm. But always, *always*, we strive to "do good to all people," even if our special focus is "the family of believers" (Gal. 6:10). So, then, in normal times, if we do good we will live well. If we greet people warmly, they will be glad to see us. If we laugh away minor problems, we will have more friends.

Third, life will be good if we "seek peace and pursue it." This theme runs through New Testament epistles. Like Peter, Hebrews 12:14 links holiness and the pursuit of peace: "Make every effort to live in peace with all men and to be holy." Likewise, Paul tells us, "If it is possible, as far as it depends on you, live at peace with everyone" (Rom. 12:18). We notice the provisos. First, it might not be possible to attain peace. Second, peacemaking requires at least two parties. We can do only our part. Sadly, it is impossible to make peace with some people. So there is a time to give up the quest. And as Proverbs 26:17 warns, "Like one who seizes a dog by the ears is a passer-by who meddles in a quarrel not his own."

To summarize, then, we find the good life when we follow Peter's five imperatives: stop evil speech, turn from evil deeds, do good, seek peace, and pursue it. The core command is to do good to others.

Then, Peter concludes, we will experience God's favor: "For the eyes of the Lord are on the righteous and his ears are attentive to their prayer, but the face of the Lord is against those who do evil" (1 Peter 3:12). This sounds much like the classic benediction of Numbers 6:24–26:

> The LORD bless you
>   and keep you;
> the LORD make his face shine upon you
>   and be gracious to you;
> the LORD turn his face toward you
>   and give you peace.

Yet we notice that there is more here than blessing. The Lord "is against those who do evil." This is vindication, not vindictiveness. For the faithful to enjoy peace, their accusers must be silenced and their enemies stopped, even judged. In *Beyond Good and Evil*, Friedrich Nietzsche derides Christianity as one of the religions or ethics with the slave morality that praises charity, piety, restraint, smallness, and submission. It has none of the life-affirming boldness of great men, but rather a pitiful hope that God will later avenge suffering believers.

But Nietzsche misconstrues the Christian ethic. We do good wherever we are, and we are realistic about the power structures of the world. We gain our freedom if we can (1 Cor. 7:21), we make peace if we can, and we entrust the results of all our actions to God, who is—this is realism—the Judge of all (1 Peter 2:23).

So Peter has explained how we might find a good and peaceful life. If we avoid evil words and deeds, do good to all, and submit to proper authorities, it will ordinarily lead to a good life in the present. That does not always happen, as Peter soon points out. We might still do good and suffer for it. If so, at least we know that the Lord's eyes see the righteous, that his ears hear our prayers, and that the same face that favors us opposes evil.

These graces are ours by the faith in Jesus that unites us to him. That faith lets us live well, speak blessings, repay evil with good, and live in harmony, sympathy, love, compassion, and humility. When troubles come, we then have the assurance that we have done what we could to avoid them. And when they come, we know that the Lord hears our cry. That should be enough to move us to live faithfully in his kingdom.

11

THE RIGHT FEAR

1 Peter 3:13–18

Who is going to harm you if you are eager to do good? But even if you should suffer for what is right, you are blessed. "Do not fear what they fear; do not be frightened." (1 Peter 3:13–14)

recent poll surveyed Americans' greatest fears. They mentioned animals such as snakes, spiders, bees, bugs, bats, and mice. Some animals can poison us, so those fears make sense. People living in the wilder parts of Africa surely list lions, hyenas, crocodiles, and hippos, which are fond of upsetting boats and attacking the people formerly in them.

Most fears are more personal. We fear enemies, armies, strangers, death, and loneliness. We fear public speaking and public singing (especially solos) not because they are intrinsically dangerous, but because they can lead to public humiliation. We fear places and spaces. We fear enclosed places (claustrophobia) and open spaces (agoraphobia). We fear crowds, bridges, tunnels, and storms.

Fears vary over the years. After a serious terrorist attack, we fear terrorism. After a nuclear accident, we fear radiation. People who lived in Communist countries were, logically, afraid of the secret police, concentration camps, and starvation. In the West, people fear job loss and economic stagnation. Our fears of cancer, flying, war, and heights, among other things, manifest our central fear of death. But we also fear bullies, broken relationships, and embarrassment. We can be afraid of safe things, such as flying, and unafraid of dangerous things, such as addictive prescription drugs. We can shed a fear of public speaking when we try it and it goes well, and we can acquire a fear, perhaps if a spider bite sends us to the hospital.

FEARLESS IN THE FACE OF TROUBLE

Peter repeatedly addresses the question of proper and improper fears in the middle section of his epistle, in 1 Peter 2:17–23; 3:1–6; 3:14–16; and 4:1–6.[1] For the first half of his epistle, Peter has stressed the necessity of an exemplary life in this hostile environment. As we saw, Peter alleviated the fear of persecution with a quotation from Psalm 34, "Whoever would love life and see good days must keep his tongue from evil and his lips from deceitful speech. He must turn from evil and do good; he must seek peace and pursue it" (1 Peter 3:10–11). It was possible to lead a good life, even in that hour. Believers could still evade trouble and live in peace, by controlling the tongue, telling the truth, and doing good to others. Peter had enough confidence that justice prevails that he could ask, "Who is going to harm you if you are eager to do good?" (3:13). If a man lives with zeal and devotion for all that is beautiful, just, and good, how many enemies can he have? The question might be translated: "Who is going to harm you if you are an enthusiast, a partisan, for the good?"[2] Again, if you are passionately committed to what is beautiful, just, and good, how many enemies can you have? Few, if any. This note of optimism is found at times in the Bible:

- Proverbs 16:7: "When a man's ways are pleasing to the LORD, he makes even his enemies live at peace with him."
- Romans 13:3: "Rulers hold no terror for those who do right, but for those who do wrong. Do you want to be free from fear of the one in authority? Then do what is right and he will commend you."

1. *Fear* as noun or verb appears seven times, but the theme continues into chapter 4.
2. The Greek is *zēlotēs*—one who is eager, avid, ardent, enthusiastic, zealous.

As a practical matter, if a believer seems to have a number of enemies, persecution could be the cause, but it's also possible that the "victim" is *earning* enemies the old-fashioned way, through selfishness or faithlessness. We must not confuse the trouble we deserve with the trouble we do not.

Nonetheless, Peter concedes, it *is* possible to suffer for doing good. At times oppression is commonplace. When corruption and deceit rule a society, the good are not welcome. For that reason, Jesus said, "Blessed are those who are persecuted because of righteousness, for theirs is the kingdom of heaven" (Matt. 5:10). Then the righteous should call to God for vindication. As David notes, "A righteous man may have many troubles, but the LORD delivers him from them all" (Ps. 34:19). First Peter 3 leads us through such a time.

THE WRONG FEARS

Peter intends to prepare the church for persecution. Ordinarily, he maintains, if we live well, life goes well. Yet he must concede that irrational persecution is possible: "Even if you should suffer for what is right, you are blessed. 'Do not fear what they fear; do not be frightened'" (1 Peter 3:14). The phrase "even if you should suffer" has a rare grammatical feature. The verb is in the optative mood, which signals that the event—the suffering—is viewed, at least for now, as a remote or doubtful possibility.[3]

Peter wants to prepare his readers for trouble by gently suggesting the possibility: "Don't *expect* anyone to harm you if you are enthusiastic about goodness, but if it *should* happen, respond this way." First, the mistreated should count themselves blessed. Second, we should neither fear the persecutors nor be troubled within. God rules the future—in the short term, at the midterm, and for eternity. If anything, we should fear God, not with craven fear, but with the fear of respect. We should fear disappointing One whom we love and revere. This is the fear that the Bible often commends. Moses said: "What does the LORD . . . ask of you but to fear the LORD your God, to walk in all his ways, to love him, to serve [him] with all your heart" (Deut. 10:12). Likewise, Solomon declared, "Do not be wise in your own eyes; fear the LORD and shun evil" (Prov. 3:7). We need to know what to fear and what not to fear, for the right fears bring sanity.

---

3. The optative mood appears just seventy times in the New Testament. A good number of them are in Peter. Roughly half appear in the stereotyped phrase "May it never be" (*me genoito*).

"Do not fear" might be the most common command in the Bible. The Bible tells us to shake off fear about a hundred times and gives a reason almost every time. It also tells us what *not* to fear. We should not fear conspiracy, shame, insults, financial loss, or loneliness. We should not fear enemies, hostility, or suffering. We should not fear death.

When Peter states, "Do not fear what they fear" (1 Peter 3:14), he means that we must question our fears. Some fears are sensible, such as the fear of heights or infections. Fear of public embarrassment drives us to prepare when we are scheduled for presentations. But, Jesus tells us, we should not fear those who slander and persecute us for our faith. In Matthew, he says that we should "beware of men" and yet "have no fear of them" (Matt. 10:17, 26 ESV). Rather, we should fear him "who can destroy both soul and body in hell" (10:28).

Echoing the word of Jesus, Peter instructs his people to be fearless even if, by ordinary standards, they had cause for fear. Indeed, Peter's people lived in a time and place—the Roman Empire, around A.D. 70—when a person could face loss of property, exile, prison, bodily harm, or even death for the faith.[4]

The command in 1 Peter 3:14 bears close study. It has been translated several ways, and each reflects important elements of the Greek text:

- NIV: "Do not fear what they fear; do not be frightened."
- ESV: "Have no fear of them, nor be troubled."
- NRSV: "Do not fear what they fear, and do not be intimidated."
- NASB: "And do not fear their intimidation, and do not be troubled."
- CEV: "So stop being afraid and don't worry about what people might do."

The key clause literally reads, "Do not fear the fear of them." The NIV, NRSV, and others take the phrase to mean that we should not fear the same things that they fear. That is, a disciple does not have the same fears as a secular person. But the ESV, KJV, NASB, and others say that we should not fear *them* as they try to frighten or intimidate us.

4. Hebrews, probably also written shortly before A.D. 70, reminds the church of an earlier time, perhaps in the reign of Emperor Claudius (around A.D. 50), when believers endured "insult and persecution . . . [and] sympathized with those in prison and joyfully accepted the confiscation of [their] property" (Heb. 10:32–34).

Translators and commentators disagree because both translations (or interpretations) are grammatically and theologically plausible.[5] That is, it's true that we should not "fear them"—those who could make Peter's people "suffer for what is right" (1 Peter 3:14). But it's also true that we should not fear "what they fear," that is, the same things that pagans fear. We should not be anxious about food and clothing, since God cares for us (Ps. 37:25; Matt. 6:25–34). We should not fear traps, plots, pestilence, or war (Ps. 91:2–6; Isa. 8:12; Jer. 30:10–11), since God cares for us. Society cannot decide what is frightening for us. We must choose our fears wisely rather than fearing what everyone else fears.

Both interpretations also make sense in context, too. We should not fear "what they fear" because disciples are "aliens" in this world and have different thoughts and different fears. Yet the idea that we should not "fear them" is even more prominent, as 1 Peter 3:15–4:6 prepares his people to endure suffering.

Even though both views have strengths, we conclude that Peter means we should "have no fear of them." First, he is quoting Isaiah 8:13, where the prophet tells flawed King Ahaz that he should fear God, not an Assyrian invasion. Second, in the immediate context, fear of persecutors is far more prominent.[6] So, then, Peter concedes that we can suffer "for righteousness' sake" even if we are "zealous for what is good" (1 Peter 3:13–14 ESV). But even if that happens, we should not be frightened by persecutors.

Rather, we should "set apart Christ as Lord" (1 Peter 3:15). "Set apart" translates the Greek word *hagiazō*. *Hagiazō* is normally translated "sanctify" or "make holy." Since God is already holy, the word has the sense of setting apart or recognizing God as holy. To set Christ apart means, first, that since Jesus is sovereign over all, we should not fear whatever might befall us. Second, since Jesus is Lord, we should fear *him*, not what any lesser person or power can do (cf. Luke 12:5). If we have the right fear, the fear of the Lord, we can overcome lesser fears.

Peter hopes his people will not even begin to fear persecution. The threat is yet distant, so they need not worry about future possibilities. But even

---

5. The Greek reads: *tōn de phobōn autōn mē phobēthete*. The debate hinges on the fourth word, the genitive pronoun *autōn*, which can mean "their" or "of them."

6. J. Ramsey Michaels, *1 Peter*, Word Biblical Commentary 49 (Nashville: Thomas Nelson, 1988), 184–87.

if persecution comes, they must not be intimidated or succumb to fear of possible harm.

Dietrich Bonhoeffer was a German pastor who had the courage to speak out against Adolf Hitler, write about it, organize opposition against Hitler, and even join plans to assassinate him. He also helped Jews to escape from Germany. Bonhoeffer persevered in all this for a decade, even though he was engaged to a woman for part of the time. The Nazis imprisoned and finally executed him. He said, "Those who are afraid of men have no fear of God, and those who fear God have no more fear of men."[7]

Living by the Right Fear

Instead of living in fear, therefore, we set Jesus apart as the *One* to fear. As we consider the prospect of persecution, we should not fear it, but prepare for it. We should always be "prepared to make a defense to anyone who asks you for a reason for the hope that is in you" (1 Peter 3:15 ESV). Of course, believers should always be ready to make a case for the faith, but Peter's term for *defense* suggests a formal event, in court, answering charges. We can prepare to defend the faith in several ways.

Peter assumes that the saints are willing to be known as God's people. Further, we should know that the way to "always be prepared" is to prepare continually. My family goes hiking in the Rockies most summers. One year, we hiked to a lake at 12,500 feet on the first day. Just as we arrived, it began to snow. We had to leave soon, but one daughter spotted a rocky promontory that promised a panoramic view of a vast valley. Although we had had no time to adjust to the altitude, she began dashing uphill, toward the rock. How could she dash uphill at that altitude, when she had lived in the flatlands all year? She had been running seven to ten miles daily for weeks, so she had the capacity to meet the challenge. So it is with us.

We prepare for unforeseen challenges by preparing daily for what we can foresee. The path is obvious. We read Scripture daily and meditate on it so that its truth sinks into mind and soul. We listen to our secular friends and to our culture. How do they object to the faith? What offends

7. Dietrich Bonhoeffer, *The Cost of Discipleship* (New York: Macmillan, 1937), 242. See also Eric Metaxas, *Bonhoeffer: Pastor, Martyr, Prophet, Spy* (Nashville: Thomas Nelson, 2010). Critics have questioned Metaxas's theological analysis of Bonhoeffer, but not his historical research.

or seems senseless to them, and what resonates? We also look for answers to the objections as we read, converse, and listen to Christian teaching. Finally, while we must not fall into mere subjectivism—who Jesus is *for me* and what he does *for me*—we should be ready to speak personally and tell people why *we* hope in Jesus.

The answer we give can be a formal self-defense; Peter's term fits a hearing, whether before Roman authorities, Communist officials, secular scholars, or neopagans. Yet we should also be ready to defend the faith informally, with friends.

Jesus supplements Peter's point in Matthew 10. As he sends his disciples out to proclaim the kingdom, he knows they are too new in the faith to prepare for every possibility. So he makes a promise: "But when they arrest you, do not worry about what to say or how to say it. At that time you will be given what to say, for it will not be you speaking, but the Spirit of your Father speaking through you" (Matt. 10:19–20). This is an immense comfort and a good word for those who are prone to dream (or worry) that the success of God's cause depends on the quality of their performance. Yet the promise that the Spirit will speak through us in crisis does not abrogate the demand that we *prepare when we can, as best we can.*

Peter urges disciples to be prepared both to defend themselves and to present the faith, to turn the tables from defense to evangelism. We see the apostle Paul doing this in his trial before King Agrippa (Acts 26:19–29). At the start, Paul defends himself as an accused man must. But by the end, he dares to question the king: "King Agrippa, do you believe the prophets? I know you do." Agrippa felt the pressure, responding, "Do you think that in such a short time you can persuade me to be a Christian?" (26:27–28). Evangelism is a gift of the Spirit, but every believer must be ready to present the reason for faith and hope. The task is by no means easy. There have been societies in which most people had a broadly Christian worldview. Even if people did not follow Christ, they knew the content of the faith. They believed that God exists and that he is personal, holy, loving, triune, and redeeming—that he is offended by sin, yet sent his Son Jesus to redeem his people. Evangelists could assume that people knew and perhaps concurred, intellectually, with leading tenets of the faith. But today, biblical ideas are largely unknown to most people, even in formerly Christianized nations. It takes time to explain the faith in terms that people can grasp, and our lives had better adorn our words.

Peter further describes this defense or answer to accusers in a second way: we should "be prepared . . . to give the reason for the hope that [we] have" (1 Peter 3:15). *Hope* does not have the sense of a wish—"I hope this storm won't spoil our picnic." For Peter, *hope* means the sound expectation of eternal life. Pagan views of the fate of the dead varied at that time, but many expected either to cease to exist or to live in a misty abode of the dead (Hades). The apostles link hope to the resurrection of Christ and his people. We rejoice and reign with Jesus, spiritually and physically renewed, in a restored creation, called the new heavens and new earth (Isa. 65:17; 66:22; 2 Peter 3:13; Rev. 21:1). Peter says that believers are reborn to "a living hope" (1 Peter 1:3) and connects this to Jesus' resurrection from the dead. In 1 Thessalonians 4:13–14, Paul proclaims:

> Brothers, we do not want you to be ignorant about those who fall asleep, or to grieve like the rest of men, who have no hope. We believe that Jesus died and rose again and so we believe that God will bring with Jesus those who have fallen asleep in him.

Our hope is not disembodied life in the clouds. We hope for a perfect physical and spiritual life, with Christ, on a renewed earth. Romans 8:11 teaches that the Father "who raised Christ from the dead will also give life to your mortal bodies through his Spirit, who lives in you." The model is Jesus' body after his resurrection. "When he appears, we shall be like him, for we shall see him as he is" (1 John 3:2).

Experience teaches that physical things are corruptible and transitory. But Scripture states that we will have a renewed physical body, as Jesus did. Our present bodies get sick, grow old, and refuse to follow orders, but our bodies will be flawless, incorruptible, and perfectly suited to a new life.[8] Jesus' resurrection body had enough continuity with his first body that he was recognizable, yet it had enough discontinuity that recognition wasn't always immediate. The form was similar and yet he had changed, as we will change (1 Cor. 15:51–52).

8. N. T. Wright, *Surprised by Hope* (New York: Harper One, 2008), 147–63.

Like Jesus' body, our resurrection bodies will have the capacity to walk, touch, and eat, yet we might have some of the new powers that Jesus showed. Hugh of St. Victor (ca. 1150) speculated that the resurrection body "will be immune from death and sorrow; it will be at the height of its powers, free from disease and deformity, and around thirty years old, the age at which Christ began his ministry. It will surpass anything we can imagine, even from the accounts of Christ's appearances on earth after his own resurrection."[9]

This hope of eternal life liberates us from fear. David, a fearless man, said, "In God I trust; I will not be afraid. What can man do to me?" (Ps. 56:11). Good question; the answer is: "People can kill us." But is that so bad? The killers will send us into God's presence earlier than we had expected. As David declared, "The LORD is my light and my salvation—whom shall I fear?" (27:1).

So Peter teaches us to choose our fears wisely. We must not share the fears of our neighbors. There is a proper fear of heights and poisonous animals. But we must evaluate our fears, for many are misguided. We fear change and uncertainty, but are they bad? We fear the loss of health, wealth, and friends. It seems sensible to fear trouble, yet when we consider the heroes of the faith, we see that trouble was essential to their stories. As Abraham enters Scripture's story, he gives up worldly wealth and security. Shortly before he exits, he gives up his treasured son. We love these stories "as long as they happen to someone else."[10] But they do teach us to live fearlessly.

LIVING FEARLESSLY

So we live in hope and we can explain that hope. But, Peter adds, we must do this "with gentleness and respect, having a good conscience, so that, when you are slandered, those who revile your good behavior in Christ may be put to shame" (1 Peter 3:15–16 ESV). This statement merits close scrutiny. First, Peter says that we should live so well that even if we suffer slander, those who malign us will know they are lying and be ashamed. Specifically, Peter tells us to be gentle and respectful. *Gentleness* (or *meekness*) is humility, a

9. Jeffrey Burton Russell, *A History of Heaven*, new ed. (Princeton, NJ: Princeton University Press, 1998), 119ff.

10. Dan B. Allender, *To Be Told: Know Your Story, Shape Your Life* (Colorado Springs: WaterBrook Press, 2005), 40.

refusal to use force or to demand rights.[11] *Respect* is literally *fear*. Curiously, a disciple can show the right sort of fear to humans because we have greater respect or fear for God (cf. 1:17). So, then, when we suffer slander or false accusations, we can reply gently and meekly because we know that God, the Sovereign, will justify us (2:23). Therefore, while a good reputation is valuable (Prov. 22:1), it is not imperative that we vindicate ourselves in the courts of men.

This is important for Christian leaders who are the targets of unjust attacks that are actually directed at Christ and his church globally. (Lest we pity ourselves, let's recall that we receive praise for things we didn't do right as well as blame for things we didn't do wrong.) Since righteousness seems bizarre to some people (1 Peter 4:4), it is impossible to silence every accuser. Therefore, sometimes it is right to stop defending ourselves and to follow Jesus as we entrust ourselves to God's judgment (2:23).

It is our task to keep "a clear conscience," a confidence that our behavior has been good (Acts 23:1; Rom. 2:15; Heb. 13:18). Our good behavior, Peter reminds us, is "in Christ" (1 Peter 3:16). Jesus defines good conduct by his commands and his example (3:18), and he is "the power and motivation for good conduct in even the most provoking situations."[12]

The disciple, wrongly accused, might suffer unjustly. Yet "it is better, if it is God's will, to suffer for doing good than for doing evil" (1 Peter 3:17). This restates, in broader terms, what Peter earlier told Christian slaves (2:19–20); he says it again in 4:13–15. If we suffer for doing evil, we merely endure just punishment. A believer cannot claim persecution when punished for wickedness or folly. But if we suffer for doing good, we demonstrate our union with Christ and can expect to join him in glory (4:13–14). Until then, we strive to live well and endure suffering "if it is God's will."[13]

First Peter 2:12 directs us to live honorably and trust God to vindicate us if slandered. Here he notes that we live so well that slander is obviously false (3:16). First Peter 2:18–20 says that slaves follow Jesus' example when they endure injustice. Here Peter explains why and how Jesus suffered. We

11. The Greek is *prautēs*; the companion adjective *praus* appears in texts such as Matthew 5:5 ("Blessed are the meek") and 21:5.

12. Peter H. Davids, *The First Epistle of Peter* (Grand Rapids: Eerdmans, 1990), 133.

13. In the phrase "if it is God's will" (1 Peter 3:17), the verb's mood is optative, suggesting that this suffering is possible, but not certain.

know that Jesus' suffering sets an example, yet 1 Peter 3:18 points out that we have more than just another case of a man who suffered for doing good.

Above all, Jesus did not merely suffer; he suffered to the point of death, for our sins.[14] That is, Jesus died a substitutionary death. He did nothing to deserve suffering or death. He was sinless and deserved nothing but God's favor. Logically, since the Father would not let an innocent man suffer and die—for that would be unjust—Jesus suffered on behalf of another. Peter teaches that Christ suffered and died "for sins once for all, the righteous for the unrighteous" (1 Peter 3:18). That is, we have a one-time, permanent, nonrepeatable substitution: Jesus, the righteous, died for us, the unrighteous. He bore on our behalf the punishment, the death that our sins deserved. As Isaiah had prophesied centuries earlier, "My righteous servant will justify many, and he will bear their iniquities" (Isa. 53:11).

Furthermore, Jesus suffered "that he might bring us to God" (1 Peter 3:18 ESV). He died to lead us from death to life, from slavery to freedom, from alienation to knowledge of God. So we passed from enemy territory into God's presence. We crossed over from death to life (John 5:24). But Jesus' death is not final. He was "put to death in the flesh but made alive in the spirit" (1 Peter 3:18 ESV). Jesus' death killed his flesh (for a time), but it did not kill him. When we are then united to him by faith, death will not destroy us either.

Careful readers notice that Peter draws on the example of Christ repeatedly—in 1 Peter 2:18–25; 3:14–18; and 4:12–14. Whenever Peter comments on injustice, the suffering of slaves, or the persecution of disciples, he turns to Jesus' life to make sense of it. He decides that if Jesus could suffer unjustly, his disciples can, too. Indeed, the force of Jesus' moral example might be more prominent in Peter than in any other epistle. Still, *moral example* is by no means Peter's prime concept of atonement. Even if Peter turns to the cross for moral reasons, he begins and ends with the cross as the source of atonement and of grace. It is the foundation for the Christian life before it is an example. Thus, 1 Peter 1 says that believers are holy because they "were redeemed" from their futile life by "the precious blood of Christ," God's spotless Lamb (1:14–19). In chapter 5, Peter calls himself "a witness

14. The Greek text varies here; some manuscripts say that Jesus suffered, others that he died. The Greek words for *suffered* and *died* are fairly similar. And the meanings overlap, since we know that Jesus shed his blood and died (1 Peter 1:3, 19).

of Christ's sufferings," which offered the grace in which we stand (5:1, 10). So Peter establishes the atonement in 1:14–19, returns to it in 2:22–24 and 3:18, and then presents it as a pattern for disciples.

Peter reminds us that the starting point for every issue that the Christian faces can be found in the gospel:

- If we commit sins, Jesus is our propitiation, our atoning sacrifice.
- If we are condemned for sin, Jesus justifies us by grace through faith.
- If sins and character flaws hold us captive, he redeems or liberates us.
- If we are estranged, he reconciles us to himself and his people.
- If we feel isolated, he adopts us into his family.
- If we feel insignificant, the gospel unites us to him.

Beyond these spiritual and soteriological issues, the gospel also speaks to our moral life, our conduct, as Peter knows:

- In society, we are humble, even as Christ humbled himself and made himself nothing.
- In marriage, we love as Christ loved the church.
- At work, like Christ, we do our duty and fulfill our calling.

First Peter 3:13–18 is a highly theological passage; nonetheless, it contains several suggestions about the conduct of life of the believer. First, 3:14 directs, we should live fearlessly. Or rather, a proper fear of God should drive out lesser fears—public opinion, human foes, tragedy, our own weakness. So we should choose our fears well. It's sensible to fear snakes and heights, but the Lord, in his awesome goodness and justice, is the One to fear. Second, 3:16 urges, we should keep a clear conscience, so that if we face unjust attacks, we will be able to defend ourselves, with gentle self-confidence and reverence for God, our Protector and Judge. Third, when an opponent speaks, we should "be prepared to make a defense" and to give a reason "for the hope that is in [us]" (3:15 ESV). This defense may be formal, in court, or informal, among friends. Finally, we remember that even if we suffer (or die!), the Lord vindicates his people. That liberates us even from the fear of death. For the love of God drives out all lesser fears, that we might live in reverent fear of him (3:15).

145

12

THE WORK OF THE LIVING CHRIST

1 Peter 3:18—22

For Christ died for sins once for all, the righteous for the
unrighteous, to bring you to God. He was put to death in the
body but made alive by the Spirit, through whom also he went
and preached to the spirits in prison who disobeyed long ago.
(1 Peter 3:18–20a)

THE CHALLENGE OF UNDERSTANDING OUR PASSAGE

First Peter 3:18b–22 is by all accounts the most difficult passage to interpret in 1 Peter—some say the entire New Testament. Lengthy academic
works aim simply to describe the history of its interpretation, or even single
aspects of it, such as Jesus' speech "to the spirits in prison" (3:19). Indeed,
since this is an expository commentary, I feel obligated to suggest that it
might be best for pastors to preach 1 Peter 3:19–22 in conjunction with the
larger passage, 3:13–22, of which it is a part.[1] However difficult 3:19–22 may

---

1. Grammatically, the sentence that starts at 1 Peter 3:18 ends at 3:20, and a grammatical connection runs to the end of 3:22, so there is continuity from verses 18 to 22. I believe it is generally
best for pastors to preach through the grammatical units of a book when possible. The mind of the
expositor is more likely to conform to the mind of the apostle and of Christ. There is less tempta-

be, if we read the passage in context and hold to the essentials of the faith, we will at least avoid major error.[2]

Taking 1 Peter 3:13–22 as a whole, we see that the *end* of the passage gives reasons for the commands stated in the *beginning*. The passage is a cousin of 1 Peter 2:18–25. Both present Jesus as the supreme example of the innocent man who endures mistreatment. In 1 Peter 2, Jesus suffers injustice and entrusts himself to God. In 1 Peter 3, Jesus suffers for doing good and experiences God's vindication. In each passage, Jesus both *illustrates and empowers* righteous action. Yet whereas 1 Peter 2 accents Jesus' sacrifice, 1 Peter 3 calls attention to his resurrection, exaltation, and power over all (3:21–22).

First Peter 3:13–18 explains that Christians who suffer are "blessed" and free from fear because they know Christ as Lord. The Christian keeps a clear conscience so that those who malign believers "may be ashamed of their slander" (3:14–16). Further, "it is better . . . to suffer for doing good than for doing evil" (3:17). No suffering can thwart God's purposes, Peter states, "for Christ died for sins once for all . . . to bring you to God" (3:18a). But after he died, God raised him in power and vindicated him, giving us strong hope of the same vindication (3:18, 22).

Scholars generally agree that 1 Peter 3:18–22 draws on an early creed or hymn, since the structure and vocabulary seem to differ from the rest of Peter, but to say more is to speculate. The texture of 3:18–19 is almost poetic:

> For Christ also suffered once for sins,
> the righteous for the unrighteous,
> that he might bring us to God,
> being put to death in the flesh
> but [being] made alive in the spirit [or "made alive by the Spirit," NIV]
> in which [or "through whom," NIV] he went and proclaimed ["preached," NIV]
>   to the spirits in prison. (ESV)

---

tion for the teacher to seize topics in the text and separate them from it. While it can be difficult to preach the entire unit when working with longer passages, it is generally feasible in New Testament epistles. A pastor could cover 1 Peter 3:13–22 in one sermon, focusing on 3:13–18, and then treat the certainties and essentials of 3:19–22. Not every congregation is ready for an entire sermon on a text as complex as 3:19–22.

2. Interested pastors may turn to reliable academic commentaries by Achtemeier, Davids, Goppelt, Jobes, and Michaels if they wish to probe riddles of the passage in detail.

Even here, in the easier part of the passage, there are riddles. Above all, it seems impossible to be sure whether the Greek means that Jesus was made alive in his human spirit or made alive by God's Spirit. Further, did he preach in his spirit or did he preach in the power of God's Spirit? Interpreters and translators are divided and uncertain. First, Greek doesn't use capital letters except for personal names, so we don't know whether *spirit* should be capitalized, to refer to the Holy Spirit, or not, to refer to Jesus's spirit. Either reading makes sense in context. Second, the word *spirit* is in the dative case, without a clarifying preposition. As a result, the sense could be that Jesus is alive *in* or *with regard to* his spirit or that he is alive *by means of* God's Spirit.

If we step back from the exegetical uncertainties, however, we see that each reading is possible grammatically and theologically because other sections of the New Testament show that both are true: Jesus is alive in his human spirit and by the Holy Spirit. Moreover, Jesus both preached in his spirit and by the Holy Spirit, since the Spirit empowered all of Jesus' life and ministry. From Luke 1–4 alone, we know that the Spirit begat Christ (Luke 1:35), entered him at baptism (3:16, 22), led him to combat Satan (4:1), and empowered his miracles and his message (4:14, 18). Let's not be dismayed that it's difficult to separate the work of the spirit of Jesus the man from the work of God the Spirit. Rather, we should give thanks for the unity in the work and persons of the triune God.

Whatever the uncertainties in 1 Peter 3:18–19, the main theme is manifest: When Jesus suffered unjustly, God vindicated him, and he will vindicate us, too. Further, there is a tight connection between verses 18 and 22, where identical aorist passive participles (all ending with the letters *-theis*) connect what humans did *to* Jesus and what the Father did *for* Jesus.

> He was put to death, by men, in the flesh (*thanatōtheis*).
> He was made alive in the Spirit [or in his spirit] (*zōopoiētheis*).
> He has gone to heaven (*poreutheis*).

This threefold declaration is the framework for the passage. Jesus was put to death, and then rose to life and ascended into heaven. Peter wants us to know that if we suffer and even die for the faith, God will raise and vindicate us, too. It is all too common for Western Christians to obsess over their pains and sorrows. But if we can discipline ourselves to lift our eyes from present troubles, we should find courage in knowing that we will follow the pattern of Christ, through suffering to resurrection and vindication.

The skeleton of 1 Peter 3:18–22 is clear, but questions abound. First Peter 3:19–20 (ESV) says that Jesus "went and proclaimed to the spirits in prison, because they formerly did not obey, when God's patience waited in the days of Noah, while the ark was being prepared, in which a few, that is, eight persons, were brought safely through water." Four questions seem prominent: (1) Where did Jesus go? (2) Who were the spirits in prison? (3) What is their prison? (4) What did Jesus say to them?

THE MISUSE OF OUR PASSAGE

If we hope to interpret this passage correctly, we cannot import 1 Peter 4:6 or Ephesians 4:9 or the Apostles' Creed ("he descended into hell") into it. The passage does *not* say that Jesus "descended," nor does it mention hell. It states that he *went*, not that he *went down*. Further, we cannot assume that *prison* (*phulakē*) means "hell." New Testament Greek had an ample vocabulary to refer to the idea of hell or the realm of the dead—*Hades, Gehenna, the abyss, the lake of fire, the outer darkness, Tartarus*—but *prison* is no part of that vocabulary.[3] Clearly, we must read Peter on its own terms.

Furthermore, the likelihood of misreading multiplies when people come looking for evidence to support their heterodox ideas. Specifically, there is interest in finding, in 1 Peter 3, evidence of a postmortem evangelistic proclamation of the gospel. That proclamation might be for those who never heard the gospel in this life or for those who heard but rejected it. At the popular level, we have *Love Wins*, by the difficult-to-categorize pastor Rob Bell. Evincing a slippery grasp on history as well as theology, Bell asserts, "At the center of the Christian tradition since the first church have been a number who insist that history is not tragic, hell is not forever, and love, in the end, wins and all will be reconciled to God."[4] Of course, to reach universal

3. See "Regions below the Surface of the Earth," in Johannes Louw and Eugene Nida, *Greek-English Lexicon of the New Testament: Based on Semantic Domains*, 2nd ed. (New York: United Bible Societies, 1998–99), 1:5–7.

4. Rob Bell, *Love Wins: A Book about Heaven, Hell, and the Fate of Every Person Who Ever Lived* (New York: HarperOne, 2011), 109.

salvation, there must be postmortem evangelism.[5] To my knowledge, Bell never actually cites 1 Peter 3. But it would be plausible for self-identified Christians to do so, since they like to appeal to Scripture.

Archbishop Hilarion Alfeyev of the Russian Orthodox Church does appeal to 1 Peter 3 in his substantive monograph, *Christ the Conqueror of Hell.* Alfeyev focuses more on patristic tradition and orthodox liturgy than on Scripture, but he does cite 1 Peter 3:19 and 4:6 as he starts his argument. He claims that Peter's words "serve as the basis for understanding" how Jesus' "preaching in hell" reached Noah's generation, described in Genesis 6:[6]

> Those who were condemned earlier "according to men in the flesh" by God who, according to the biblical expression, "was sorry" that he had created them, did not perish eternally. Christ descended into hell, granting them another chance of salvation by preaching to them the Gospel of the kingdom so that they might live "according to God in the spirit."[7]

Alfeyev wants to draw on Scripture, and for about three pages he mentions seven or eight passages that "serve as the basis" for his assertion that the patristic and orthodox tradition, especially in its liturgy, has long claimed that Christ descended into hell and preached, postmortem, to those who had not believed in him while on earth. Further, his tradition says that Jesus "freed all who were held captive" and "emptied hell" so that no mortals remained. Thus, Jesus descended into hell as Conqueror, to mortify death and destroy hell.[8]

A scholar such as Alfeyev chooses his words carefully, so that the phrase "serve as the basis" is telling. The New Testament texts that he cites indeed "serve" his argument. He cites them but does not attempt to make his case from them. Indeed, he gives just three pages on the New Testament, but grants fourteen pages on apocryphal literature, sixty on the patristic tradition, and fifty on the liturgy of the Orthodox Church. Alfeyev will hardly be the only person to see whether 1 Peter can serve his purposes, cite him

---

5. Fans of C. S. Lewis must acknowledge that he at least made it possible to read *The Great Divorce* as a guess at how that might occur.

6. Hilarion Alfeyev, *Christ the Conqueror of Hell: The Descent into Hades from an Orthodox Perspective* (St. Vladimir's Seminary Press, 2009), 19.

7. Ibid., 18–19.

8. Ibid., 203–18.

briefly, and move on. For Alfeyev, like others in the Roman and Orthodox tradition, tradition has as much weight as Scripture—more in some cases, since the tradition teaches us how to interpret Scripture. In that tradition it is acceptable to argue this way:

- Scripture could indicate X.
- While Scripture isn't clear regarding X, our tradition affirms X with certainty.
- Therefore, we affirm X with certainty.

Let no evangelical Protestant follow that pattern of reasoning. It is fine to say, "Scripture is not clear, but our confession says," and then show respect to a confession that captures the wisdom of godly leaders past. But those who profess the supreme authority of Scripture should never argue: "Scripture is not clear, but our confession is. Therefore, we affirm and *require* adherence to the confession." Instead, let the many bodies that affirm the Westminster Confession appreciate the genius of its assertion that Scripture is infallible but councils are not. And let us require supreme allegiance to God and his Word. No human artifact merits such loyalty.

THE GOSPEL PROCLAIMED TO THE "SPIRITS IN PRISON"

The task of the faithful expositor is clear. If we cannot plumb the mysteries of the passage, we can (1) state the main, clear points and (2) avoid major error by refusing to base novel doctrines on an obscure passage.

So, then, Peter states that Jesus "preached" (NIV) or "proclaimed" (ESV, NASB) something. The Greek verb is not *euaggelizomai*, "to preach the gospel or good news," but *kērussō*, "to make a proclamation." Like other words, *kērussō* has a range of meanings, and it can be used for evangelistic proclamations (e.g., Rom. 10:8–15; Gal. 2:2), but it typically means "to make an official announcement or public declaration," not "to evangelize" (e.g., Mark 1:45; Gal. 5:11; Rev. 5:2). So we need not think that Jesus *evangelized* the spirits in prison.

Next, who are these "spirits in prison"? Theories abound. They could be the demons that Jesus cast out during his ministry in Israel, as they await a final reckoning hinted at in Luke 8:26–33. But there is barely a scrap of evidence for this interpretation. They could be all the saints of old, waiting for Jesus to liberate them from Sheol or the bonds of death. But the efficacy of Jesus' sacrifice is not bound by time. There is no need to believe that Old Testament saints were separated from God from the day of their death to the day of Jesus' resurrection. The spirits could be the antediluvian generation of humans who lived in the darkness of Noah's day. But why would they be singled out to hear Jesus' words? Or they could be fallen angels, perhaps those mentioned in Genesis 6 and imprisoned by God (2 Peter 2:4; Jude 6). The last option, that Jesus made a proclamation to fallen angels, is most widely adopted, for several reasons.

First, in the New Testament, the word *spirits* (plural) "always refers to non-human spiritual beings unless qualified." It calls deceased humans *souls* (*psuchē*).[9] So unless this passage is the lone exception (and it would be special pleading to claim that it is), *spirits* does not mean "humans" here either. Typically, *spirits* refers to evil spirits or fallen angels.

Second, we can identify the spirits who "disobeyed . . . in the days of Noah." In Peter's time, the most common Jewish understanding of Genesis 6 held that fallen angels played a great role in corrupting humans in Noah's generation. These fallen angels are prominent in 1 Enoch 12–21. Of course, Enoch is not authoritative, but it was a widely known and revered book at the time, so we can expect readers to pick up an allusion to it.[10] First Enoch 21:6–10 says that fallen angels "transgressed the commandment of the Lord" and so were bound to prison.

Third, as we saw earlier, *prison* probably does not refer to hell, since the New Testament uses many other terms for the location of dead, unre-deemed humans. We notice that no location for Peter's prison is given. It seems wise (if not certain) to take *prison* as a metaphor for God's control over evil spirits. Jesus' domination of evil spirits is certainly a pervasive theme in the Gospels and Acts, as both he and his apostles break their power and force them to submit to his will. Indeed, the Synoptics' prin-cipal explanation of Jesus' power over demons uses a similar metaphor for his control of Satan:

9. Peter H. Davids, *The First Epistle of Peter* (Grand Rapids: Eerdmans, 1990), 139–40.
10. We may say that an allusion to Enoch in that day might be picked up much as an allusion to C. S. Lewis's Aslan might be picked up today.

But if I drive out demons by the Spirit of God, then the kingdom of God has come upon you.

Or again, how can anyone enter a strong man's house and carry off his possessions unless he first ties up the strong man? (Matt. 12:28–29)

We cannot know what Jesus told the spirits in prison, but several New Testament themes would be appropriate: Their realm is now under his dominion. Every knee will bow to him. Their doom is sealed, since Jesus' death and resurrection concludes and demonstrates his control over evil in all places and forever. Martin Luther supposedly said that if Jesus descended into hell, he spent three days thumbing his nose at the devil. There may be truth to the gibe. After all, demons seem confused about Jesus' life and ministry. In the beginning, when Satan tempted Jesus, he offered bloodless paths to glory (Matt. 4:1–11). But at the end, he prompted Judas to betray Jesus to death (John 13:27). Perhaps Jesus proclaimed that his death, resurrection, and exaltation sealed their defeat and doom. We cannot now know. But we do know that nothing in 1 Peter 3 promotes the idea that Jesus evangelized humans after their deaths.

Indeed, if we want to guard against uncertainty by asserting what is certain, let us affirm this: If the essence of hell is separation from God, then Jesus "descended into hell" on the cross. He experienced separation from the Father while on the cross. The Apostles' Creed declares that Jesus was crucified, dead, and buried and that he descended into hell. What the creed says is true, but the order of two phrases should be reversed to read, "He was crucified, descended into hell, was dead and buried, and rose again on the third day." Jesus' main descent into hell occurred on the cross. After his death, Scripture notes, he did not join the devil in hell; he joined the Father in paradise (Luke 24:34, 46).

God gives people ample opportunity to repent in this life. Indeed, Peter relates, during the long years when Noah built the ark, "God waited patiently," but no one responded to the call to repent. Sadly, Peter says, "in it only a few people, eight in all, were saved through water" (1 Peter 3:20). With this segue to baptism, Peter presents a similarity between Noah's family and the family of Christians. The senses are different, but both are saved through water. Yet whereas a *few* were saved through water in Noah's day, now, Peter asserts, baptism saves *you* through the resurrection of Christ.

"Saved through Water": Claiming the Promise of Baptism

Whatever the differences between Noah's clan and the family of Christ, in each case God's people cling to his covenant promises by faith and the Lord rescues his flock. According to Peter, Noah's family was "saved through water" (1 Peter 3:20). He continues, "Baptism, which corresponds to this, now saves you, not as a removal of dirt from the body but as an appeal to God for a good conscience, through the resurrection of Jesus Christ, who has gone into heaven" (3:21–22a esv). If we streamline 1 Peter 3:21a, we hear the words "baptism now saves you" (the nasb uses the exact sequence). The church has long debated these words.

In the early church, many thought baptism to be essential for salvation and embodied that conviction in the emergency baptism of dying infants. Later, Augustine stated that infants were incorporated into the faith and life of the church by their baptism. Others focused on the long preparation of adult converts for baptism. They linked baptism and the confession of faith, by which one shares in the death and resurrection of Christ. In the Middle Ages, Thomas Aquinas and others stressed that God dispensed his grace through the seven sacraments. In that system, baptism had the essential role of removing the guilt of original sin.

Protestants, as we know, debate whether baptism is rightly applied to children and, if so, what it signifies and what it accomplishes. Risking over-simplification, we can say that most Protestants aim to avoid two errors. First, mindful of the passages that declare what baptism *does*, they do not want to reduce baptism to a mere sign of graces already received. For Scripture says that baptism unites us to Christ (Rom. 6:1ff.), clothes us with Christ (Gal. 3:27), and joins us to the body of Christ (1 Cor. 12:13).

But second, we also know that the action of baptism does not, in itself, save. (We deny the Roman concept of *ex opere operato*—"by the work, worked.") Scripture says that *the Lord Jesus saves*, by grace through faith, in climactic texts such as Acts 2:21; 15:11; 16:31; and Romans 10:9–10. Further, it is all too obvious that many of the baptized eventually reject the Lord and his covenant.

Therefore, Protestants affirm that God gives grace in baptism and yet deny that it guarantees salvation or necessarily regenerates unto eternal life. We want to stand between two errors. We deny that baptism is a *mere* sign and we deny that baptism is an *intrinsically efficacious* sign. But what does baptism accomplish?

The Westminster Confession of Faith seems both to avoid our two dangers and to state the positive role of baptism. In 28.1, it states that baptism is a sacrament "ordained by Jesus Christ" for the admission of the "party baptized into the visible Church" and "a sign and seal of the covenant of grace, of his ingrafting into Christ." The confession turns to the efficacy of baptism in 28.5–6:

> 28.5. Although it is a great sin to contemn or neglect this ordinance, yet grace and salvation are not so inseparably annexed unto it, as that no person can be regenerated, or saved, without it: or, that all that are baptized are undoubtedly regenerated.

> 28.6. The efficacy of Baptism is not tied to that moment of time wherein it is administered; yet, notwithstanding, by the right use of this ordinance, the grace promised is not only offered, but really exhibited, and conferred, by the Holy Ghost, to such (whether of age or infants) as that grace belongs unto, according to the counsel of God's own will, in His appointed time.

At a minimum, this is a classic Protestant statement on baptism. If baptism is "a sign and seal of the covenant of grace," then it is a means of saving grace. The confession accents the grace promised in the covenant and union with Christ. There is strong warrant for both themes. Romans 6:1–4 says that we are baptized into union with Jesus in his death and resurrection (cf. Gal. 3:27). And Acts 2:38–41 links baptism and covenantal grace when Peter, at the climax of his Pentecost sermon, tells his convicted listeners, "Repent and be baptized . . . . The promise is for you and your children."

Still, the principle of *sola Scriptura* nudges us to lay down the confession and consider other Scriptures. We begin with the source and starting point of Christian baptism, Jesus' Great Commission in Matthew 28:18–20. There, Jesus places baptism in the context of disciple-making (theological debates tend to focus on regeneration and salvation, which are related but distinct). In the Great Commission, Jesus tells the apostles to "make disciples of all nations, baptizing them in the name of the Father and of the Son and of the Holy Spirit, and teaching them to obey everything I have commanded you." In this case, teaching and baptizing are means or instruments of discipleship.

For adults, baptism is a confirmation of their faith and an instrument of their union with the triune God. For children, the Spirit may or may not impart new life at the time of baptism, but baptism can surely be a means for discipleship. For instance, when a child witnesses an infant baptism during worship, parents (or others) can remind the child of his or her own baptism:

> We baptized you when you were little, too. We promised to raise you to trust Jesus. The pastor put water on you, too. We use water for washing, and when we baptized you, we asked God to wash away your sins. The pastor also said, "In the name of the Father and of the Son and of the Holy Spirit" for you. That means that he asked God to be your God. Now you belong to him. We all want you to believe in God for yourself, but baptism means that you are never all by yourself. See how the family always comes to baptisms and how the whole church is there? Our family came, too, and we pray for you. The people of the church promised to care for you as well. We teach you and pray for you so that you will belong to God and follow him all your life. [Friends in the Baptist tradition can adopt this outlook, with necessary adjustments, since infant dedication shares substantial common ground with infant baptism.]

Is all of this consistent with 1 Peter 3? Yes, although it is not immediately obvious. To quote the ESV, which offers an essentially literal, word-for-word translation: "Baptism, which corresponds to this [the baptism of Noah's family], now saves you, not as a removal of dirt from the body but as an appeal to God for a good conscience, through the resurrection of Jesus Christ" (3:21).

We still hear the words "baptism . . . now saves you." Yet Peter is clear that neither water nor baptism, per se, can save. The act itself does not save. What saves is the "appeal to God for a good conscience." What saves, to paraphrase, is the proper awareness of God that leads someone to seek and find peace with him. This occurs, however, not on the basis of the interest or effort of the person in question, but "through the resurrection of Jesus Christ, who has gone into heaven and is at the right hand of God, with angels, authorities, and powers having been subjected to him" (1 Peter 3:21–22 ESV). The risen and reigning Christ saves and is the basis of our appeal to God. Water baptism represents all this.

So Peter returns to the conquering power of Jesus' resurrection and ascension and the assurance it brings. Jesus "suffered once for sins, the righteous for the unrighteous, that he might bring us to God" (1 Peter 3:18 ESV). To atone for sin, Jesus had to endure the pain and shame of the cross. Still, just as Jesus' openness to dangerous obedience is our model, his ascension and exaltation are our hope, for God raised him from the dead and seated him "at God's right hand" (3:21–22). Peter assures us that just as the Father vindicated Jesus, so he will vindicate us if we suffer for him. That ought to motivate the fearlessness Peter advocated in 3:14. If we have the mind of Christ, we can and should put it into practice.

Peter has already described how the mind of Christ galvanizes us for courageous living. We fear God, not humanity (1 Peter 2:17; 3:15). We commit to make God's grace visible (3:15–16). In troubles, we await vindication and entrust ourselves to God, who judges justly (2:23). Because Jesus conquered death, nothing can keep us from joining him at God's right hand. We lay hold of God's power by the faith that unites us to him, so his character and his deeds become ours. Naturally, all of this is easier said than done. We need the means of grace to lay hold of the courage that is ours—prayer, Christian community, praise (alone and in public worship), meditation, repentance, and the right use of the sacraments, including baptism. Whatever we find uncertain in life or in the message of 1 Peter 3, this should be clear. "Christ died for sins once for all, the righteous for the unrighteous, to bring you to God" (3:18). Now he "has gone into heaven and is at God's right hand—with angels, authorities and powers in submission to him" (3:22).

13

BREAKING WITH SIN

1 Peter 4:1–6

*Therefore, since Christ suffered in his body, arm yourselves
also with the same attitude, because he who has suffered in his
body is done with sin. As a result, he does not live the rest of his
earthly life for evil human desires, but rather for the will of God.*
(1 Peter 4:1–2)

GOALS FOR LIFE

The pilgrims who settled New England came to America, from one perspective, because they felt alienated from their own culture. They first left
England for Amsterdam, then Leiden, and then the New World, in a search
for religious freedom. They left England because laws required attendance
at the Church of England, which they considered corrupt. In Amsterdam
and Leiden, some pilgrims found no work. When they saw their children
becoming ever more Dutch, they decided to go to America. There they met
cold, hunger, disease, hostility (since the natives had already met slavers), and,
all too often, death. The pilgrims sacrificed so much because they wanted
to pursue a life of purity and devotion to God. Their dedication shows that
strong goals, rigorously pursued, can lead almost anywhere. But "anywhere"

could entail suffering, and suffering tempts some to abandon their goals. Yet if we give up when we face hardship, life becomes dull. There is less pain, but less meaning. Whether someone wants to start a new society or a new company, great goals are costly and demand sacrifices.

Mihaly Csikszentmihalyi is a champion of goals. Well-chosen goals, he declares, leave us no time to be unhappy. Challenging and engaging goals leave us "little room . . . for noticing the entropy of normal life." At a minimum, therefore, goals are a superb diversion. But how are we to choose the right goals? Adults cannot assume that meaning comes through traditional roles—woman as wife and mother, man as worker and provider. So, then, Csikszentmihalyi asks, "How do we know where to invest psychic energy?" No one can show us the goal that deserves our energy, so each person must discover his or her purpose independently, through trial and error and self-knowledge.[1]

Is Csikszentmihalyi right? Do we examine *ourselves* so that we can find or create meaning? Can we find the equilibrium between action and contemplation, so that we can pursue the right goals? How many have aimed at a goal, reached it, and then realized that it was a mistake? Further, we often choose noble goals and fail to reach them. We can choose marriage and suffer betrayal. We can choose a sensible career and watch it explode for reasons outside our control. Unfortunately, in order to be sure that we have chosen the right goals, we would need to be omniscient. And even if we choose the right goals, if we select the wrong means, we court disaster.

I have spent many days working on projects or goals that I never envisioned. As a young man, I wanted to be a teaching professor, introducing students to the glories of Christian theology and philosophy. I expected to lead vibrant seminars that periodically ended with a cookout and Wiffle ball in my backyard. But for a decade, I led a large urban church where I raised money, solved communication problems, trained new staff, and wrote when time permitted. I never envisioned giving myself to the first three at all or giving so much to the last.

Maybe I lost my way, maybe not. We make plans as best we can, staying within God's revealed will. We measure our abilities, passions, and opportunities, yet we say "Lord willing" because Scripture teaches us to hold our

1. Mihaly Csikszentmihalyi, *Flow: The Psychology of Optimal Experience* (New York: Harper & Row, 1990), 225–27.

goals loosely. The Lord is free to overrule our plans: "To man belong the plans of the heart, but from the LORD comes the reply . . . . In his heart a man plans his course, but the LORD determines his steps" (Prov. 16:1, 9). That is, we can have goals, but must keep them open to revision.

Perhaps we should think less of "my goals" and more of following God's call to Christ and to holiness. Then we can take account of our gifts, training, and experiences. We know that we are on the right path if we say with Paul, "I want to know Christ and the power of his resurrection and the fellowship of sharing in his sufferings . . . . Forgetting what is behind and straining toward what is ahead, I press on toward the goal to . . . which God has called me" (Phil. 3:10, 13–14). The principal goal is to know Christ. Then we search for personal goals, which are secondary and provisional, open to God's midcourse adjustments.

God himself pursues goals, above all the redemption of humanity through the work of Jesus. And he assigns goals to some of his servants. He chose Moses to lead Israel from Egypt (Ex. 3:9–10) and Paul to proclaim the gospel to the Gentiles (Acts 9:15). We see the same thing in Peter himself. Still, because we see dimly, we might not perceive our God-given assignments. We might also think a task is ours when it is not. We must remember that David wanted to build the temple and that Nathan initially approved David's desire (1 Chron. 17, 22).

This shows, again, that we must maintain some critical distance or detachment from our plans. Our self-appraisals are always somewhat inaccurate and sometimes flatly erroneous, so we remain open to correction. And as long as we love and obey God, our tactical errors will be less damaging. Personal goals are less important if we do the good that lies before us and trust the results to God. Yet we dare not drift through life, taking whatever others thrust upon us, squandering our gifts because we fail to hone them. We may imagine ourselves as travelers on a great overland journey, from Cairo to Cape Town. We plan to visit places familiar from an earlier stint in East Africa. We know that parts of the trip—a cruise up the Nile, perhaps—will be safe and pleasant. Other phases will take us to semiclosed borders and to roads of dirt and sand that are more theoretical than substantial. Yet in all the uncertainty, there is a launch point and a terminus, and a sense of the way from one end to the other.[2]

2. Paul Theroux took this journey in 2001, as recounted in *Dark Star Safari: Overland from Cairo to Cape Town* (Boston: Houghton Mifflin, 2003).

This image can provide a lens on 1 Peter as a whole. Clusters of specific commands are found in 2:13–3:7 and 5:1–5, but large stretches have none. Rather, Peter offers a condensed epitome "of the Christian life and of the conduct that it inspires."[3] He describes the work of Christ and the life that follows in ideal terms. Readers must discover how his general principles manifest themselves daily. Take Peter's description of the atonement: "He himself bore our sins in his body on the tree" (2:24). He tells us that Jesus' willingness to suffer and entrust himself to God sets us an example, but he adds no specifics. We need to apply it to ourselves.

First Peter 4:1–6 is another case in point. It begins: "Therefore, since Christ suffered in his body, arm yourselves also with the same attitude, because he who has suffered in his body is done with sin" (4:1). The passage assumes that, as Peter said earlier, God's people are exiles and sojourners (1:1, 17; 2:11). It then labels the price we pay for that status. Old friends will not be pleased with a disciple's new life. They will be startled, they will accuse, and they might graduate to physical violence (4:4, 12–19).

Peter had already noted this danger and encouraged his people to endure it: "Even if you should suffer for what is right, you are blessed" (1 Peter 3:14). He stressed the conquering power of Jesus' resurrection and the assurance that comes with it. Jesus "suffered once for sins, the righteous for the unrighteous, that he might bring us to God" (3:18 ESV). To atone for sin, Jesus had to endure the cross.[4] To follow Jesus, Peter's people also need to forfeit their safety, entrusting themselves "to him who judges justly" as they endure opposition (2:23). Still, just as Jesus' openness to dangerous obedience is our model, his ascension to God's right hand is our hope (3:21–22).

In the end we have one broad goal—to live "for the will of God" (1 Peter 4:2). There is a point of departure, the debauchery and idolatry of our pagan past (4:3). And there is a goal—the day we meet the Judge and account for ourselves (4:5). Other than that, the course of life is open as we leave sin behind and follow Christ.

---

3. Edmund Clowney, *The Message of 1 Peter: The Way of the Cross* (Downers Grove, IL: Inter-Varsity Press, 1988), 15.

4. Hebrews concurs with Peter: "Let us fix our eyes on Jesus, the author and perfecter of our faith, who for the joy set before him endured the cross, scorning its shame, and sat down at the right hand of the throne of God" (Heb. 12:2).

A FEARLESS LIFE

Harking back to 1 Peter 3:18, "Christ died for sins once for all," Peter promises that just as the Father vindicated Jesus, he will vindicate us if we suffer. That should supply the fearlessness that Peter advocated in 3:14. Here Peter commands, "Since Christ suffered in his body, arm yourselves also with the same attitude, because he who has suffered in his body is done with sin" (4:1). To survive persecution faithfully, we must prepare like soldiers, armed with the mind or insight of Christ.[5] Peter has already described that insight: We fear God, not humanity (2:17; 3:15). We commit to make God's grace visible (3:15-16). In troubles, we have "a steadfast hope for vindication" and entrust ourselves to God, who judges justly (2:23).[6]

First Peter 4:1 adds, cryptically, that "he who has suffered in his body is done with sin." The Greek verb translated "is done" means "to stop, cease, or have finished" with something.[7] That means that when we identify with Christ in his suffering, we break with sin globally. A willingness to suffer for the faith, for our convictions, is galvanizing. It is *empowering* to suffer for the Lord. A willingness to suffer proves our faith real. One secular historian noted, "A religion of compromise would not . . . have been a Christian religion."[8] When we stay with Jesus at the cost of physical or material suffering, we follow him. The very willingness to suffer shows that we have made a break with sin in its essential selfishness. We see that there is more to us than rhetoric, that we *do* put the Lord ahead of self.

The danger of suffering might seem far removed from pluralistic societies, but most nations remain hostile to the faith. (According to recent surveys, Christians are liable to persecution in well over a hundred nations.) Even in allegedly free nations, there are places where it is dangerous to own Christ. Peter's people faced prison, beatings, or death. Around A.D. 50, Claudius expelled Christians from Rome and seized their property. Around 64-65,

5. *New International Dictionary of New Testament Theology*, s.v. "Reason" (Grand Rapids: Zondervan, 1975), 3:125.

6. Scot McKnight, *1 Peter*, NIV Application Commentary (Grand Rapids: Zondervan, 1996), 224.

7. Frederick W. Danker, ed., *A Greek-English Lexicon of the New Testament and Other Early Christian Literature*, 3rd ed. (Chicago: University of Chicago Press, 2000), 638; Johannes Louw and Eugene Nida, *Greek-English Lexicon of the New Testament: Based on Semantic Domains*, 2nd ed. (New York: United Bible Societies, 1998-99), 1:660. The Greek *pauō*, especially in the middle voice, means "to cease doing something" or to stop oneself; cf. Luke 11:1; Acts 14:18.

8. Robin Lane Fox, *Pagans and Christians* (New York: Knopf, 1987), 441.

Nero shed their blood. Hebrews 10 refers to lighter oppression: "Sometimes you were publicly exposed to insult and persecution; at other times you stood side by side with those who were so treated. You sympathized with those in prison and joyfully accepted the confiscation of your property, because you knew that you yourselves had better and lasting possessions" (Heb. 10:33–34). But it could get worse, the author of Hebrews says. He foresees bloodshed (12:4).

Peter also sees heavier suffering approaching: "Dear friends, do not be surprised at the painful trial you are suffering, as though something strange were happening to you" (1 Peter 4:12). So he reminds them that Jesus suffered in the flesh, hinting that we should be ready for the same (4:1). When Jesus submitted to death on the cross, he defied the instinct of self-preservation. We can and must make the same break, even if we don't face a clear test such as persecution. We make a similar break when we sacrificially give money, time, or personal peace in order to advance the cause of Christ.

We distinguish a babysitter from a parent by this: In an emergency, she calls the parents and is free to leave when they arrive. Parents do not leave. The willingness to suffer with and for a child shows that a parent has broken with the life of the childless. So the believer who suffers for righteousness has broken with the easy life. The commitment to ease and pleasure is the source of so much sin. A faith that endures suffering is done with that.

Imagine a man who, after a string of reversals, examines himself and decides that he is angry, cynical, lazy, and arrogant, despite a singular lack of achievement. He resolves to change, to become a decent human. Yet he knows that mere resolve is insufficient. He must *do* something. That night he takes his wife to a play he hates, because *she* likes it. On the way home, he gives $90 to a homeless man, keeping just $10 for himself. He knows it's foolish, but he had to give something away that day, to seal his break with the old life.[9] A willingness to sacrifice, to suffer loss, proves that he has changed.

Arm yourselves with this willingness to suffer, Peter urges, "so as to live for the rest of the time in the flesh no longer for human passions but for the will of God" (1 Peter 4:2 ESV). Our "time in the flesh" is our allotted time on earth, whether long or short. It is our span of days, our "time of exile,"

9. Based on Nick Hornby, *How to Be Good* (New York: Viking, 2001).

whether filled with joy or sorrow (Ps. 90:9–17; 1 Peter 1:17). Our lifestyle and our passions can be good or bad. We can indulge evil passions or pursue good ones, but disciples live "for the will of God."

AN INDULGENT LIFE

In 1 Peter 4:3, Peter explains that his people should live well from that time onward: "For you have spent enough time in the past doing what pagans choose to do—living in debauchery, lust, drunkenness, orgies, carousing and detestable idolatry." This is ironic understatement. One day is more than enough time for debauchery and idolatry, and Peter's readers had spent their lives at these things until they received the gospel.

Peter's list of sins fits the times. Debauchery, lust, drunkenness, orgies, and carousing are sensual sins. Many pagans gave themselves to such things, to liaisons with slaves, concubines, courtesans, and lovers, to drinking and feasting, as far as their resources and their need to protect their reputation permitted.[10] Idolatry was the norm, but we need to purge certain contemporary concepts if we want to understand it. The principal religions of the time, emperor worship and the veneration of local patron deities, had scant doctrine or moral instruction. Those duties fell to philosophers. The popular religions emphasized public celebrations, in which everyone was expected to participate. Everyone came together to honor the emperor and swear by his genius, or to pay homage to the city's patron gods. This promoted social unity and (allegedly) maintained the favor of the gods. Imagine mandatory celebrations of Independence Day as a proof of loyalty to nation and neighbor, and we start to see polytheism and emperor worship as Greco-Romans did. Peter calls all of it "lawless idolatry" (1 Peter 4:3 ESV), since these gods had no laws of their own and violated the law of God.

The vices of Peter's day have parallels today. We spend enough time satisfying our greed and lusts, getting drunk or stoned, and following newer deities. Peter exhorts us that it's time to change, to stop wasting our lives.

Yet when people do change, it might displease old friends. They "are surprised when you do not join them in the same flood of debauchery, and they malign you" (1 Peter 4:4 ESV). Old friends notice that the believer no

10. Bruce W. Winter, *After Paul Left Corinth: The Influence of Secular Ethics and Social Change* (Grand Rapids: Eerdmans, 2001).

longer (literally) "runs" or "travels with" them. The believer has a new crowd, and the old crowd doesn't like it. It upsets the equilibrium. The woman who lives for her lusts feels threatened or judged by the woman who lives differently. The secular man is baffled. Why doesn't his friend want to have fun?

Change is unsettling, and that includes constructive moral reform. The secular person attacks. The church is still maligned for its moral positions. When a culture abandons biblical standards, when extramarital sex, cohabitation, and birth outside of marriage become normal, people attack the church for its moral snobbery and judgmentalism. While the church might deserve criticism if it constantly scolds, we surely invite reproach if we commit the very sins we condemn and if we blast one sin and tolerate another. Still, there is a time to stand up and say, "That's wrong." Peter warns us that if we do take a stand, we need to expect slander, not applause.

A Life Conducted in God's Presence

Disciples might feel defenseless, but according to Peter, their foes "will have to give account to him who is ready to judge the living and the dead" (1 Peter 4:5). God is ready to judge all flesh. "The living and the dead" represent all humanity, past and present. If God is ready to judge, we should be ready, too, for "the end of all things is near" (4:7). James likewise says that "the Lord [is] coming," that his coming is "near," and that "the Judge is standing at the door" (James 5:8–9; cf. Rom. 13:12). This teaching originates with Jesus, who makes four essential points. First, no one knows the day or hour of his coming (Matt. 24:36, 42, 50). Second, he will come personally, in a manner that is visible to all (24:26–27, 30–31). Third, his coming ends the history of fallen humanity (24:37–40; 25:31–46). Fourth, we should always be prepared for Jesus' return (24:42–25:13). If we are, we will have joy in his presence and will receive his blessing (25:14–46).[11]

Peter's statement that "the end of all things is near" (1 Peter 4:7) is puzzling *if* we assume that *near* means "soon, by the clock." But 2 Peter 3 explains that God's scale of time differs from ours. For him, "a thousand years are like a day" (2 Peter 3:8). To the Lord, we might seem like little children who

11. This follows a summary of New Testament eschatology outlined in my commentary, *James*, Reformed Expository Commentary (Phillipsburg, NJ: P&R Publishing, 2007), 278–80.

start asking, "Are we there yet?" when a fifteen-hour trip is fifteen minutes old. Besides, an apparent delay grants sinners more time to repent (3:9).

Jesus tells us that he will come suddenly, without warning, like a thief in the night (Matt. 24:43–44; cf. 2 Peter 3:10). As a thief slips in without forewarning, so Jesus will come unexpectedly (Matt. 24:50). Each day could be the day. Therefore, everyone should prepare for Jesus' return. Scripture promotes the question "*Will you be ready* when he returns?" rather than "*When* will Christ return?" We should always be ready to give an account of our life.

First Peter 4:6 has been the subject of extensive debate because of lexical, grammatical, and theological questions.[12] The great question is the meaning of the gospel proclamation to the dead. Some have cited 4:6 and 3:19 to support the concept of a postmortem gospel proclamation by which many, perhaps even all, humans eventually believe.[13] Others believe that the "dead" are the spiritually dead and that they will receive either judgment or life, depending on their response to the message. We can get a hint of some interpretive issues if we quote both the NIV and ESV, noticing the differences:

> For this is the reason the gospel was preached even to those who are now dead, so that they might be judged according to men in regard to the body, but live according to God in regard to the spirit. (NIV)

> For this is why the gospel was preached even to those who are dead, that though judged in the flesh the way people are, they might live in the spirit the way God does. (ESV)

As always, the literary and cultural contexts offer the surest path to understanding. The literary context shows that the "dead" are the physically dead. The previous verse, 1 Peter 4:5, has just mentioned "the living and the dead,"

12. For more detailed exploration of the issues, consult any of the technical commentaries by Davids, Goppelt, Jobes, Marshall, and Michaels. While I have drawn on many writers, I most follow Karen H. Jobes, *1 Peter* (Grand Rapids: Baker Academic, 2005), 270–73.

13. See Hilarion Alfeyev, *Christ the Conqueror of Hell: The Descent into Hades from an Orthodox Perspective* (St. Vladimir's Seminary Press, 2009). Alfeyev studies the history of the doctrine of Christ's descent into hell. In the East, he found widespread belief that Jesus preached, postmortem, to those who did not believe in him during their lifetime. The West generally held a narrower view—perhaps applying Jesus' preaching to Noah's generation. Many in the East held that Jesus "freed all who were held captive" and "emptied hell" so that no mortals remained. Thus, Jesus descended into hell not as victim but as Conqueror, to mortify death and destroy hell. See ibid., 203–18.

where Peter certainly means the physically dead. It would be most surprising if he changed meanings so abruptly in tightly connected lines. The literary and cultural contexts also come together here. In the immediate context, Peter's first point, as Karen Jobes notes, is that "death does not exempt a person from God's coming judgment." Pagans rarely taught personal accountability after death.

> With that assumption, a pagan critic could reasonably question what good the gospel is, since it seems so restrictive of behavior in this life, and then the believer dies like everyone else. Peter, however, teaches that *because* people will be judged even *after* physical death, contra pagan expectation, the gospel message of forgiveness and judgment . . . is still efficacious. Death does not invalidate either the promises or the warnings of the gospel of Jesus Christ.[14]

This preaching is therefore not connected to the preaching "to the spirits in prison," mentioned in 1 Peter 3:19. Although English translations often use *preach* for both verses, the Greek of 3:19 is *kērussō*, which means that Jesus made a proclamation, while 1 Peter 4:6 uses *euaggelizomai*, which means that Jesus preached the good news.[15] Further, 3:19 says that *Christ* made a proclamation; 4:6 says that "the gospel was preached." Acts and many of Paul's epistles show that the apostles and their coworkers did this preaching.

The point is straightforward and fits the context perfectly: The people who malign Christians (1 Peter 4:4) will have to give an account to God for their actions (4:5). First Peter 4:6 begins: "For this reason"—that is, because judgment is coming—the gospel was preached widely, "even to those who are now dead," that is, people who have died since they heard the gospel while they still lived. Peter points out that the goal of evangelism is to prepare humans for the day when they stand before God and "give account" to him as Judge. Death exempts no one from this judgment, nor does death remove any believer from Jesus' care.[16] His work as Deliverer is not always visible to us in this life, yet Jesus' "redemption is not void . . . for his power extends to the dead."[17]

---

14. Jobes, *1 Peter*, 270–71.

15. As we noted in the previous chapter, *kērussō* and *euaggelizomai* inevitably overlap in meaning, but a distinction remains.

16. Jobes, *1 Peter*, 272–73.

17. John Calvin, *Calvin's Commentaries*, trans. John Owen, vol. 22, *The First Epistle of Peter* (Grand Rapids: Baker, 1999), 126.

This passage has several teachings that we must take to heart. Above all, it makes a claim about Christ. His gospel is essential for all and is no fleeting, provincial social construct. The people who mock it need it, lest they face the judgment with nothing but their sin. Everyone needs the gospel, and all who believe it "live according to God in regard to the spirit" (1 Peter 4:6).

Everyone dies. Everyone is judged in the flesh, "according to men." That is, everyone is guilty and everyone fails, even by human standards. We condemn others for sins that we know to be wrong, and then we do the same things, and so condemn ourselves (Rom. 2:1–3).[18]

The idea of judgment is offensive today. The Bible teaches that God is love; we reduce that to the idea that he is nice to people. C. S. Lewis observes that we want "not so much a Father in heaven as a grandfather in heaven—a senile benevolence who likes to see young people enjoying themselves and whose plan for the universe was simply that it might be . . . said at the end of each day 'a good time was had by all.'"[19]

But God aims for something greater than our happiness; he aims for our goodness. No one wants to be condemned by God, but we should not want a God who is so soft that he doesn't care what we do so long as we feel good while doing it. God is holy, a consuming fire. He deserves our reverence and awe. The thought of facing him and accounting for life in the body ought to motivate us to embrace the gospel, which was preached that men might live forever with God.

This returns us to our first thought. We certainly may pursue individual goals for life, trying to find God's design for us. Yet life is full of disruptions, and they easily erase the lines we wrote into the script. We can trust God to write new lines and let the story unfold as he wills. That begins with the substitutionary sacrifice of Christ, and then to his exemplary life that shows the way. It continues with Jesus' resurrection and ascension. These grant us the boldness that lets us break with our old life. The world may slander, but it is more than enough compensation to share the attitude of the Lord who broke the power of sin on the cross, that we might break the power of sin day by day.

18. J. Ramsey Michaels, *1 Peter*, Word Biblical Commentary 49 (Nashville: Thomas Nelson, 1988), 154–55.

19. C. S. Lewis, *The Problem of Pain* (New York: Collins Fount Paperbacks, 1977), 28.

14

GIFTS FROM GOD, GIFTS FOR GOD

1 Peter 4:7–11

Each one should use whatever gift he has received to serve others, faithfully administering God's grace in its various forms. If anyone speaks, he should do it as one speaking the very words of God. If anyone serves, he should do it with the strength God provides, so that in all things God may be praised through Jesus Christ. To him be the glory and the power for ever and ever.
(1 Peter 4:10–11)

One summer I spoke at a family camp in Pennsylvania's Nittany Mountains. Our eldest daughter was seven, and we gave her the run of the place, including the rolling woods on the edge of the camp. For hours, she explored fallen logs and thin streams, capturing small creatures. One day, she burst into our room with a box of plants, bugs, and red-spotted newts and declared, "I was *made* for this."

The label for that sensation—*I was made for this*—is *optimal experience* or *flow*. Mihaly Csikszentmihalyi described *flow* as complete immersion in an activity "for its own sake. The ego falls away. Time flies. Every action, movement, and thought follows inevitably from the previous one . . . .

Your whole being is involved, and you're using your skills to the utmost."[1] A professor once said, "I teach for free; they pay me to grade papers." For him, teaching was an optimal experience. During optimal experiences, self-awareness fades. The hours speed by, yet time also slows down as we concentrate on the moment. For athletes, balls seem large and opponents seem slow. For speakers, each word proceeds with both logic and passion from the one before and there is oneness with the audience. Hunger, thirst, and weariness cannot interrupt, and distractions fade away. Blessed is the man who often experiences flow.[2]

We can feel that we are made for something when we exercise our God-given gifts. Gifts equip believers for service in God's kingdom—for the church first, but also for work in the wider world. For the sake of discussion, let me propose that God grants *abilities* to all people, believers and doubters alike. These abilities become *gifts* when we dedicate them to God and the Spirit wills to make them fruitful for his purposes. But before we explore a New Testament theology of gifts, we need to locate them in the message of 1 Peter 4:7–11.

LIVING FAITHFULLY IN COMMUNITY

Since 1 Peter 4:5–6 says that all flesh must render an account to God, who judges "the living and the dead," Peter easily shifts, in 4:7, to the end of all things. More importantly, this passage concludes the long middle portion of 1 Peter, stretching from 2:11 to 4:11, describing the social conduct of a disciple. First Peter 2:11–12 is the overture, as the apostle urges his beloved readers to "abstain from sinful desires, which war against your soul," and to "live such good lives among the pagans that, though they accuse you of doing wrong, they may see your good deeds and glorify God on the day he visits us." The outline is simple: abstain from evil, do good, and remember the last day. First Peter 4:7–9, similarly, urges that disciples keep a clear mind and do good, while remembering the times.

---

1. Mihaly Csikszentmihalyi, interview by John Geirland, "Go with the Flow," *Wired* 4.09 (1996), http://www.wired.com/wired/archive/4.09/czik.html.
2. Mihaly Csikszentmihalyi, *Flow: The Psychology of Optimal Experience* (New York: Harper & Row, 1990), 53–60, 143–60.

The Greek has an untranslated conjunction, *de*, that loosely connects 1 Peter 4:6 and 4:7: The gospel is proclaimed because all humanity will be judged (4:6), and this is significant because "the end of all things is near" (4:7). The world as we know it, fraught with ambiguity at best and misery at worst, will not continue forever. When this age ends, Jesus will return to overthrow sin and establish his new order. Then creation will reach its proper end. This end "is near" not chronologically but theologically. Peter asserted that the end was near almost two thousand years ago, and he was right, because we have been brought into the final phase of God's plan of redemption by the resurrection of Jesus and the gift of the Spirit.[3] Peter already noted that we are in the last times in 1:20, saying that Jesus "was revealed in these last times for your sake." When this age ends, Jesus will return to overthrow sin and establish his new order. That day is near in the sense that it could happen at any time (cf. Matt. 3:2; 4:17; 10:7; 24:44; Mark 1:15).

"Therefore," Peter says, we must live in light of Jesus' return and be clear-minded, self-controlled, prayerful, and full of love and forgiveness (1 Peter 4:7–8). Because we are in the last phase of God's plan of redemption, because the end is near, certain conduct follows. These commands are the backbone of the passage:

- Be clear-minded and self-controlled so that you can pray (4:7b).
- Love each other persistently and unfailingly, and so cover sins (4:8).
- Offer hospitality to one another without complaining (4:9).
- Use the gracious gifts that God has bestowed to serve one another (4:10).

One could argue that Christianity is the most intellectually demanding of the faiths. It has robust and complex doctrines, and it regularly summons believers to be mindful of the implications of the faith and to let God's truth govern their lives. Peter's twin command, "be clear minded and self-controlled," seems to be a hendiadys, with the two verbs functioning as one. To be clear-minded is to see things as they are and to act appropriately. The root of the verb translated "self-controlled" comes from a term that originally

---

3. The word *telos*, translated "end," can signify the last stage of a process as well as the termination of a process.

meant "sober" rather than "drunk," but came to mean "alert, sound-minded, and mentally disciplined."[4] This promotes the life of prayer (cf. 1 Peter 3:7). This is no generic prayer, "but the prayer that calls upon and submits to God in the light of reality seen from God's perspective and thus obtains power and guidance in the situation."[5]

The word *all* links 1 Peter 4:7 and 4:8. Because "the end of all things is near," believers should, "above all, love each other deeply, because love covers over a multitude of sins" (4:8). A disciple loves everyone, even his enemies, but Peter focuses on love within the Christian community. The reference to "grumbling" in 4:9 underscores the need to maintain Christian unity. The word *deeply* (Greek *ektenēs*) can describe an attitude of perseverance, earnestness, and eagerness, even devotion. Such love "covers" many sins not by covering them up, and not by atoning for them, since Jesus does that (1:18–19; 2:24). Rather, we cover sins by forgiving them. This is first taught in Proverbs 10:12: "Hatred stirs up strife, but love covers all offenses" (ESV). The phrase also appears in James 5:20, and we see the concept in Matthew 18:21–22; Luke 17:3–6; and 1 Corinthians 13:7. Further, such forgiveness is vital to Peter's interest in preserving Christian community.

Why does Peter claim that such love is "above all"? Because the church is a society of sinners, redeemed by grace. Because we are sinners who both offend each other and take offense when no real offense is given. We cannot hope for a strong Christian community if we fail to extend to one another the grace that the Lord first gave us. Church splits, at local and national levels, give sad testimony to the evil effects when such grace is missing. But Paul exhorts, "Be kind and compassionate to one another, forgiving each other, just as in Christ God forgave you" (Eph. 4:32). Love *includes* feelings (Rom. 12:10), but it is more than a feeling. Love is a resolve to do good to others, including the good of forgiving their sins.

When Peter instructs, "Offer hospitality to one another without grumbling" (1 Peter 4:9), he shifts from the general principles of 4:7–8 to particulars in 4:9. Hospitality is a form of the love mentioned in 4:8. Indeed, the Greek term for *hospitality, philoxenos*, is a compound formed from *philos* (*love*) and *xenos* (*stranger*). Hospitality is a specific form of love: caring for strangers, who might be part of the Christian mission. Of course, believers

---

4. Paul J. Achtemeier, *1 Peter* (Minneapolis: Fortress, 1996), 294.
5. Peter H. Davids, *The First Epistle of Peter* (Grand Rapids: Eerdmans, 1990), 156–57.

with larger homes are most capable of offering hospitality. The little phrase "without grumbling" reminds us that hospitality can be burdensome. Yet hospitality is necessary, given the imperative of Christian mission and the lack of decent lodging, in that day, for travelers. This implies that all the service we offer each other should be humble and joyful.

Throughout, Peter stresses mutuality, as we see in the repeated use of "one another." He says that Christians must "keep loving one another" (1 Peter 4:8), "show hospitality to one another" (4:9), and exercise our gifts to "serve one another" (4:10, all ESV). These are universal obligations, but we are most likely to help one another cheerfully—"without grumbling"—and effectively when we act within our God-given endowments.

Peter speaks to every Christian, not just elite believers or church officers, when he urges, "Each one should use whatever gift he has received to serve others" (1 Peter 4:10). We serve others because our gifts ultimately belong to God, not to us. We are "good stewards of God's varied grace" (4:10 ESV; cf. Rom. 12:6). God's gifts are gracious in two senses: (1) they are given widely and freely, and (2) they are bestowed apart from human merit.

Because we *receive* gifts from God, they are never simply *ours*. Gifts in some senses do, and in some senses do not, belong to us. We receive them from God, but they are not our possession or trophy. There is no room for pride, and we have no right to view them as a windfall.

Paul says that those who hold office are stewards of God's grace (e.g., 1 Cor. 4:1–2; Titus 1:7). But 1 Peter 4:10, like Romans 12 and 1 Corinthians 12, asserts that every believer is a steward of God's grace. For Peter, *grace* usually means the gift of salvation awaiting all who believe in Jesus (1 Peter 1:10, 13; 3:7). And to be sure, every gift, rightly exercised, *points* to God's grace, but this passage is not saying that we steward or manage God's *saving* grace. The grace of 1 Peter 4:10 is the grace that gives abilities and ministries to all.

For most gifts, there is no office, so Peter speaks to all disciples, not office-holders. Nonetheless, the two main categories of gifts, speaking and serving, do correspond to the two principal church offices: "If anyone speaks [as elders do], he should do it as one speaking the very words of God. If anyone serves [as deacons do], he should do it with the strength God provides, so that in all things God may be praised through Jesus Christ. To him be the glory and the power for ever and ever. Amen" (1 Peter 4:11). Teaching and ruling elders lead the ministry of words, and deacons lead the ministry of deeds.

Peter says that speakers should act as if they utter "the very words [or *oracles*] of God" (1 Peter 4:11; *logia theou*). This is the exact phrasing of the Septuagint of Numbers 24:4, 16, where Balaam's words are God's words or oracles (cf. Rom. 3:2; Acts 7:38). Historically, church leaders and scholars have taken this as a comment on preaching. Chapter 1 of the Second Helvetic Confession famously says, "The preaching of the word of God is the word of God." Earlier, Martin Luther said, "Every honest pastor's and preacher's mouth is Christ's mouth . . . and the Word which he preacheth is likewise not the pastor's and preacher's but God's."[6] Similarly, John Calvin said, "When a man has climbed up into the pulpit . . . it is [so] that God may speak to us by the mouth of a man."[7] So preaching is God's Word in some sense, yet the preacher's words are human, too, and therefore often garbled, weak, or even false. But the Spirit "makes the broken human words become . . . a living word of God to the hearers."[8] Hebrews states that this happens in the church, and not only through the apostles: "Remember your leaders, who spoke the word of God to you" (Heb. 13:7; cf. 1 Thess. 2:13; 1 Peter 1:25). Preachers can and must prepare, yet we must pray that the Lord will excise what is false, improve what is true, and apply all the truth, even things hinted at rather than articulated, to receptive hearts. At best, when a congregation hears Christ proclaimed, according to the pattern of Scripture itself, they hear more than explanation and application; they hear Christ himself, imploring them to believe and to live by grace. (At worst, a preacher knowingly contradicts Scripture.)

Although we traditionally apply 1 Peter 4:11a to preaching, dialogical teaching that is Scripture-based and prayer-bathed can have the same "very words of God" status. Suppose a man strikes and threatens his wife and children. The wife, ashamed and afraid of a humiliating scandal, tells her pastor, "If I pray fervently and do nothing upsetting, I believe I can overcome my husband's anger and violence." A wise pastor might reply, "Mrs. Smith, I admire your endurance and devotion, but it is very likely that he will strike and threaten again, no matter what you do or how you pray. This case requires church leaders and, quite likely, civil authorities to stand with

6. Quoted in Karl Barth, *Church Dogmatics*, ed. G. W. Bromiley and T. F. Torrance, vol. 1.1 (New York: T. & T. Clark, 2009), 107.

7. T. H. L. Parker, *Calvin's Preaching*, sermon 22 on 1 Timothy 3:2 (Louisville, KY: Westminster/John Knox, 1992), 24.

8. C. E. B. Cranfield, *I & II Peter and Jude* (London: SCM Press, 1960), 117.

you. God appointed church authorities to rebuke sin, and he summons civil authorities to strike fear in evildoers and punish them as necessary" (cf. Rom. 13:3–4). Strong pastoral counsel of this kind may also be God's very Word.

First Peter 4:11 also mentions those who serve. They give to the poor and needy, feed the hungry, welcome the stranger, and visit the sick and the prisoner. Some of them do the work; others organize it. Servants are also stewards of grace. Our service has greatest effect when it is performed not with grim resolve but "with the strength God provides" (1 Peter 4:11). If servants know that their strength and resources come from God, they will not condescend or patronize. Whether we speak or act, we focus on God, who is the source of all strength and every accomplishment. Then "God may be praised through Jesus Christ. To him be the glory" (1 Peter 4:11; cf. Phil. 4:13; Rev. 5:12; 7:12).

This passage harks back to 1 Peter 2:12. There Peter sees evildoers glorifying God (perhaps not willingly) on the day that God "visits" mankind, for they must acknowledge the good deeds of believers. In this chapter, Peter sees believers doing good and willingly giving God all praise and glory. This passage also looks to the end of Peter. A united, gifted, and God-centered church will endure fiery trials. It will live together well under Jesus, the Good Shepherd, and will await the day when Christ exalts us (4:12–5:10).[9]

Although we could stop here, the biblical theology of gifts is both important and somewhat misunderstood. We can therefore profit from an extended meditation on the biblical teaching.

A THEOLOGY OF GIFTS

The theological conviction behind the concept of gifts is simple: we "do not all have the same function" (Rom. 12:4). From the beginning, God created mankind for diversity within unity. Some serve, some teach, some lead (12:7–8). Christianity has a point of contact with pagan thought here: Aristotle said that a city-state is made of different kinds of men and finds life in its diversity.[10] Paul says that the church is like one body with many

9. J. Ramsey Michaels, *1 Peter*, Word Biblical Commentary 49 (Nashville: Thomas Nelson, 1988), 254.

10. Aristotle, *Politics*, in *The Basic Works of Aristotle*, ed. Richard McKeon (New York: Random House, 1941), 2.2.

parts or members (1 Cor. 12:12–30). We don't all sing the same note. God created us for harmony.

When God created this world, he cast his powers on the waters of humanity. He expected us to use our strength and creativity to give him a return on his investments (Eccl. 11:1). We each love some part of God's creation and exercise our abilities within it. Each person reflects the character of God and the grace of Christ in a distinct way, so that we make a personal contribution to God's design for our world, even while our work overlaps with that of many others. Each of us has tastes and insights. Each sees something discrete in a landscape. One regards a desert as dead and frightening; another rests in its austere beauty. Many love to see an unbroken succession of sunny days; others love mist and rain in the valley. At any point, our capacities, experiences, and tastes can lead us to unique service. Jesus promised, "To him who overcomes, I will give . . . a white stone with a new name written on it, known only to him who receives it" (Rev. 2:17). Because each of us has a unique name, insights, capacities, and interests, each can make a unique contribution to God's work.

A Survey of Spiritual Gifts: Biblical Principles, Lists, and Terms

God bestows a persona and graces that equip each one to herald his kingdom and serve him. He has distributed gifts to every believer. Peter lists the gifts of the Spirit in 1 Peter 4:10–11. Paul's lists appear in Romans 12, 1 Corinthians 12–14, and Ephesians 4. These lists vary in size and content. Together, they mention about twenty gifts. Several cite teaching, prophesying, serving, encouraging, leading, giving, and healing, but no two lists are identical and none is exhaustive. None tries to enumerate and categorize all classes of God-given talent.

Careful reading suggests that the lists are partial. First, each list diverges from the others. Even short lists can have terms that are missing in long ones. Second, some terms are listed as gifts in one place and a result of a gift in others: Encouraging is a gift in Romans 12:8, but a result of prophecy in 1 Corinthians 14:3. Knowledge is independent in 1 Corinthians 12:8 and a result of prophecy in 1 Corinthians 14:6. Third, music appears *with* the gifts of teaching, tongues, and interpretation in 1 Corinthians 14:26, but is never listed *as* a gift. Similarly, hospitality is mentioned near gift lists (Rom. 12:13; 1 Peter 4:9), and it aids church life (Rom. 16:23; 1 Tim. 5:10; 3 John 8), but is never called a gift. Again, Moses reports that God gave Bezalel and Oholiab artistic skill to construct the tabernacle (Ex. 31:2; 35:30; 36:1–2), but artistry appears in no New Testament inventory. Thus, we miss the point if we try to specify the precise number and categories of gifts. The main lesson is simple: we have diverse gifts and must find and use them.

Curiously, the phrase we use most, "spiritual gifts," never appears in the original Greek, although it appears in English translations of 1 Corinthians 12:1 and 14:1. Paul calls our spiritual abilities "gifts" (Eph. 4:7–8),[11] "service," and "working[s]" (1 Cor. 12:5–6), "manifestation[s] of the Spirit" (1 Cor. 12:7), "spiritual things" (1 Cor. 12:1; 14:1; the Greek is *pneumatika*), and "measure of faith" (Rom. 12:3). Paul's favorite term *charismata* (Rom. 12:6; 1 Cor. 12:9, 29–31) is a cousin of *grace* (*charis*) and means "gracious gifts."

Scripture calls our capacities *graces* because they are more than abilities. God gives them graciously, and they are *means* of grace for others. Peter says that the gifted "serve others, faithfully administering God's grace in its various forms" (1 Peter 4:10). At best, gifts empower us to do God's work and focus our attention on him and his grace (1 Cor. 12:7–11; 14:12). We distinguish the abilities possessed by the godless from the gifts of believers this way: we seek the glory of God as well as "the common good" (1 Cor. 12:7).

All gifts are important. Just as the human body needs every part, so the body of Christ needs every member. We pay more attention to the head than to the lungs, but life requires both. We pay more attention to hands than feet, but need both (1 Cor. 12:14–21). Paul does mention "greater gifts," but "greater" refers to more strategic service, not service that pleases God more (12:31; 14:1–5).

The Nature and Use of Gifts

Therefore, to discover our gifts, we can ask, "Am I fundamentally a speaker of words or a doer of deeds?" We all speak and act, but most of us do one

---

11. Ephesians 4:7–8 uses two similar words for *gift*: dorea and doma. New Testament language is usually plural: *gifts*. But Paul does exhort Timothy to stir up the "gift" given to him with prophecy (1 Tim. 4:14; 2 Tim. 1:6).

more than the other. We should ask, "What do I do best? Where do I sense God's pleasure? What do wise people ask me to do again and again?"

A gift begins with a capacity that resides at the core of our being. It starts with something we can do with skill and joy. God distributed gifts and designed roles for all his children. As we add friends and mentors, we find opportunities to use our capacities. An individualized and possibly almost unique set of abilities may develop. We can discover a basic capacity and then refine it. A musical child might start on the piano but move on to the violin or trumpet. A child with an early interest in numbers, properly encouraged, might find a career in a specialized aspect of math.

We discover our skills as we grow older, as we work with peers and superiors. I often found myself explaining lessons to my friends while in school and suspected that I might become a teacher. One day, when I was twenty, a campus ministry leader asked me to address our college group. When I stood up to speak, I felt energetic and intense, yet calm and connected to my fellow students. When I finished, a friend whispered, "I didn't know you could do *that*." I replied, "I didn't either." Whatever *that* is, I've been doing it ever since.

My experience is common enough. Basic skills start to emerge at an early age. Observant adults see something, some knack. They invite a young person to work beside them. The youth thinks, "Yes! I want to try that." He tries it and it works. Sometimes the success is partial, sometimes surprisingly advanced. The adult invites him to try it again, offering some coaching, and the skill ripens.

It's possible to present this visually. A core interest or ability spurs a disciple to do something beneficial for others. The desire leads to action, and the action leads to good results. Perceptive people then invite the gifted man or woman to serve again. In time, something formal might emerge, whether it be through regular, paid work or in a recognized volunteer position. Ideally, the more someone exercises a skill, the more the skill and pleasure grow. Thus we learn what we can and should do. Anyone can find a skill this way. It might or might not lead to a job and a paycheck, but if a spiritual gift is present, there will be spiritual fruit.

Some wonder whether they are called to a form of Christian ministry that requires theological training. The church ought to give men and women opportunities to explore that. But every believer needs to pursue his or her passions and abilities. The exploration of possible gifts leads to more than self-realization.

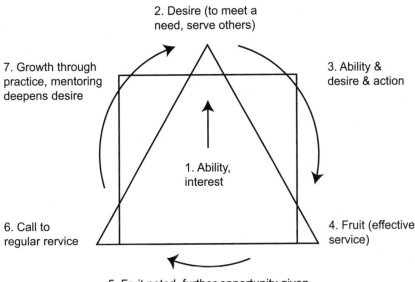

Fig. 14.1 Gifts and Calling

The discovery of our gifts can start with a question: "*Do I have a passion* to right a wrong or to remedy a deficit?" It can be an evil that we have seen first-hand. Eventually the passion gets legs. We create a plan, and then dive into messy reality. We realize that we need training to go further, and we get that training.[12]

We also ask, "*What people will I serve?*" Godly dreams aren't selfish. They serve people who have suffered a wound or who face a deficit that we can remedy. Next, we can ask, "*Where shall I serve?*" Even if our work reaches across the globe, even if we travel constantly, there is a primary location and a specific group that most counts on us. We must know who they are.

Finally, we ask, "*What burden will I bear?*" Every lasting call will bring glory and suffering, self-fulfillment and self-denial. We should aim to relieve suffering, do justice, restart a stagnant group, or tackle a tough project.

12. Dan B. Allender, *To Be Told: Know Your Story, Shape Your Life* (Colorado Springs: WaterBrook Press, 2005), 113–17.

If we meet a clear need, whether physical, financial, legal, psychological, educational, spiritual, or relational, it will bring both satisfaction and pain.

There should be a focal point, a core activity in our service. Jesus himself showed this. Because Jesus is Creator and Lord of all, all things belong within his sphere of interest. Still, he came in *one place, at one time, to serve one people*. He did many things: he healed, taught, made disciples. But above all he lived in perfect righteousness, died in perfect innocence, and rose perfectly restored, that he might bear the punishment for our sins, defeat death, and grant us eternal life.

None of us has gifts and a calling as splendid as Jesus. Few become glorious leaders. Yet every role is important. In the 2008 Olympics, Jason Lezak was a relay specialist on the U.S. men's swim team that was led by Michael Phelps, who was pursuing an unprecedented eight gold medals. When Lezak arrived, he owned four medals from prior Olympic relays, but had never won an individual medal, and some opined that he couldn't win a big race. Lezak was the anchor of the 400-meter freestyle relay. The U.S. freestyle teams had won the silver in the last two Olympics. In this race, the favored French team gave a 0.6-second lead to Alain Bernard, the world's best freestyle swimmer, for the final leg.

If Lezak failed to catch Bernard, Phelps, who had swum the first leg of the relay, would fail, too. When Lezak entered the pool, no one gave him a chance to catch Bernard. Indeed, Bernard's half-body lead grew to a full-body lead. But Lezak kept working. "You're at the Olympics," he told himself. "You can't give up." (Apparently, Olympic athletes think about quitting *during their greatest races*. Yet the internal compulsion given by their gift and the external discipline gained by training enable them to persevere.)

Lezak started gaining with thirty meters to go. Bernard was losing steam, pressing to honor his prerace boast of smashing the Americans. With ten meters to go, Lezak was almost even. People were screaming, "He's catching up!" With five meters left, the race was a dead heat as Lezak swam toward his bellowing teammates.

Lezak and Bernard seemed to touch the wall simultaneously. Then the scoreboard flashed Lezak's triumph. The man who couldn't win the big race had won the gold with the fastest 100 meters *of all time*. The Americans had crushed the world record by four seconds and won on the strength of a relay specialist. Fans remember Phelps, who would eventually win eight gold medals, and the image of him roaring at the finish line, every muscle straining. But Phelps, the greatest swimmer in the world, needed Lezak, the relay specialist, to win that race. Indeed, Lezak sealed the eighth gold with another relay victory that set a world record yet again. The world also has more relay specialists than independent stars. This applies in the church, too.

Frederick Buechner observed, "The place God calls you to is the place where your deep gladness and the world's deep hunger meet."[13] If Buechner is right, then our call and work are provisional, for the world's hungers shift. We might have core abilities and interests that remain through life, but as we grow, our interests and capacities change, so that our call may change, too. We need to ask, "Where can I do the most good? Where can I, broken and restored as I am, bring restoration to this broken world?" If we finish a task, having contributed what we could, we might need to move on, if God issues a new call.

KEY CONCEPTS

A gift is a capacity and desire for ministry, given by God for regular use, to bear fruit in the church. Capacity means gifted people's ability to advance God's kingdom. Gifted leaders mobilize people for causes. Gifted teachers are clear and compelling, so people learn. Encouragers listen, speak, and act to lift spirits.

Desire means the ordinary pleasure that we take in our gifts. Yes, prophets might need to deliver bitter words. But there is usually joy in prophecy. Leaders govern diligently. Those who show mercy do it cheerfully. Givers do so generously. Paul's phrase "let him give generously" literally reads "let him give *with simplicity*" (Rom. 12:8). That is, if someone has the gift of giving, he or she needs no return, but simply gives. Giving itself is the reward. Givers say, "Please take this money. Please borrow our car. You will minister to us if you take our gift." So it should be with all gifts. Leaders find satisfaction in helping people to accomplish their goals. The merciful are *glad* to help others. The gifted feel alive when they exercise their talents, even if doing so brings hardships, as apostleship did for Paul. If someone has a skill and dislikes using it, it probably is not a gift in the fullest sense.

Fruit results when the exercise of a gift strengthens God's church, bringing maturity and edification to the body of Christ (Eph. 4:12–13).

13. Frederick Buechner, *Wishful Thinking: A Theological ABC* (New York: Harper & Row, 1973), 95.

Conversely, a talented musician or speaker will not bless the church if he or she seeks to entertain rather than inspire worship. Gifts are God-centered.

CATEGORIES OF GIFTS

The gifts are diverse, yet we can classify them.[14] Let me propose three categories. First, there are gifts of speaking and service, gifts of word or deed (table 14.1). Second, gifts can be more and less obviously supernatural (table 14.2). Third, gifts can be more public or more private (table 14.3).

Gifts of Speaking and Serving

Peter says, "*If anyone speaks*, he should do it as one speaking the very words of God. *If anyone serves*, he should do it with the strength God provides." Through words and deeds, we administer God's grace (1 Peter 4:10–11). This holds for everyone, not just elite believers or officeholders.

Speaking Gifts	Speaking and Doing Gifts	Doing Gifts
Apostleship	Faith	Administration
Discernment	Leadership	Creativity
Encouragement		Giving
Evangelism		Healing
Knowledge		Hospitality
Prophecy		Mercy
Shepherding		Miracles
Teaching		Service
Tongues		
Tongues interpretation		
Wisdom		

Table 14.1 Speaking and doing gifts

14. Some gifts are listed, but neither defined nor described, so our knowledge is limited.

Gifts More Natural or More Supernatural

All gifts are supernatural, but gifts such as miracles, prophecy, and tongues are more obviously so. With gifts such as leadership, encouragement, and teaching, God heightens or consecrates common abilities. As gifted teachers prepare lessons, they use normal human skills.[15] But we do not prepare, or follow procedures, to perform a miracle. That power comes immediately from the Spirit.[16]

More Supernatural	Natural and Supernatural	More Natural
Discernment	Evangelism	Administration
Healing	Faith	Creativity
Miracles	Mercy	Discernment
Prophecy		Encouragement
Tongues		Giving
Tongues interpretation		Hospitality
		Knowledge
		Leadership
		Service
		Shepherding
		Teaching
		Wisdom

Table 14.2 More supernatural and more natural gifts

Gifts More Public or More Private

We differentiate between public gifts, used in leadership, and private gifts, used with individuals or small groups. Apostles, evangelists, teachers, and leaders exercise gifts publicly. Serving, encouraging, and contributing are

15. Scripture doesn't define the relation between natural gifts and spiritual gifts or explain the role of training, but we perceive a link. Jesus prepared the Twelve for apostleship by teaching them and setting an example. Paul's rabbinic training, Roman citizenship, resiliency, and intellectual ability prepared him to be the apostle to the Gentiles.

16. We can pray for healing, but healing comes directly from God in a way that sermons do not.

more private gifts. In Corinth, tongues were for private use and prophecy was for public speech (1 Cor. 14).

More Public/ Authoritative	Potentially Public or Private	Less Public/ Authoritative
Administration	Discernment	Creativity
Apostleship	Encouragement	Giving
Leadership	Evangelism	Healing
Miracles	Faith	Hospitality
Prophecy	Knowledge	Mercy
Teaching	Service	Shepherding
	Tongues	
	Tongues interpretation	
	Wisdom	

Table 14.3 More public/authoritative and less public/authoritative gifts

Gifts as Heightened Forms of Regular Duties

A second look at the gift lists shows that God expects all believers to participate, at least occasionally, in exercising most gifts. Most gifts of the Spirit label qualities or activities that are required of all believers. Wisdom, knowledge, discernment, faith, evangelism, teaching, generosity, and mercy are all gifts, yet believers should pursue all of them.

Typically, therefore, gifts entail a *heightened* capacity for something that others can do to a lesser degree.[17] We might call this the *Principle of Participation*. One implication is that no one should use a theology of gifts to dodge mundane tasks such as nursery duty, claiming, "That's not my gift." Anyone can serve.

For example, wisdom is a gift, but the Bible says that all should pursue wisdom. We should listen to the wise and ask God for it (Proverbs; James 1:5). Similarly:

17. There are exceptions to this. For example, miracles and speaking in tongues are all or nothing.

- Discernment is a gift, but Paul tells us that everyone should "test everything. Hold on to the good" (1 Thess. 5:21 ESV).
- Evangelism is a gift, but all should be able to give a reason for the faith that is in them (1 Peter 3:15).
- Faith is a gift, but all should believe in the Father and the Son (John 14:1).

We can develop the Principle of Participation by distinguishing between functions, roles, and offices in ministry. Christians may briefly exercise almost any spiritual *function*. Everyone can serve and should occasionally function there. A crusty old grump might see a sad person and say an encouraging word. A traveler can share her faith on an airplane even if she is no evangelist.

When someone has skill and desire for a task, when his labors meet needs, so that wise people ask him to serve again, he moves beyond a function. Regular, fruitful service is a *role*. When work becomes customary, joyful, and effective, it might express a gift that leads to regular tasks in the kingdom.

People can also fill a role, perhaps for a long time, even if they are not especially gifted. To speak personally, my main gifts are teaching and preaching, but leadership roles seem to pursue me. Either I have a leadership gift but can't quite admit it, or I don't have the gift but accept the role because I'm in the vicinity of a leadership deficit. Either way, I keep heeding calls to lead. Still, my work as leader (true to my nature) has a teacherly texture. Thus, my angle on leadership is cognitive rather than administrative. I have no interest in administration per se, yet administrative tasks impose themselves on me, since administration must occur if ideas and plans are to become realities. I might delegate the administration to others with greater gifts there, but I can't ignore it. In this way, as needs arise, people with modest abilities might find vital but ill-fitting roles thrust upon them. Ideally, a gifts/service conversation goes like this:

Leader: We need help with XYZ, and someone suggested that I call you.
Servant: Wonderful. I've been praying for an opportunity to help with XYZ.
Leader, later: Great job, servant! You really have a knack for it.
Servant: You don't need to thank me. I love to do it.

On the other hand, some needs do not find eager servants. We can't refuse to attend to them simply because they fail to match an internal sense of call. A person with modest interest and ability might take a role sacrificially. That person might find that it fits better than he or she imagined, and stay there. Or the person might shift out of it as soon as a gifted person surfaces.

With gifts such as giving and encouraging, there is nothing more than a long-standing role. There is no office of encouraging. But a *role* can become an *office* if the church recognizes, calls, and consecrates someone for a formal leadership position. Officers meet known criteria for positions described in Scripture. An office is a formal position, formally bestowed. Officers are first tested, and then consecrated to lead God's people (1 Tim. 3:10; 5:22). In the past, there were prophets, priests, kings, and apostles. Today, offices include elder, deacon, and perhaps evangelist. God equips elders to teach, lead, and shepherd. The technical name for a pastor in some traditions is *teaching elder*, since his emphasis lies there, but he leads, shepherds, and evangelizes, too. Yet to lead well, officers must *function* in many areas. Tough guys must encourage and shy folk must learn to speak. And many should be willing to move into areas of clear and urgent need, such as cleanup after a natural disaster.

When we serve others, we get close to the character and plan of God. For when sin shattered his world, he came in space and time, among particular people, to solve our problem. After returning to the Father, he commissioned us, in all our diversity, to finish his work. At best, the redeemed have a name, and a set of gifts that let us bring God's healing to this broken world. When the work is done, we don't even need thanks. We say, "I was made for this."

15

God's Way to Endure Trials

1 Peter 4:12—19

Dear friends, do not be surprised at the painful trial you are
suffering, as though something strange were happening to you.
But rejoice that you participate in the sufferings of Christ,
so that you may be overjoyed when his glory is revealed.
(1 Peter 4:12–13)

rom the beginning of his epistle, Peter has told the disciples in his churches that they are strangers, outsiders, and aliens in this age. At best, he says, believers can live an exemplary life, so that their good deeds will silence false accusations (1 Peter 1:2; 2:12). The themes of alienation, suffering, and persecution never seem far away in 1 Peter. Each section contributes something to the apostle's teaching on suffering and injustice. First Peter 2:18–23 tells disciples to bear mistreatment patiently and to entrust themselves to God, the Judge. We must never return evil for evil. If we must suffer, we should suffer for doing what is right.

A Final Word on Persecution

But 1 Peter 3 begins a more sustained and challenging discussion of the topic as the apostle warns his people to prepare to "suffer for what is right" and to "suffer for doing good" (3:14, 17). He begins by asking, "Who is going to harm you if you are eager to do good?" (3:13). In the Greek, the question is phrased to invite the answer: "No one." Yet, he says, you *might* suffer because you are good: "But even if you should suffer for what is right, you are blessed" (3:14). The Greek verbs in 3:13 and 3:17 use the rare optative mood, a verb form typically used for remote or theoretical possibilities. Ordinarily, Peter says, no one will harm you "if you are eager to do good." Nonetheless, he implies, it could happen, and believers should be prepared.

Perhaps Peter meant to ease his churches into the hard truth, or perhaps, as some scholars speculate, Peter received bad news even as he wrote. Whatever the reason, Peter's tone shifts in chapter 4. Suffering was a possibility; now he urges his readers to expect trouble.[1] In 1 Peter 3:13–17, Peter tells us that persecution will possibly happen and that disciples must be prepared if it does. In 4:12 he says, "Do not be surprised at the painful trial you are suffering." The Greek verb (*xenizesthe*) is a present imperative, which suggests that they *are* surprised by this development and should not be.

First Peter 4:12–19 is Peter's final word on suffering and persecution. The apostle makes six points. First, the disciples in the church should not be surprised by fiery trials (4:12). Second, they should rejoice, for they share in the sufferings of Christ (4:13). Third, no one should suffer *deservedly*—as a murderer, thief, or even a meddler (4:15). Fourth, no one should be ashamed to "suffer as a Christian." Rather, we should praise God that we bear the name of Christ (4:16). Fifth, we should be prepared to meet the Lord (4:17–18). Sixth, those who do suffer should entrust themselves to their faithful God (4:19). We will consider these commands one by one.

DON'T BE SURPRISED AT TRIALS

Peter opens starkly: "Do not be surprised at the painful trial you are suffering, as though something strange were happening to you" (1 Peter 4:12). "Do not be surprised," Peter says, because trials are not strange. Peter predicts them. Jesus also told his disciples to expect them: "In this

---

1. Commentators speculate that the situation changed for the worse even as Peter wrote, so that his warnings grew more urgent. But there is no external evidence of such a change. It is possible that Peter chose to ease his readers into a difficult discussion.

world you will have trouble" (John 16:33b). Happily, Jesus also encourages: "Take heart! I have overcome the world" (16:33c).

Further, in God's economy, the *result* of trials is positive. When we endure persecution, it demonstrates that we belong to God, our King. Jesus said, "Blessed are those who are persecuted for righteousness' sake, for theirs is the kingdom of heaven" (Matt. 5:10 ESV). Persecution proves that we are united to Christ: "Rejoice that you participate in the sufferings of Christ." For that reason we have a reward in heaven "when his glory is revealed" (1 Peter 4:13; cf. Matt. 5:12). If Jesus suffers hostility, we should expect to follow our Master's path (Matt. 10:24–25).

First Peter 4:12–19 marks the third time that Peter told believers that they must endure suffering. The leaders of the Roman Empire were not necessarily hostile to religious divergence, but new religions, exclusive religions, and rapidly growing religions were viewed less favorably. The apostle warns of trouble because he sees it coming and wants to shepherd his people. If they are prepared for adversity, they can endure, possibly even thrive. As we read Peter, we hear an urgent personal word. He wants to warn his "dear friends" of an imminent danger (4:12).

Since Western Christians generally live in times of relative ease, we might feel that Peter's warnings have no purchase here. Western believers might face mild mockery or dismissive remarks. Our arguments might not be taken seriously and our campus ministries might lose the right to meet on campus while the gay-lesbian-transgender-bisexual club doesn't, but this is marginalization, not red-blooded persecution. Of course, there is no guarantee that this peace will last. Still, we don't feel the need for counsel about trials and suffering in easier days. Whatever hostility Western believers endure, as I write, it barely compares to the troubles of believers in Rome in Peter's day.

Let us remember how many believers in Asia and Africa suffer for the cause of Christ every day. A friend of mine helps to lead a Christian training center for exiled Eritreans living in Sudan, one of the most oppressive nations on earth. In vast areas of Sudan, a family can be in mortal danger simply for being Christians. Nonetheless, life in Eritrea is so much worse that Eritrean Christians flee to Sudan for refuge. The number of Christian leaders who are imprisoned and martyred for the faith has never been higher than it is today.

Although Western Christians face no direct persecution as I write, we never know when the situation might change. Apart from that, every nation experiences times of war, economic distress, and upheaval, so we can identify with the problem of suffering. When our jobs disappear and savings dwindle, not because of dereliction or sin, but because of the mistakes of powerful people in distant places, we feel some of the sting of persecution. Whenever we suffer for actions beyond our control, we taste the life of the first Christians, who suffered even if they did no wrong. They suffered because they did something right; they repented of the follies of pagan polytheism. So even if our experience is far from Peter's, we can hear his message for those who suffer unjustly.

"Do not be surprised at the painful trial you are suffering, as though something strange were happening to you" (1 Peter 4:12). This world is full of tribulation of many kinds, and it strikes for many reasons. First, we suffer because we live in a fallen world. We taste pain and brokenness even when no human does evil. Flocks of birds strike planes so that they crash. We battle illness, disease, storms, and floods. Sadly, humanity sometimes compounds these ordinary disasters. We mismanage lands and rivers so that heavy rains become floods. War can multiply the effects of a light harvest so that it becomes famine.

Second, we suffer because we are united to evil men. We endure leaders, teachers, and coaches who, at one end of the spectrum, are careless, lazy, or unfair. At the other end, some are malicious, oppressive, and abusive. Heedless political leaders and generals start pointless wars and the foot soldiers die, leaving widows and orphans in their wake. Family members and so-called friends say and do cruel things.

Third, we suffer because of our own sins. According to Proverbs 5:22, "the evil deeds of a wicked man ensnare him; the cords of his sin hold him fast." We suffer when friends break their promises, but when we break promises, we suffer, too—the decay of a relationship.

First Peter 4 addresses the worst evil: deliberate malice. A few try to harm Christians because they are hostile to the faith. Others seize the opportunity to rob or crush the weak, and if Christians happen to be weak, predators will attack the same way they would attack any other defenseless minority.

Whether we suffer true persecution or for another reason, everyone needs Peter's message about suffering. Therefore, as long as we live in this fallen world, this magnificent ruin, we should expect to suffer. It is neither strange nor surprising. The more we expect trouble, the better we will be prepared for it.

We should be prepared because suffering is a "fiery ordeal" or "fiery trial" (1 Peter 4:12 NASB, NRSV, ESV). The event tries or tests us. The phrase *fiery trial* is from Proverbs 27:21 (LXX), which reads, "A man is tested [or *judged*] by his praise." This can mean either the praise we receive—our reputation—or the praise we give, what we choose to praise. Both make sense in context. If we endure trials, we should be praised. And if we praise God during the trial of unjust suffering, then we have surely passed a test of character.[2]

Yet we can see why suffering took Peter's people by surprise. They had never been cultural outsiders, so they had never faced irrational prejudice. Recently they had turned to God, so they might have expected his favor to lead to an easier life. But when life got harder, they were surprised.

Langdon Gilkey's memoir, *Shantung Compound*,[3] tells the story of two thousand Europeans and Americans whom the Japanese kept in an internment camp in Shantung for the entire length of World War II. Their imprisonment surprised them because they had committed no crime. They were missionaries, businessmen, travelers, or educators who simply happened to live in north China when the war broke out. We can suffer simply for belonging to the wrong group at the wrong time. It should not surprise us; we should be prepared for it.

Rejoice That You Are United to Christ

Jesus *predicted* that we would face persecution, and he *showed* that God's agents will suffer. As a result, Peter says, disciples should "rejoice that you participate in the sufferings of Christ, so that you may be overjoyed when his glory is revealed" (1 Peter 4:13). Suffering is a product of our union with Christ.

I once preached a guest sermon in a city known for its rudeness. Afterward, two men surprised me with their comments. One remarked that it was the second-best sermon he'd ever heard (I didn't ask). The other told me that the message was "a stench in the nostrils of God." The man seemed

2. Bruce K. Waltke, *The Book of Proverbs* (Grand Rapids: Eerdmans, 2005), 2:387.
3. New York: Harper & Row, 1966.

arrogant, so I tried to discount it, but it is never easy to be blasted when we do our best to please God and neighbor.

But Peter tells us not to be surprised at trials or rejection. If Jesus, in all his perfection, could be rejected, so will we. If his life followed a pattern of suffering before glory, so will ours, since he expects our life to resemble his (1 Peter 2:23–25; 3:14; 5:1). Indeed, we should rejoice, not in suffering per se, but in the pain that demonstrates our participation in his suffering. So we rejoice if (and only if) we suffer innocently, as he did. Then we will rejoice when Jesus returns, in glory, appearing to all flesh, to judge and renew creation, beginning with this world (4:13).

Therefore, "if you are insulted [or *reviled*] because of the name of Christ, you are blessed, for" it proves that "the Spirit of glory and of God rests on you" (1 Peter 4:14). In a hostile, pagan environment, a reproach can be proof that God's Spirit shapes us so completely that our life disturbs the pagan, who responds by reviling. Opposition might therefore be proof that God is so differentiating us from the culture that we cannot be ignored.

Around A.D. 400, a monk named Telemachus felt God compelling him to travel to Rome to preach against the city's corruptions, especially against the gladiatorial games. He preached on a street corner, but no one paid him heed. Then came a day for the games. As the crowds bounded to the amphitheater, Telemachus decided to walk with them. He entered, saw, blanched, and acted. He leaped into the arena and shouted to two combatants to cease their bloody contest.

There are two accounts of what happened next. One says that the combatants briefly stopped fighting each other, killed him, and then resumed their battle. The second reports that the crowd picked up loose stones from the crumbling Colosseum and used them to stone him to death. Either way, his protest so challenged the proceedings that he was slain.

It *seemed* that Telemachus's protest had failed. But in Matthew 5:10–16, Jesus says that four things can happen when godly character manifests itself. We might be "persecuted because of righteousness" (5:10); we might be "the salt of the earth," retarding its decay (5:13); we might be "the light of the world," enlightening all who see it (5:14); and that light might shine so clearly that witnesses "see your good deeds and praise your Father in heaven" (5:16).

Telemachus was persecuted for righteousness that day, but the story of Telemachus's protest spread. His "salt and light" strengthened those who protested the games. For centuries, most people had seen the games as a spectacle and entertainment. It took a long time, but eventually, with the help of Telemachus, the world came to view the games as a crime and an abomination. In God's providence, the prosperity of the empire was crumbling, making it harder for governors to sponsor the contests. By A.D. 450, to God's glory, they had essentially ceased.[4]

Today, young adults who abstain from sexual encounters before marriage are viewed as antiquarians at best, fools at worst. Why, a highly regarded advice columnist asks reproachfully, would *any* couple want to get married without first assuring themselves that they are sexually compatible? We believe that total *physical* self-giving belongs in the marital context of total *personal* self-giving—heart, soul, body, mind, will, and strength. Outside marriage, sexual intimacy is intrinsically deceptive—a life-uniting act without a life-uniting intent.[5] There will always be areas where Christian ethics so clash with a given culture's ethic that Christians will endure reproach for following God's ways.

It is miserable to endure mockery, scorn, and character assassination, and every sane person recoils from physical persecution. Yet we want to be like Jesus, who loved us and gave himself for us as a sacrifice (Eph. 5:2). He is the supreme case of an innocent man unjustly persecuted. Like Jesus, we neither *seek* persecution nor *retreat* from it. We accept it if it comes, and when it does come, it proves that we have allied ourselves with the suffering Christ. Paul states, "I want to know Christ and the power of his resurrection and the fellowship of sharing in his sufferings" (Phil. 3:10–11).

When we belong to Christ, we experience a real union with him. My wife and I have been married for over thirty years. For some years, people have treated us as though we shared each other's attributes. They pepper her with biblical and theological questions, even though she has no formal training. Even more astonishing, because she is delightfully friendly and remembers everyone's name, people assume that I'm friendly and remember their names, too. There are good reasons for these assumptions. *We become like the people with whom we are united.* Husbands and wives, in real marriages at least,

---

4. Philip Schaff, *History of the Christian Church* (Peabody, MA: Hendrickson, 1996), 3:122–25.

5. Lewis B. Smedes, *Sex for Christians: The Limits and Liberties of Sexual Living* (Grand Rapids: Eerdmans, 1994), 110–11. See also Timothy Keller, with Kathy Keller, *The Meaning of Marriage: Facing the Complexities of Commitment with the Wisdom of God* (New York: Dutton, 2011), 224–27.

do become similar. Because of our marriage, I am friendlier and my wife knows more theology.

If we are united to Christ, we become more like him. Our life path resembles his more and more. Our suffering recapitulates his suffering. So our suffering shows that we belong to him now and will share in his coming victory. So we will "be overjoyed when his glory is revealed." If we share in his suffering, we will share in his victory over death and enjoy God's reward in heaven.

Peter teaches, "If you are insulted because of the name of Christ, you are blessed, for the Spirit of glory and of God rests on you" (1 Peter 4:14). Jesus likewise told his disciples that they were blessed if they suffered evil "because of righteousness" or "because of me" (Matt. 5:10–11). That is, we are blessed if we suffer for God's principles, and we are blessed if we suffer for God's Son.

Persecution also links us with the prophets, who suffered the same thing. If we suffer for Jesus' sake, we are in good company. We join the prophets who suffered because they challenged their age. When we engage the world, clashing values inescapably create conflict. When Jeremiah confronted the idolatry and corruption of his age, they called him a traitor, burned his writings, and shut his mouth by tossing him into a pit. Ahead of his time, he participated in the sufferings of Christ. We should expect the same, for "a student is not above his teacher." If opponents slander the master, they will also slander his followers (Matt. 10:24–25). Jesus doesn't hide bad news; he repeats it:

> If the world hates you, keep in mind that it hated me first. If you belonged to the world, it would love you as its own. . . . I have chosen you out of the world. That is why the world hates you. Remember the words I spoke to you: "No servant is greater than his master." If they persecuted me, they will persecute you also. (John 15:18–20)

The Bible never blesses suffering in itself. No one should take direct pleasure in pain. Threats, insults, and slander hurt, even if the slanderer is a great fool. Nonetheless, Peter insists, "If you are insulted because of the name of Christ, you are blessed, for the Spirit of glory and of God rests on you" (1 Peter 4:14).

NEVER SUFFER FOR EVIL DEEDS; AVOID WELL-DESERVED SUFFERING

When the Spirit of glory so rests on us that we become more like Christ, we participate in his life, and insults suffered for the sake of righteousness prove that. But the progress of the disciple is always partial, so that Peter is compelled to add a caveat: "If you suffer, it should not be as a murderer or thief or any other kind of criminal, or even as a meddler" (1 Peter 4:15). Peter requires that we avoid criminal acts meriting punishment. He assumes that we will shun the foolishness that earns us displeasure.

Refraining from murder also means no displays of anger, no resentment. No harsh judgment—scorning, scoffing, despising, or belittling. Refraining from theft also means no envy or greed, no manipulation or abuse of funds, no unpaid debts, and no waste of wealth or creation.

It is obvious that disciples should avoid criminal activity, but the ban on meddling is a subtle notion. The term translated "meddler" (*allotriepiskopos*) is a rare compound word that means "an overseer of another's affairs." Meddlers interfere, usurping roles not properly theirs. They might even scheme to gain influence outside their sphere. They nose into matters that are not their proper concern and offer unwanted opinions. They speak when protocol calls for silence. No one gladly listens to a meddler; most are irritated. If a child is misbehaving at the grocery store, how many parents will welcome child-rearing tips from the nearest cashier?

The Lord disapproves when we violate reasonable social standards. He does not bless tactlessness or folly, even if they are somehow connected to the faith. A worker cannot claim persecution if, while proselytizing a fellow laborer, he talks beyond the lunch hour and is rebuked for it. If we bark out corrections whenever our peers speak crudely, we can expect rejection. Leaders have a right to set standards for their organization, but ordinary employees should keep their judgments private. God does not bless tactless behavior, and it is not persecution when obnoxious acts earn wrath. There is a time for silence, as Solomon declared and as Jesus and Paul showed (Eccl. 3:7; Luke 23:9; John 19:9; Acts 19:30).

When we receive harsh treatment, we should ask, "What have I done to deserve this?" rather than "Why do they persecute me?" For example, if we freely share pointed opinions in person or in blogs and Internet posts, we should not be surprised if people disagree with us and criticize us. And if the critic's language is harsh, we should not call it *persecution*, but a predictable consequence of sharp debate. On the other hand, both David and Peter say that, ordinarily, we suffer no harm if we do good (1 Peter 3:10–13, quoting Ps. 34:12–16).

DON'T BE ASHAMED TO SUFFER AS A CHRISTIAN

"Yet if anyone suffers as a Christian, let him not be ashamed, but let him glorify God in that name" (1 Peter 4:16 ESV). Translators debate whether the phrase "glorify God in that name" means that we praise God that we bear the name of Christ (NIV), or that we praise God in the name of Christ (NASB). A common interpretation takes Peter to say, "Even if the name 'Christian' is hurled at you in derision, wear the name proudly, for you do belong to Christ." In a common variant reading, the text reads "let him glorify God *in this matter*," that is, let him glorify God while it happens.[6] At any rate, it seems that the term *Christian* was a slur, an insult, much as certain English-men coined the term *Puritan* to mock English believers who had a zeal for purity. In each case, believers eventually decided to take the slur as a positive name. If that happens, Peter says, praise God in it. Don't be ashamed; take your eyes off yourself. In today's terms:

- If called a *fundamentalist*, think, "Yes, I believe the fundamentals."
- If called a *Bible-thumper*, think, "Yes, I do read and honor God's Word."
- If called a *Puritan*, think, "Yes, I do aim for purity and integrity."
- If called a *Christian*, think, "Yes, I do follow Jesus."

In Peter's day, Christians were exiled, arrested, tried, even slain for their faith. If any believer so suffers, he or she should count it an honor to suffer for Jesus' name.

In the West, where religious freedom has long been respected, we might think this discussion pointless. But we should be prepared. In Russia, after the Communist revolution, and in Germany, during the later stages of Nazi

---

6. The chief difference is that the text normally adopted has "name" (*onomati*), whereas the common alternative reading has "matter" (*merei*). See J. Ramsey Michaels, *1 Peter*, Word Biblical Commentary 49 (Nashville: Thomas Nelson, 1988), 269–70.

rule, it suddenly became dangerous to be an evangelical Christian. Most recently, Christians in Iraq and Sudan, who had been safe minorities for decades, even centuries, suddenly found themselves at risk. The same could happen in many other lands, in time.

BE PREPARED TO MEET THE LORD

Peter says that his people must be ready to live faithfully, for each person must render an account of his or her life before God the Judge: "For it is time for judgment to begin with the family of God; and if it begins with us, what will the outcome be for those who do not obey the gospel of God?" (1 Peter 4:17). Peter has already mentioned judgment several times (1:17; 2:23; 4:5–6). The original says that "it is time for *the* judgment," which can only mean the final judgment. The Old Testament prophets said that this judgment must begin with God's people (Jer. 25:15–33, noting 25:29; cf. Ezek. 9; Mal. 3).[7]

Peter's readers might be surprised to hear that believers will face judgment. After all, it is challenging enough to be a Christian. And after suffering for Jesus in this life, we still face judgment. This teaching should neither surprise nor dismay us. First, it is the consistent testimony of Scripture. Jesus said, "When the Son of Man comes in his glory, . . . all the nations will be gathered before him, and he will separate the people one from another as a shepherd separates the sheep from the goats" (Matt. 25:31–32). The goats are unbelievers; the sheep are believers, to whom he will say, "Come, you who are blessed by my Father; take your inheritance, the kingdom prepared for you since the creation of the world. For I was hungry and you gave me something to eat, I was thirsty and you gave me something to drink, I was a stranger and you invited me in" (25:34–35). The Bible consistently teaches that God will examine us and will do so through our works when we stand before him. We will account for them all on the last day (Ps. 62:12; Jer. 17:10; Matt. 16:27; 2 Cor. 5:10; 1 Peter 1:17; Rev. 20:12).

But this judgment should not alarm us for a second reason: we will not be condemned. This is not according to works. Our works do count, but they count because they *follow our heart commitments.* This is clear in Psalm 62. David declares, "My soul finds rest in God alone . . . . He alone is my rock and

---

7. Peter H. Davids, *The First Epistle of Peter* (Grand Rapids: Eerdmans, 1990), 170.

my salvation . . . . You, O God, are strong, . . . you, O Lord, are loving. Surely you will reward each person according to what he has done" (Ps. 62:1–2, 11–12). Because David trusts the Lord, he is confident that his life, his works, reflects that trust. He knows the Lord will see his loyalty in his deeds.

The believer's sins and failings will be forgiven, yet—what a gift—our noble words and deeds will attest our heart commitment to the Lord on judgment day. Deeds supply public, verifiable evidence of the heart's condition (Matt. 7:17–18; 12:33–35; James 2:14–26). Therefore, we should examine ourselves and ask what our words and deeds reveal. Do they show that Jesus is our King and that his grace and reign have transformed us? Peter directs us to expect that day and prepare for it, living according to our identity as members of "the family of God"—the Father's sons and daughters.

Now, Peter continues, if judgment day is a serious matter even for disciples, "what will the outcome be for those who do not obey the gospel of God? And, 'If it is hard for the righteous to be saved, what will become of the ungodly and the sinner?'" (1 Peter 4:17–18). That is, if someone does not love and obey God, it will be clear, and it will lead to judgment. Again, this is not judgment according to works in a narrow sense. Rather, the corrupt heart also proves itself in actions. Jeremiah put it this way: "The heart is deceitful above all things and beyond cure. Who can understand it? I the LORD search the heart and examine the mind, to reward a man according to his conduct, according to what his deeds deserve" (Jer. 17:9–10). So the direction of the heart and mind leads to deeds that God rewards or punishes.

The priority of the heart's direction, a person's faith or the lack of it, is clear in the question that closes 1 Peter 4:17: "What will the outcome be for those who do not obey the gospel of God?" When the phrase "obey the gospel" appears in the Bible, it is clear that to *obey* the gospel means to *believe* the gospel of Jesus (Rom. 10:14–16; 2 Thess. 1:8–10). Peter is therefore speaking of those who hear and reject the gospel and persecute Christians for the faith (1 Peter 2:8; 3:14–17). If the judgment is a serious thing for "the family of God . . . , what will the outcome be for those who do not obey the gospel of God? And, 'If it is hard for the righteous to be saved, what will become of the ungodly and the sinner?'" (1 Peter 4:17–18). It is hard even for believers to be saved. God must preserve the elect (Matt. 24:22–24). The gate is narrow (Matt. 7:13–14). Our faith is tested and proved genuine (1 Peter 1:6–7; 4:12). We must remember whom to fear (3:14).

If the believer must be so careful to persevere and stay ready to meet the Judge, even in our union with Christ, what will come to the person who has spurned Christ, oppressed the weak, and lived for himself? We should then be sober-minded and give thanks that we face the judgment vindicated by the good deeds that come from faith.

Let us therefore be ready for that day. Many call on the Lord, but not all call sincerely (Matt. 7:22). We prepare by praying and telling Jesus, "I sincerely believe in you as you are presented in the gospel. I will fail often, but I do resolve to love, follow, and obey you, even if that should bring me persecution, for I know how you loved me and gave yourself for me."

This passage begins and ends with suffering; suffering divides those who truly call on Jesus from those who dabble in religion for a season. Suffering clarifies things. If we endure at a cost, it shows that we know the Lord and are preparing daily to meet him and render an account for our life.

COMMIT YOURSELF, THEREFORE, TO THE FAITHFUL GOD

"So then, those who suffer according to God's will should commit themselves to their faithful Creator and continue to do good" (1 Peter 4:19). We suffer according to God's will when we suffer for the sake of righteousness, not our sin or folly. At the same time, we accept that our suffering is his will, his decree, as he continues to govern the world.

Peter also tells us how to endure suffering. Curiously, he does not command us to be faithful; he reminds us that God is faithful. So we should continually commit or entrust ourselves to the faithful Creator.[8] The word translated "commit" means "to entrust or to hand over something to the care of another." The "thing" that we commit to God is our very life, and we do so because we believe he is faithful. That is why David told the Lord, "Into your hands I commit my spirit; redeem me, O LORD," and it is why Jesus said the same words even as he died on the cross (Ps. 31:5; cf. Luke 23:46). The command is in the present tense, which means that we continue to

8. The Greek is *paratithēmi*. The verb is a present imperative, signifying an ongoing disposition. "Ourselves" translates *hē psuchē*—literally, "the soul." This is not meant to contrast with the body. It means the whole person, perhaps with the connotation that persecutors can harm the body but not the whole person. See Matt. 10:28; Davids, *1 Peter*, 173; Michaels, *1 Peter*, 273.

commit ourselves to God, knowing that he is faithful. And while we suffer and trust, we do good, as he defines it in Scripture.[9]

There is a time to flee persecution and run to another place, Jesus noted (Matt. 10:23). But while we might run by abandoning our home, we cannot run by abandoning our faith, our vows, or our Lord. Many do abandon their vows. Pastors administer vows fairly often—at weddings and baptisms, to new church members and church officers. A few take their vows in vain and begin to abandon them almost at once. All of us fail partially. But God does not. That is why we entrust ourselves to him instead of entrusting ourselves to ourselves.

Summary

To review, Peter has suggested some means to remain true during suffering and persecution. First, we must be ready when trials come (1 Peter 4:12). Second, we should rejoice that we are united to Christ (4:13). If we suffer insults, it shows that the Spirit of God rests on us (4:14). Third, we should suffer for the faith, not because we merit punishment (4:15). Fourth, no one should be ashamed to suffer because we bear the name of Christ (4:16). Fifth, we remember that we will stand before God the Judge (4:17–18). Finally, when we suffer, we should commit ourselves to our faithful God and continue to do good (4:19).

In Psalms 26:1; 35:24; 43:1; and 54:1, the singer pleads, "Vindicate me, O Lord." Psalm 135:14 seems to answer the petitions: "For the Lord will vindicate his people." Jesus is the archetype of the one who is falsely accused and then vindicated by God, above all in his resurrection (1 Tim. 3:16; see also Rom. 1:1–4 [which has the concept, not the word]). Because of our union with Christ (1 Peter 4:13), we will be vindicated with him. Knowing this, we can persevere.

The sixfold counsel of 1 Peter 4:12–19 deserves our careful attention, but we must remember that the Bible is never essentially about lists of duties. To live by lists is as appealing as cotton candy—and just as nourishing. The Bible starts with the covenants and the character of God. He created us, he redeemed us, and he is worthy of our trust. If Jesus was willing to suffer in the flesh, we should be, too. And if the Father vindicated Jesus by raising him from the dead, he will vindicate us, too. That future, in God's presence, that future, sharing in his glory, teaches us to persevere.

---

9. The Greek phrase *en agathopoia* could mean "*by* doing good" or "*while* doing good." *While* fits better, for Peter is urging his readers to continue to do good as they suffer.

16

JESUS SHEPHERDS HIS CHURCH THROUGH SERVANT LEADERS

1 Peter 5:1–4

To the elders among you, I appeal as a fellow elder, a witness of Christ's sufferings and one who also will share in the glory to be revealed: Be shepherds of God's flock that is under your care, serving as overseers—not because you must, but because you are willing, as God wants you to be; not greedy for money, but eager to serve; not lording it over those entrusted to you, but being examples to the flock. And when the Chief Shepherd appears, you will receive the crown of glory that will never fade away.
(1 Peter 5:1–4)

THE PARADOXES OF LEADERSHIP

Leadership is a paradox—a glory and a ruin, a privilege and a torment. People look *for* leaders, who are in short supply, and look *to* leaders, whose skills are often exaggerated. People assist and advise them, favor and flatter them, haunt them and hover over them. But others suspect, criticize, and condemn. They drown their leaders and delight in their demise. It's so much easier to review a book (or movie) than it is to write (or direct) one. And it's so much easier to rail at a leader than to be one. Every step up is simultaneously a step down.

Every leader knows the paradoxes of headship, sees them, hears them, smells them coming, in the way that fits his realm. A judge has great power. He ferrets out the truth, protects the defenseless, and punishes evildoers. He fines petty miscreants, jails the wicked, and acquits the innocent. But every sound judgment disappoints someone a little, and a few earn a leader full-blooded enemies. Headless chickens on the porch and slashed tires are one thing, death threats on wives and children another. Presidents and prime ministers are the most-loved and the most-detested persons in their lands, the objects of fevered adulation and plotted assassination. In the circle of fawning admirers, every wish is a command; but in the circle of foes, every gesture is reviled. The boss, the coach, the director, the governor—all loved, all scorned. Every privilege gained is a freedom lost.

Few bear the mantle of authority with ease. One type is too quick to decide, too eager to lead, even to dominate, and readily abuses power. Another sort is too reluctant to command, too thin-skinned to endure. Rare indeed is Plato's reluctant-but-willing philosopher king.

Like the sad fish that daily ingest but never expel mercury until the concentrate cripples them, the leader never even hears of the easy problems. Only the toxic stuff reaches his desk, only the problems that no one else conquers.

What sane person would want to be a leader? The deluded and power-hungry want it, the naive and grasping hunger for it. More importantly, those whom God has called and gifted to lead desire it. They want to change the world, to bring truth, peace, and grace to bear in churches and cities so that people find healing and life. They want to improve some part of creation and believe they know how to do it.

Through Scripture, godly leaders have witnessed Jesus' sufferings. Depending on their age and course of life, they see, whether dimly or fully, what it means to suffer with him. They also hope to share in his glory, and depending on their age and experience, they have either robust or guarded optimism about their chances. But whatever their expectation, they hope to shepherd God's flock by their teaching and a godly example.

Peter comes to the subject of leadership late in the epistle. He has already taught that we are God's beloved people, raised to a living hope and an unfailing inheritance. We endure hardship, follow God's Word, and live by God's mercy. By his blood Jesus ransomed us from a futile way of life and called us to be holy (1 Peter 1:1–16). Believers are a holy priesthood, a holy nation set apart for God by their faith in Jesus and their determination to follow him in their social relations, in their marriages and their homes (2:5–4:19). When we follow Jesus we change, and change can create problems (4:1–4). When a sinner reforms, he leaves his old ways and old companions, who might resent the departure. Peter's people had been pagans, and when they forsook pagan ways, they became outsiders, exiles in their own culture. The government also had suspicions, since the disciples refused to worship the emperor, an attitude that looked subversive. These social and political problems, taken together, convinced Peter that trials and persecution were inevitable for all who will to suffer with Christ rather than renouncing him: "Do not be surprised at the painful trial you are suffering, as though something strange were happening to you. But rejoice that you participate in the sufferings of Christ" (4:12–13, passim).

The church needs stalwart shepherd leaders in such times.[1] Elders should not hesitate to lead the church, even though they might make themselves a target for persecution. In this willingness to suffer, Peter stands with Jesus and, calling himself a "fellow elder," invites church leaders into solidarity with him.[2] Strong and steady hands are essential during a crisis.

Yet churches need shepherds even in the best times. Even the saints can wander into sin, and the immature need a godly example (1 Peter 5:2–3). And however much individual Christians may progress, the church needs men to lead and to harness its diverse gifts (4:10–11). The greater the talents, the greater the need for leaders. It is the most gifted orchestra, comprising musicians with the greatest capacities and the most fertile imaginations, that needs the strongest conductor.

Apart from the challenge of enduring persecution, all Scripture testifies that the church will also experience trouble from internal sources, from (1) *the heretical,* (2) *the immoral,* and (3) *the envious.* Peter's prescriptions for elders answer all three problems. We begin with heresy and the antidote, experiential knowledge of true doctrine.

---

1. Although this turn of thought is not explicit, 1 Peter 5:1 does begin with *oun,* "so" or possibly "therefore." The conjunction points to a thought process. The church needs leaders for a reason.
2. Karen H. Jobes, *1 Peter* (Grand Rapids: Baker Academic, 2005), 300.

THE BASIS OF PETER'S LEADERSHIP AND MESSAGE

Peter speaks elder to elder: "To the elders among you, I appeal as a fellow elder, a witness of Christ's sufferings and one who also will share in the glory to be revealed" (1 Peter 5:1). We know that Jesus himself appointed Peter as an apostle and herald of the gospel, that Peter was one of the inner three, and that he was often a spokesman for the disciples. Yet with touching modesty, he calls himself a "fellow elder" rather than "apostle." He locates himself with that band of elders who labor in the church. He stresses his equality with others and his empathy with their position, not his supremacy or even his authority.

Nonetheless, elders (*presbuteroi*) *do* possess authority over the congregation. *Elder* was the customary term for a community leader in the Old Testament and in the Judaism of the Hellenistic age. Peter does not call the others "fellow elders" in a play at humility; he "makes the elders aware of their commission." They now fulfill part of the work of the apostles themselves—the need to shepherd and care for all the congregations (2 Cor. 11:28; 1 Peter 5:2).[3]

Peter is "a witness of Christ's sufferings" (1 Peter 5:1). Peter heard the words of Jesus and beheld his deeds, from the beginning (Acts 1:21), by the appointment of Jesus (Mark 3:14–16). He stood at Jesus' side, both watching events and hearing Jesus' explanation of them, so Peter, in turn, could declare both what happened and what it meant.

No, Peter did not see *everything* with his own eyes; he fled before the crucifixion (Matt. 26:56). Nonetheless, he is a witness in the secondary sense that he *testified* to Jesus' suffering. Thus, Peter partially shares the position of elders who proclaim the work of Jesus by drawing on the eyewitness testimony of others. In this limited sense, all elders are witnesses alongside the apostles.

Further, Peter is "a partaker in the glory that is going to be revealed" (1 Peter 5:1b ESV). So Peter stands beside the church's elders, not above them. All witness to Jesus and wait to participate in Jesus' glory. From the position of "fellow elder," he exhorts the elders of the church. This is no condescension, no rhetorical subterfuge. He is not acting as though his fellow elders

---

3. Leonhard Goppelt, *A Commentary on 1 Peter*, trans. John E. Alsup (Grand Rapids: Eerdmans, 1993), 341.

were his peers; he is elevating them to his level. All witness to Christ. All share in his sufferings and glory, for Jesus' life is a pattern for ours, as Peter has said before (2:21ff.).

Peter is not denying his unique role as a witness of Jesus. As he proclaims in 2 Peter 1:16, he was and therefore is an eyewitness of Jesus' majesty. But Peter wants to stress his solidarity with his fellow elders, and he can legitimately do so. After all, Peter was hardly a perfect leader. He contributed to Jesus' suffering. He fell asleep when Jesus asked him to stand beside him in his anguish in Gethsemane, as he faced his death and separation from the Father. Hours later, after Jesus' arrest, Peter denied that he even knew Jesus. Hours like these could lead one to ask how Peter (far from putting on humility) dares to present himself as a fellow elder.

Indeed, Peter's case can explain how anyone dares to be called or to call himself an elder or leader. In a way, the church has leaders because God appointed "some to be apostles," prophets, evangelists, pastors, and teachers, as well as elders (Eph. 4:11; cf. Acts 14:23). Yet Peter illustrates the principle that no one, not even an apostle, *deserves* to lead. Again, Peter denied that he even knew Jesus. He did so in Jesus' darkest hour, despite Jesus' prior warning, despite promising that he would never betray Jesus, and despite his position as a leader and example.

Beyond doubt, Peter's actions disqualified him for church leadership. Yet here he is, an apostle and elder, shepherd and overseer (1 Peter 1:1; 5:1). He regained his position because Jesus reinstated him after his failures. After the resurrection, Peter and the other fishing disciples returned to the Sea of Galilee, and Jesus met Peter there (John 21:2–5).

Jesus asked him, "Simon, . . . do you truly love me . . . ?" (John 21:15). The question was fair. Peter had claimed that he loved Jesus more than anyone else did: "Even if all fall away on account of you, I never will." Yet Peter did fall away, even swearing an oath that he had never known Jesus (Matt. 26:33, 72).

Peter had *denied* Jesus three times, so Jesus *questioned* him three times: "Do you love me?" Jesus wasn't mocking Peter's failure. Rather, Peter had denied Jesus three times, so Jesus asked three times, "Do you love me?" This allowed Peter to declare three times: "I love you, Lord; you know I love you." That in turn lets Jesus reinstate Peter three times: "Feed my lambs," "take care of my sheep," "feed my sheep" (John 21:15–17). This was Peter's restoration.

Someone called this sequence Peter's ordination exam. Jesus' questions were quite different from our (perfectly valid) questions about forms of church government and adherence to confessions of faith. Jesus' questions were also quite different from our half-solicitous, half-accusatory inquiries: "Have you learned your lesson? Do you promise never to do that again? Are you really sorry?" Jesus simply asked, "Do you love me?" That remains the great question for every church leader. Apart from our union with Jesus, whom we love, our labors can bear no fruit.

The lessons are clear. First, no Christian leader is self-qualified, morally or spiritually. No one deserves to lead the church. Jesus forgives, appoints, and qualifies his apostles and elders. Second, the core of an elder's qualification is the love of Jesus, both experienced and returned.

The love of Jesus creates the essential desire to lead and care for God's people. Despite the threat of persecution, leaders do so "because you are willing," as Peter puts it (1 Peter 5:2). Elders must also hold to the faith with a clear conscience. They should be apt to teach and lead. They should be tested and proved faithful. They must have godly character. They must care for people inside and outside their church. They should lead their own families well and so gain a good reputation (Acts 20:17–35; 1 Thess. 5:12–15; 1 Tim. 3:1–13; 5:17–19; Heb. 13:17). But above all, they are beloved of God and must love God in return.

THE PROBLEM OF HERETICAL TEACHERS

This foundational knowledge of Jesus and love for him is the antidote to the first internal challenge to the church and its leaders, the challenge of heretical teachers. In the New Testament, Paul says most about heretics and false teachers. Instead of leading in love, they are violent (spiritually) and quarrelsome (1 Tim. 6:3–5; cf. 2 Tim. 2:23–26).

False teachers are "confident" and want to be recognized as "teachers of the law, but they do not know what they are talking about or what they so confidently affirm" (1 Tim. 1:7). Elders, by contrast, are "able to teach" (3:2). False teachers "have shipwrecked their faith" (1:19), whereas elders and deacons have been tested and are above reproach (3:1, 7, 10).

Some false teachers are former church leaders. Paul foretold this in his final address to his beloved Ephesian elders: "Even from your own number men will arise and distort the truth in order to draw away disciples after them" (Acts 20:30). In 1 Timothy 1:20, Paul names two of them—Hymenaeus and Alexander, whom he has "handed over to Satan." This seems like the sort of public rebuke Paul requires when an elder is caught in sin (5:17–20).

The greatest danger is that heretics will preach "a different gospel—which is really no gospel at all" in the truest sense of the word (Gal. 1:6–7). The "alternative" gospel is contrary to the word Paul preached and utterly defective: "If anybody is preaching to you a gospel other than what you accepted, let him be eternally condemned!" (1:9). These teachers miss the central gospel, and shift their interest to matters that are, at best, peripheral. They major in genealogies, myths, speculations, and vain discussions (1 Tim. 1:4–6). Today they burrow into the interpretation of creeds and catechisms, rather than Scripture itself. They try to distinguish between the early and late phases of thought leaders instead of asking whether they are right or wrong. Second Peter 2 further addresses false teachers. Speaking of the old covenant era, Peter says:

> But there were also false prophets among the people, just as there will be false teachers among you. They will secretly introduce destructive heresies, even denying the sovereign Lord who bought them . . . . Many will follow their shameful [or *sensual*] ways and will bring the way of truth into disrepute. In their greed these teachers will exploit you with stories they have made up. (2 Peter 2:1–3)

Second Peter shows that the twin internal challenges of false teaching and immorality are linked. Peter explains that false teachers deny the Sovereign Lord so that they can claim to believe and yet live for selfish pleasure. They "carouse in broad daylight . . . , reveling in their pleasures while they feast with you. With eyes full of adultery, they never stop sinning; they seduce the unstable; they are experts in greed" (2:13–14). The antidote to such false and corrupt teachers is the holiness of the true Shepherd.

THE MANNER OF A GODLY LEADER

Peter commands elders to "shepherd the flock of God that is among you"—that is, under the elder's charge—"exercising oversight, not under compulsion, but willingly, . . . not for shameful gain, but eagerly" (1 Peter 5:2 ESV).[4] This compressed

---

4. The phrase "exercising oversight" translates the single participle *episkopountes*, which does not appear in all early manuscripts. But most do include it, and there is no convincing reason to doubt that it is original.

statement describes the duty, manner, and motives of godly leaders. First, they willingly shepherd and watch over the flock. In the agrarian world, everyone knew that sheep stray, find trouble, and cannot extricate themselves from it. Unless they receive constant care and oversight, they perish.

Psalm 23 pictures the Lord as a shepherd to his people. In John 10, Jesus calls himself the Good Shepherd, the Lord who feeds his sheep, seeks the lost, gathers the scattered, and heals the wounded. Then he commissions men to become shepherds under him. God told David, "You will shepherd my people Israel" (2 Sam. 5:2). Jesus commanded Peter to be a shepherd, and now Peter commands elders to be shepherds. What the Lord did for them, they must do for others.

Peter hints that an elder's first task is to witness to Christ's sufferings and glory (1 Peter 5:1). But he explicitly charges elders to watch over that part of God's flock that is right in front of them (literally, "among you") as their charge. Good shepherds care for *their flock*, not for the whole world.

OVERSEEING THE FLOCK OF GOD

Yet Peter first says that the people are "God's flock" (1 Peter 5:2). We are, above all, *God's* flock. That flock is under the care of elders and shepherds who watch out for and prevent trouble. We should take comfort that the flock belongs to God, not to man, for if we falter, God is the Chief Shepherd and will never forsake his people.[5]

C. S. Lewis noted that humans sometimes make strange claims to ownership. We talk about "my body" as if we had created the pulsating energy within us. We use the word *my* for ownership but fail to notice that *my* cannot possibly mean ownership most of the time. We use these phrases very differently: *my shoes, my coworker, my wife, my father, my church, my country,* and *my God*. We cannot reduce all these relationships to ownership, as in *my teddy bear*. For an unpleasant child, *my teddy bear* can mean "the bear I can pull to pieces if I like."[6] Surely we cannot do what we like with *my church*. At worst, *my church* means "the church that ought to do what I want."

5. C. E. B. Cranfield, *I & II Peter and Jude* (London: SCM Press, 1960), 127.

6. C. S. Lewis, *The Screwtape Letters and Screwtape Proposes a Toast* (London: Geoffrey Bles, 1961), 97 (in chapter 21, for those working with other editions).

We should have a home church, and we may call it *my church*. But the church is God's people and family before it is ours. Therefore, *my church* should mean the part of God's family that is my spiritual home—the one I love, warts and all, and the one that loves me, warts and all.

The church is often so disappointing, so far short of God's ideal. Particular churches hurt many people and many people *feel* hurt—which is *not* the same thing. Yet the church, as God sees the whole, is a glorious family that stretches across all lands and all centuries and leads to eternity. Sadly, even good churches—the better parts of the whole—are regularly places of shallow relationships, weak teaching, dull worship, and lazy prayers. Worse, some particular churches are breeding grounds for wounding relationships and heretical ideas, where worshipers are critics and it seems that everyone is either angry or asleep. Clearly, we need God to shepherd us even in our spiritual activities.

The church will inevitably disappoint perfection-demanding attenders, if only because no style of music, liturgy, preaching, and serving suits everyone. More important, every church is entirely composed of sinners. (The church is the one organization in which all who join first declare themselves unworthy to join.) Since sinners do act the part, the church will inevitably fail its members. But the church's failure is not equivalent to God's failure. When the church fails, we must look past it to the Lord of the church.

Pastors, elders, and shepherds must strive to represent the Lord well. All the while, we must remember that the church is his, not ours. He can accomplish what our plans and skills do not.

The Conduct of an Elder

Serving Willingly, Not Grudgingly

These caveats notwithstanding, Peter still has standards for leaders. He states three principles for the *way* in which leaders conduct themselves. He states them in a series of three contrasts in 1 Peter 5:2–3 (esv). Elders serve:

- "not under compulsion, but willingly";
- "not for shameful gain, but eagerly";
- "not domineering over those in [their] charge, but being examples to the flock."

209

Clearly, elders must care for God's people willingly, not coldly or grudgingly. "Willingly, not grudgingly" is a good ideal for every calling. The willing shepherd embraces God's will and makes it his own, as a task freely chosen. This does not mean that we are always in the mood for every task. Every calling has its drudgery. There is a time to do our duty, as Jesus teaches in the parable of the unthanked servant (Luke 17:3–10). In a way, all ministry is a God-given duty or obligation, and not simply a result of our choice (1 Cor. 9:16). So, however willing our service, there is a time to do our duty, whether we feel like it or not.

But the main motive must be neither duty nor the compulsions of expectations, reputation, or social status, nor the thrall of models or precedents. We should act willingly and cheerfully, for "God loves a cheerful giver" (2 Cor. 9:7). Good cheer for our work makes us glad to get up and go to work in the morning.[7]

Serving Eagerly, Not for Personal Gain

The call to serve "not for shameful gain, but eagerly" is best understood if we realize that the practice of compensating church leaders arose early in church history (1 Cor. 9:7; Gal. 6:6; 1 Tim. 5:17). But abuse of the privilege arose quickly, so that Peter, Paul, and postapostolic leaders all had to warn about "love of money" (1 Tim. 3:3; Titus 1:7; see also Paul's refusal to take money in Acts 20:33).[8] To serve the church for the sake of money rather than the Lord and his people is shameful and akin to fraud.[9]

Sadly, what begins as willing service can become service rendered for the sake of rewards such as wealth and status. Leaders must examine themselves for this. The ancient Japanese tale of the crane wife hints at the way this

7. Sadly, those who do have passion for their work often fall into overwork and problems such as Sabbath violation, exhaustion, and frayed relationships.

8. J. Ramsey Michaels, *1 Peter*, Word Biblical Commentary 49 (Nashville: Thomas Nelson, 1988), 284–85; Jobes, *1 Peter*, 305. Polycarp, writing around A.D. 140–50, urged the church to "avoid the love of money." With the failure of an apparently well-known presbyter (elder) named Valens in mind, he asks, "But how may he who cannot control himself in these matters preach self-control to someone else? If any man does not avoid love of money, he will be polluted by idolatry." Polycarp, "The Letter of Polycarp to the Philippians," trans. Joseph Lightfoot, in *The Apostolic Fathers*, ed. Michael W. Holmes, 2nd ed. (Grand Rapids: Baker, 1992), 217 (11.2; cf. 5.2).

9. Frederick W. Danker, ed., *A Greek-English Lexicon of the New Testament and Other Early Christian Literature*, 3rd ed. (Chicago: University of Chicago Press, 2000), 29, renders the Greek *aischrokerdōs*, translated "shameful gain," as "in fondness for dishonest gain, greedily."

can happen: A poor but honest man finds a stricken crane on his doorstep, wounded by an arrow and unable to fly. He takes it in, cleanses the wound, nurses it to health, and releases it, thankful for the chance to do good. That very night a mysterious and beautiful woman appears at his doorstep, and they soon marry. Knowing her husband's poverty, the wife soon begins to weave wondrous clothes out of silk that sell at a great price in the market. So she eases their poverty. The wife has one stipulation, to which her husband agrees: he must never watch her making her cloth. But he becomes greedy and presses her to weave more and more. Her health begins to falter, but his avarice blinds him. He eventually peeks into her secret room and sees her weaving the cloth from feathers she plucks from her own body. The crane, seeing him, flies away and never returns.

Thus, slow-growing greed can corrupt good motives. Paul, by contrast, says, "We work with you for *your* joy" (2 Cor. 1:24). Peter notes that our service should also bring us joy, as we labor willingly, eagerly teaching, preaching, and counseling. By contrast, I knew a student at a heterodox seminary who seemed to have no love for Jesus, the Bible, or the church. When I asked why he planned to become a pastor, he replied that the work is secure, respectable, not especially taxing, and something of a family custom.

It is no evil for shepherds to be paid for their labors, as 1 Corinthians 9:1–14 shows. If an elder left his regular work, it was fair for the church to pay him, especially if he worked long and well (1 Tim. 5:17). The problem is not payment; it is service for the sake of payments that bring personal gain.

It's one thing to *make* money, another to *serve* it. Let us take care not to follow the money, to choose work simply because it offers more payment or status. Let us pray, "Lord, show me if money or popularity is too much a motive in my life."[10]

Not Domineering but Setting an Example

To review, Peter sets up the manner of elders' service through three contrasts: "not under compulsion, but willingly . . . ; not for shameful gain, but eagerly; not domineering over those in [their] charge, but being examples to the flock" (1 Peter 5:2–3 ESV). Peter's third lesson is that leaders should operate more by setting an example than by wielding power. They lead

10. Scot McKnight, *1 Peter*, NIV Application Commentary (Grand Rapids: Zondervan, 1996), 272.

their portion or share of God's flock, their share of the universal church, the group they actually know.

When Jesus said that Gentile rulers lord it over their subjects, he described the way of the world (Matt. 20:25).[11] In ancient times, people measured status by the number of servants or slaves they possessed. Today, we ask how many people take a man or woman's orders, how many attend this church or sign up for that class. But Jesus says, "Not so with you" (20:26). Rather, "Whoever wants to become great among you must be your servant." Jesus exemplified that principle by coming not "to be served, but to serve, and to give his life as a ransom for many" (20:28).

So godly leaders don't domineer; they set an example. This, of course, generally happens apart from any design. We speak and act according to what lies in our heart. So we become examples by accident. Yet we should stay alert to observe and learn from the examples that others set for us. One pastor showed me how effective a hospital visit by phone can be, when everyone knows that a personal visit is daunting. Another taught me to let agitated people talk themselves out (time permitting) before venturing a reply. Take some time to label and remember the lessons you have learned from exemplary leaders.

THE PROBLEM OF IMMORALITY

The exemplary life of elders and shepherds is the antidote to the church's second internal source of trouble: immorality (the others, again, are heresy and envy). Jude 4 describes the immoral this way: "Certain men whose condemnation was written about long ago have secretly slipped in among you. They are godless men, who change the grace of God into a license for immorality and deny Jesus Christ our only sovereign and Lord."

Jude 4 says that they "slip in" or infiltrate the church. Operating from within, they advocate a truncated gospel. They want the *grace* of Christ without the *lordship* of Christ. They love the *idea* of a gracious God who forgives whatever they do. They claim to know Jesus and ask for mercy, dreaming that the *idea* of grace, not sincerely embraced, somehow leads to the forgiveness of every sin, no matter how calculating. They

11. The Greek in both 1 Peter 5:3 and Matthew 20:25 is *katakurieuō*. The term can be descriptive rather than pejorative.

see Christian doctrine as a "Get out of hell free" card, but they do not know Jesus (Matt. 7:21).

It is the character of heresy to take a biblical idea and isolate it from all true doctrine, so that the idea can be stretched to accommodate almost anything. As the saying goes, every heretic has his verse—or half-verse. Jude's heretics seem to love 1 John 1:9: "If we confess our sins, he . . . will forgive us." They lop off the last phrase, "and purify us from all unrighteousness."

Jude 12 says that these miscreants "boldly carouse together, looking after themselves" (RSV). Literally, they are "shepherds who feed only themselves" (NIV). That is, they shepherd or care for themselves only. As long as they are satisfied, all is well. They declare that they are their own shepherds and stand under no one's authority. But even pastors and shepherds need pastors and shepherds. Everyone needs an authority in his or her life, even the authorities themselves.

THE PROBLEM OF ENVY

Another source of trouble in the church is envy. We can approach it through further reflection on Peter's point that elders lead by example.

The Shepherd as Example

Perhaps because of naive and legalistic misuses of the concept, Protestants are reluctant to embrace the notion of imitation, even though it pervades the New Testament (e.g., Matt. 10:24–25; Luke 6:40; John 15:20; Rom. 8:29; Eph. 5:25–27; Phil. 2:3–8; Heb. 2:5–14; 1 John 3:2–3).[12] On most occasions, disciples hear that they are or will be like Jesus. But Paul establishes himself as an example in Philippians 3:17: "Join with others in following my example, brothers" (cf. 2 Thess. 3:9). He also tells the next generation of leaders to set an example for their people. Timothy must "set an example for the believers in speech, in life, in love, in faith and in purity" (1 Tim. 4:12). He commands Titus, "In everything set them an example by doing what is good" (Titus 2:7).

Peter also affirms that all believers should imitate Jesus and that leaders will be faithful enough that they can set a secondary example.

12. Daniel M. Doriani, *Putting the Truth to Work: The Theory and Practice of Biblical Application* (Phillipsburg, NJ: P&R Publishing, 2001), 201ff.

First Peter 2:18–25 declares that believers should follow Jesus' example, enduring mistreatment and trusting God for deliverance, just as he did. Now 1 Peter 5:3 says that godly leaders, with their eye on Christ, become examples or patterns for others.[13]

The Roots of Envy

Sadly, the more exemplary the leader, the more likely that he or she will be both admired and attacked, adored and scorned. A beautiful life, filled with light, will attract a host who aspire to share in it, follow it, or imitate it. Admirers want for themselves what they admire, and that wanting easily becomes envy. Any prosperity, any success, will stimulate at least mild envy. But deep resentment aims to destroy every light that shines brightly, for the resentful believe that they suffer and grow dim when another prospers and shines. They reason: "Who does he think he is? He's no better than we are! Let's bring him down to size."

Resentment fuels senseless hate for athletes, speakers, politicians, business leaders, entertainers, artists, even elders and shepherds. Every day, the news offers a fresh version of mankind's strange delight in the collapse, even humiliation, of some prominent person. Envy *can* spur people to work harder, to do the right thing, even if for the wrong reason. As Solomon puts it, "And I saw that all labor and all achievement spring from man's envy of his neighbor" (Eccl. 4:4).[14]

But a great deal of envy is unalloyed malice. In Jesus' case, the very teaching, miracles, and compassion that led the crowds to flock to Jesus led the Pharisees to envy, hate, and kill him. At Jesus' trial, Pontius Pilate—hardly a sensitive man—readily saw that "it was out of envy that the chief priests had handed Jesus over to him" (Mark 15:10).

Public figures and leaders constantly receive praise, gratitude, and adulation on one hand, and criticism and envy on the other. Envy is a wasting and self-destructive disease. It wants whatever others have, if they *seem* to be stronger, smarter, prettier, wealthier, more cool, more powerful, more *anything*. Envy is the bitter negative to the awesome and alarming positive of setting an example for God's people.

---

13. Peter uses different terms for "example"—*hypogrammon* in 1 Peter 2:21 and *tupos* in 5:3—but the sense is the same.

14. See also Joseph Epstein, *Envy* (New York: Oxford, 2003).

Like others, I find this adoration/scorn polarity painful at both ends. Only a madman enjoys irrational hatred, but adulation is just as alarming. We should think, "They are imitating me, a man afflicted with sores?"

Sadly, James tells us that envy is universal: "Or do you think Scripture says without reason that the spirit he caused to live in us envies intensely?" (James 4:5).[15] Scripture certainly testifies that envy is a pervasive malady. Cain envied the favor that God showed Abel, but instead of seeking God's favor himself, he sought to destroy the favor that Abel enjoyed by killing him. Saul envied David's praise (1 Sam. 18), and Absalom envied David's throne (2 Sam. 15). But the destructive character of envy of an ordinary man is never more clear than in the case of humble Moses.

God chose Moses over his protests. As soon as his confrontation with Pharaoh ended with success, the people of Israel doubled his distress with rebellion, doubts, and demands. And as soon as that ended, lesser leaders decided that they wanted Moses' seat. The voice of envy asks, "Are you any better than we are?" Moses' own siblings, Aaron and Miriam, said those very words. They criticized Moses, ostensibly because they disapproved of the woman he had married. But envy lurked behind the accusation. They asked, "Has the LORD spoken only through Moses? . . . Hasn't he also spoken through us?" (Num. 12:2). God himself defended Moses:

> When a prophet of the LORD is among you,
>   I reveal myself to him in visions,
>   I speak to him in dreams.
> But this is not true of my servant Moses;
>   he is faithful in all my house.
> With him I speak face to face,
>   clearly and not in riddles;
>   he sees the form of the LORD. (Num. 12:6–8)

It is the lot of leaders to endure burdens in hard times and to suffer envy when life is easy. The wise prepare for this. Blessedly, God also promises to reward faithful leaders.

15. The proper translation of the Greek is debated; I have argued for the NIV translation in my commentary, *James*, Reformed Expository Commentary (Phillipsburg, NJ: P&R Publishing, 2006), 136–38, 143–44.

THE REWARD FOR LEADERS

Leaders aim to be faithful stewards of the portion God assigns. It is a privilege to be God's agent, and the harder the work, the greater the honor. We serve for the Master's sake, not for pay, recognition, power, or rewards. Nonetheless, God promises a reward in 1 Peter 5:4: "And when the Chief Shepherd appears, you will receive the crown of glory that will never fade away." The Chief Shepherd, also called "the great Shepherd" in Hebrews 13:20, cares for the universal church, and the elders shepherd their local congregations.

When Jesus appears in the glory and victory of his second coming, the elders will receive an unfading crown of glory. The word translated "receive" (*komizō*) here means to receive what is owed, a payment, compensation, or reward.[16] Let us summarize the biblical teaching about such rewards.

First, the doctrine of rewards is compatible with justification by grace, through faith. The Bible often remarks that we must render an account for every word and deed (Ps. 62:12; Jer. 17:10; Matt. 16:27; 2 Cor. 5:10; 1 Peter 1:17; Rev. 20:12). The beauty of the gospel is that, for believers, God does not treat us as our sins deserve (Ps. 103:10), but he does remember our good deeds and rewards us for them.

Second, the leaders' labor for the Lord's eternal reward contrasts with the error (even sin) of greediness. Greed seeks rewards in this life; Peter promises an unfading crown that lasts forever.

Third, the crown of glory confers neither power nor riches. The crown confers glory and honor. Thus, it is like the victor's wreath in the Greek athletic festivals, not the king's royal circlet of gold. To be precise, in the phrase "crown of glory," *crown* is the metaphor and *glory* the reality.[17]

Fourth, this crown does not confer glory onto one individual rather than another. Rather, as 1 Peter 5:1 just noted, all of Peter's fellow elders "will share in the glory to be revealed." Indeed, every believer shares God's incorruptible blessing. When Jesus appears in all his glory to re-create all things,

---

16. Danker, *Greek-English Lexicon of the New Testament*, 557; Johannes Louw and Eugene Nida, *Greek-English Lexicon of the New Testament: Based on Semantic Domains*, 2nd ed. (New York: United Bible Societies, 1998–99), 1:572.

17. Michaels, *1 Peter*, 287. From the perspective of Greek grammar, the phrase "crown of glory" is appositional or epexegetical. The crown is or consists of glory. The phrase "crown of life" is identical. See James 1:12; Rev. 2:10.

we will share his joy, and our unfading, imperishable crown of glory will reflect his glory (1 Cor. 9:25; 2 Tim. 4:8; Rev. 3:11).

Let shepherds therefore follow Jesus and serve God's flock. As he did, let us do so willingly, not grudgingly; eagerly and not for personal gain; not domineering, but setting a good example. In all, let us look back to Christ's sufferings, which atoned for our sins. And let us look forward to his appearing, when he will grant us an unfading crown of glory.[18]

18. It could be sensible to discuss 1 Peter 5:5 here, for it is the last word about leadership. Yet it is also the first word in a series of closing exhortations, running from 5:5–11.

17

HUMBLE YOURSELVES

1 Peter 5:5–6

Young men, in the same way be submissive to those who are older. All of you, clothe yourselves with humility toward one another, because, "God opposes the proud but gives grace to the humble." Humble yourselves, therefore, under God's mighty hand, that he may lift you up in due time. (1 Peter 5:5–6)

THE GLOBAL NEED FOR HUMILITY

The pioneering missionary William Carey wrote a letter to one of his sons on the occasion of Carey's birthday:

I am this day 70 years old, a monument of Divine mercy and goodness, though on a review of my life I find much, very much, for which I ought to be humbled in the dust; my direct and positive sins are innumerable, my negligence in the Lord's work has been great, I have not promoted his cause, nor sought his glory and honor as I ought. Notwithstanding all this, I am spared till now, and am still retained in his work. I trust for acceptance with Him to the blood of Christ alone.[1]

1. Letter to Jabez Carey, in James Culross, *William Carey* (New York: A. C. Armstrong and Son, 1882), 208.

This is an astonishing statement, given the scope of Carey's devotion and labor. He went to India in 1793 and worked without respite, with scarcely a tenth of the resources or support he needed. He hardly rested as he evangelized, taught, and translated the Bible, in whole or in part, into forty languages or dialects. How could Carey possibly fault himself for sinfulness and sloth? Did he suffer from poor self-esteem, morbid self-inspection, or the ancient battle with age and mortality?

Carey's letter seems strange today because so many people succumb to pride. Just as some physical diseases are treated but never cured, so spiritual pride is treated but never fully removed. Pride is also a malady that resists treatment. Flaws such as an explosive temper and procrastination are hard to deny because the evidence is public. But some sins are hidden, even from those who suffer them. Pride and self-righteousness are cases in point because awareness of sin is precisely what the proud lack.

If someone points out a sin, the proud plead special circumstances or a misunderstanding. If a friend points out that the very refusal to admit any sin is pride, and that pride is the root of the problem, the proud protest that, too: "But I haven't done anything wrong. Why are you picking on me? You are so critical." The proud examine themselves and say, "Very good."

Again and again, the Scriptures tell us that God opposes the proud and brings them low, even as he exalts the humble. According to 1 Samuel 2:7–8, "The Lord makes poor and makes rich; he brings low and he exalts. He raises up the poor from the dust; he lifts the needy from the ash heap to make them sit with princes and inherit a seat of honor." David agrees: "Though the Lord is on high, he regards the lowly, but the haughty he knows from afar" (Ps. 138:6). Job 5:11 declares that God "sets on high those who are lowly." And Isaiah 2:11 agrees: "The lofty pride of men shall be humbled, and the Lord alone will be exalted in that day" (all esv).

With tiny variations, Jesus says the same thing on three separate occasions: "Everyone who exalts himself will be humbled, and he who humbles himself will be exalted" (Luke 14:11; 18:14; Matt. 23:12; cf. Matt. 18:4; Luke 1:52). Both 1 Peter 5:5 and James 4:6 quote the Septuagint of Proverbs 3:34 almost verbatim, saying, "God opposes the proud but gives grace to the humble." Clearly, the call to humility pervades Scripture. In 1 Peter, it is the apostle's last word on leadership and the first in his series of closing exhortations for the church.

The Need for Humility before Leaders

In 1 Peter 5:1–4, Peter told the church's elders—its leaders—to shepherd and oversee the flock in three ways. They must serve eagerly, not for personal gain; they must serve willingly, not grudgingly; and they must not domineer, but set an example. If these are the duties of the elders, then the prime duty of the younger is to be submissive, to yield, to follow, to defer, even to obey (see chapter 8).

Peter teaches that elders must lead and that young men must be submissive (1 Peter 5:1–5). But he quickly moves to the whole church: "All of you, clothe yourselves with humility toward one another, because, 'God opposes the proud but gives grace to the humble'" (5:5).

In 1 Peter 5:5, the NIV says that "young men" must be submissive, but the original is simply "the younger" (see ESV). A few interpreters believe that "the younger" means younger *leaders*, who should defer to older leaders, but there is no real evidence that the early church had a recognized body of younger leaders. Rather, Peter shifts from the duty of shepherd to flock to the duty of flock to shepherd. "The younger" might seem like an unusual term for the whole church. Peter does call his readers "dear friends" twice (2:11; 4:12), but he doesn't have a favorite term of address as, for example, the epistles of James ("brothers") and John ("beloved") do. Further, Peter has already used "in the same way" (NIV) or "likewise" (ESV) to introduce reciprocal duties in 3:1, 7. So it makes sense to match the duties of "the elders" (5:1) with the duties of "the younger."

It is human nature for adults, especially "the younger," to pick and choose what we like in the style and direction of our leaders. But we need to question ourselves. If we constantly judge our leaders, deciding what we do and don't like, what we will and won't heed, we aren't truly following them. The songwriter Jeff Tweedy illustrates the point. He leads a band, Wilco, that one critic called peaceful on the outside, demented on the inside. The band plays soft ballads with jazzy chords, then scorching, cacophonous guitar licks. Laid-back country rock plays beside electric distortion that hides simple melodies. The band changes styles radically between albums and sometimes even within a song. Some suspect that they *aim* to befuddle their fans. Their song "Side with the Seeds" addresses the issue. It starts bluesy, tuneful, and slow. It picks up speed, until two guitars race to a dissonant, exhausted coda.

The lyrics lament that some fans of trees "side with the leaves" and some "side with the seeds." To side with the seeds is absurd, since trees need leaves and seeds alike. People try to choose between the two sides of Wilco—the tuneful band and the experimental one. But Wilco is both, and it's impossible to choose between them. The song's last line says, "I'll side with you, if you side with me." So Tweedy asks fans to side with him and his band as a whole, not to choose between the parts that they love or hate. True loyalty goes to whole persons, in both their winsome and difficult aspects. That is true in friendship, in marriage, and in leader-follower relationships.

Good leaders are loyal to the whole church, even the people and policies they dislike. Wise followers yield to the church and its leaders as a whole, even if certain decisions seem flawed. Jesus loves both sides of us, the beautiful and the ruined. We can do the same for each other and the church.

The Need for Humility in All Church Relationships

By chapter 5, Peter has already spoken of subjection to authorities several times (1 Peter 2:13, 18; 3:1), so he can quickly shift from his words on church leadership to the first of his closing exhortations for his church. While the younger should especially submit to their elders, everyone should be humble: "All of you, clothe yourselves with humility toward one another, because, 'God opposes the proud but gives grace to the humble'" (5:5b).

By definition, a church is a gathering of the humble. Disciples are confident of their worth, since we know that God created us in his image and valued us enough to send his Son for us. Yet every believer is aware of his sin and need. Every disciple has repented, and when we repent, we both confess particular sins and admit that we are selfish and rebellious to the bone. Knowing that we are incapable of self-reform, we trust in Christ to forgive and restore us. This is the conviction of every Christian.

For this reason, Peter says, "God opposes the proud." This is a global principle, often repeated in Scripture. It is a gospel principle, essential for a saving relationship with God. Yet it is vital for human relationships, too. Peter wisely leads with it as he offers his guidance for a church that needs to survive constant pressure, even persecution.

It is human nature—fallen human nature—to be proud. Left to ourselves, we will be the center of our universe and our own chief concern. We trust ourselves and our resources. If we succeed, we crow, "Behold what I have done." If we falter, we rationalize, "I had no resources! What could I do?"

Self-reliance, a sense of our merit, runs strong in humanity. Yet believers are humble in principle because we know and confess that we sin. More important, we are *sinful* and too weak to reform ourselves. Therefore, we should be humble.

In Psalm 51:5, David confessed that he sinned because sin dwells deep within: "Surely I was sinful at birth, sinful from the time my mother conceived me." After twenty-five years of daunting service to the Lord Jesus, the great apostle Paul confessed that he was still "a slave to sin" in Romans 7:14.

> For we know that the law is spiritual, but I am of the flesh, sold under sin. For I do not understand my own actions. For I do not do what I want, but I do the very thing I hate. . . . For I know that nothing good dwells in me, that is, in my flesh. For I have the desire to do what is right, but not the ability to carry it out. (Rom. 7:14–15, 18 ESV)

This means, first, that we deserve none of God's favor, that his salvation is entirely gracious. We could easily keep our attention there, but we must hear the exhortation to practical humility: "All of you, clothe yourselves with humility toward one another, because, 'God opposes the proud but gives grace to the humble'" (1 Peter 5:5). It is illuminating to outline the passage:

5:5 Command: "Clothe yourselves with humility toward one another,"
　　Reason: "because God opposes the proud,"
　　Promise: "but gives grace to the humble."
5:6 Command: "Humble yourselves, therefore, under God's mighty hand,"
　　Promise: "that he may lift you up in due time."

The Christ-centered theologian might focus on 1 Peter 5:6 and the gospel. Yet at the moment, Peter uses the gospel to motivate conduct. Given the context, we realize that Peter wants believers to obey their spiritual leaders. Beyond that, Peter urges the reciprocity between all believers that lets Christian community thrive.

This reminds us of Peter's prior statement of the need for mutuality in 1 Peter 4. There, in similar language, Peter said that believers should "keep loving one another earnestly, . . . show hospitality to one another without grumbling," and "serve one another" with our God-given gifts (4:8–10 esv). In 1 Peter 5, the common motif in the commands lies with motivation, not mutuality. If we remove some subordinate clauses, the interest is clear (following the niv):

5:5 "Clothe yourselves with humility... because 'God opposes the proud....'"
5:6 "Humble yourselves . . . that he may lift you up."

So Peter offers theological motives for his instruction. The command "Clothe yourselves with humility" imagines humility as a garment that believers fasten to themselves. The root of "clothe yourselves" refers to an apron that a slave or herdsman tied over his tunic to keep it clean. In Greek culture, humble-mindedness "meant an attitude expected of slaves but unworthy of free people." Our word *humiliation* has similar emotional heft. Yet believers should wrap themselves in humility because "God opposes the proud."

God does indeed oppose the proud, as the Bible often says (Isa. 26:5; Lam. 1:5; Ezek. 17:24; Hos. 14:9). Well-known narratives show how pride operates and how pride toward God ruins relations with neighbors. For example, Cain and Abel both brought gifts to God in Genesis. Abel brought the first and best from his flocks. Cain brought whatever he pleased from his fields. When God preferred Abel's gift of the first and the best ("fat portions") to Cain's featureless offering of "the fruits of the soil," Cain took umbrage (Gen. 4:1–5). Instead of repenting, Cain stuffed himself with false rage, then murdered his innocent-but-envied brother Abel. When God confronted him, he denied everything. "Am I my brother's keeper?" When God rebuked Cain for this, he refused to repent, and the Lord banished him, for he opposes the proud (4:6–13).

Peter himself illustrates God's grace to the humble. Before the crucifixion, Peter proudly insisted that he, unlike the other disciples, was ready to go with Jesus to prison and death. Jesus told the disciples, "This very night you will all fall away" (Matt. 26:31), but Peter boasted, "Even if all fall away on account of you, I never will. . . . Even if I have to die with you, I will never disown you" (26:33, 35; cf. Luke 22:31–33). In his pride, Peter trusted himself, wandered into temptation unprepared, and denied Jesus three times. Yet afterward, Peter wept, repented, and declared anew his love for Jesus. So the Lord gave grace to him, a humbled man (Luke 22:62; John 21:15–17).

First Peter 5:6 continues, "Humble yourselves, therefore, under God's mighty hand, that he may lift you up in due time." Peter does not say, "The Lord will humble you," but "Humble yourselves." The command "Humble yourselves" signifies that we don't wait for God, an adversary, or the hardships of life to humble us. We must act on ourselves. Peter doesn't specify *how* we humble ourselves, but the phrase "under God's mighty hand" supplies a hint. The phrase "mighty hand" is common in Exodus, where God's power delivered Israel from slavery and oppression in Egypt. God's mighty hand defeated Pharaoh and humbled him, although he did not humble himself (Ex. 6:1; 13:3–16; Deut. 3:24; 4:34).

God's strong hand also showed itself in the ministry of Jesus—in the miracles and above all in Jesus' saving death and resurrection (Acts 4:28–30). As with Jesus, so also with the church, suffering leads to glory. God already has power to do what he now promises, that he will lift up his people at the right time.

The "due time" (1 Peter 5:6) or right time (Greek *kairos*) can be the moment that suits God's purposes (Eph. 5:16). Or it can be the time of God's great acts of redemption, including his return. First Peter 1:5b uses *time* in the second way. Even if we are uncertain *when* God will act, in this lifetime or later, when this age ends, he promises to restore the humble.

This was an essential promise as Peter's churches endured the threat of harm. It remains a strong promise for Jesus' people in every nation as they face hostility. We can respond to hardships, sorrows, and delay in God's action in one of two ways. We can grumble and accuse God, or we can trust him. Peter exhorts his readers to take the second path. "Cast all your anxiety on him because he cares for you" (1 Peter 5:7). Israel, sadly, often took the wrong path by grumbling against God. Consider the episode recounted in Exodus 17:1–7. Shortly after the Israelites crossed the Red Sea, they ran out of water when they camped at Rephidim. The people quarreled with Moses, accusing him of bringing them out of Egypt to kill them. They also tested God, demanding that he act at once, when they issued a foolish ultimatum: "Is the LORD among us or not?" That is hardly the voice of someone who humbly waits for God to act. Of course, we can tell the Lord about our pains and losses. But we must remember that the Lord has a mighty hand, that he cares for us, and that he acts on *his* schedule. Believers wait for the Lord; they do not *demand* that he act at our word.

PRIDE AND HUMILITY

God granted humans dignity at creation, but that dignity is threatened by internal and external forces. If we grew up in an abusive home, or if our spouses, coworkers, or friends belittle us, we might need to reassert and restore our honor. But sin and selfishness readily corrupt the proper desire for respect. We seek glory, adulation, and domination. We become proud.

Peter spoke to the church in time of trial, to believers who knew the gospel. In their trial, Peter urged them to stay together and to clothe themselves with humility. The New Testament tells us to "put on" virtue several times (Rom. 13:12; Eph. 6:11–14; 1 Thess. 5:8). Peter's term means "to tie something on"—as we tie on an apron to protect our clothes (see above). So we should wrap or drape ourselves in humility.

People are prone to feel slighted when their honor is questioned. Athletic teams constantly protest: "We get no respect. We're going to show the world . . ." Political debates constantly play upon slights, real or imagined. A U.S. senator derides an amendment to a bill. Instead of saying, "Nothing substantive changed, so it's as bad as ever," he says, "That's like putting lipstick on an ostrich." Immediately, his rival declares that his state's ostrich farmers are offended. When people ask, "Why wasn't I chosen, informed, called, invited?" it could be the voice of pride complaining, "But I'm an important person!"

Pride can have more complex roots. A young man once told me about his battle with pride, saying something like this: "I grew up in a rough home. My parents constantly shouted and threatened. Sometimes they tried to hit us and sometimes they connected. My father was talented but addicted, so he was always losing one job, getting another, and moving on. That meant a new school, so I was an outsider. And since I was small, I was also a target for bullies. Between my parents and the bullies, I learned to give off a 'Don't mess with me' aura. I acted tough and threatening, and got tattoos with knives and skulls. It became my identity. After I graduated and became a professional, the attitude seemed useful, even if I was shaking with fear. It was a facade, but I never tried to change until I met the Lord." However our lives differ from this man's, we get the point. To preserve our honor (or pride), many of us pretend to be someone we are not. We strike poses that convey strength and confidence. We might persuade others, but it's dangerous if we persuade ourselves.

The gospel brings us low and lifts us up. The gospel brings us low because it leads us to confess that we are sinners. We have no hope, except in God's sovereign mercy. It brings us low because it says that we can do nothing to redeem ourselves. We must wholly depend on Jesus, the Son of God, who died for our sins and was raised for our justification (Rom. 4:25). By his wounds we have been healed (1 Peter 2:24). The gospel exalts us because it demonstrates that the Lord sets great value on us and loves us. To come to the Lord as he is offered in the gospel is to be humbled and exalted. We become children of God, called with a purpose, and heirs of life. So let us wrap ourselves in humility. In that way we own the gospel and let it permeate our lives. As Peter says, "Humble yourselves, therefore, under God's mighty hand, that he may lift you up in due time" (5:6).

18

Counsel and Blessing

1 *Peter* 5:7–14

And the God of all grace, who called you to his eternal glory in Christ, after you have suffered a little while, will himself restore you and make you strong, firm and steadfast. To him be the power for ever and ever. (1 Peter 5:10–11)

 certain company attracts customers to its health products by offering to test people's "real age." The test allegedly compares a person's chronological age to his body's real age. If someone eats fruits and vegetables, sleeps enough, and exercises daily, the test declares that his real age is less than his birth certificate indicates. But if he sleeps three hours per night, smokes cigarettes, devours cheeseburgers, and commutes by helicopter, the test says, "Because of your risk factors, your life expectancy is less than anticipated." It then delivers counsel that, if followed, will lead to a longer life.

First Peter 5 presents the apostle's counsel to people who have a great risk factor: they resolved to follow Jesus in a world that was hostile to the faith. The Christians in Peter's churches no longer worshiped pagan deities, no longer bowed to the emperor or participated in pagan revelry. That brought danger. Change upsets people. Friends questioned these believers, and the empire entertained suspicions.

Peter's counsel aims at a *faithful* life more directly than a *long* life. He commands the church to "humble yourselves" (1 Peter 5:6), "cast all your anxiety on him" (5:7), "be self-controlled and alert" (5:8, a double command), and "resist" the devil (5:9). Peter's commands rest on a theological foundation, as his last passage begins and ends with God. His hand is mighty (5:6), he cares for us (5:7), and he is gracious (5:10a). He has called us to glory and promises to restore us (5:10). He can make good on his promises because he possesses eternal power (5:11). Clearly, the character of God is the basis for our faithfulness and confidence.

The Might and Care of God

As we saw in the previous chapter, Peter commands his people, "Humble yourselves, therefore, under God's mighty hand, that he may lift you up" (1 Peter 5:6). In the exodus, the mighty hand of God liberated Israel from Egypt's oppression (Ex. 13:9; Deut. 3:24; 7:19). The New Testament describes the work of Jesus as a second exodus. At the transfiguration, as Luke 9:30–31 says, Moses and Elijah spoke to Jesus "of his departure [literally, *exodus*], which he was about to accomplish at Jerusalem" (esv). As an Israelite, Peter knew the blessings that God gave Israel when he established the new nation after the exodus. Peter claimed and applied those blessings to his Gentile converts in 1 Peter 2:9–10. If Jesus accomplished a new exodus for the Gentiles, then they enjoy God's power and compassion, just as Israel did. Because God is strong, because he has a "mighty hand," Peter tells his people, "Cast all your anxiety on him because he cares for you" (5:6–7).

Peter asserts that God's favor depends on both his grace and his power: "the God of all grace, who called you to his eternal glory in Christ, . . . will himself restore you and make you strong." He will fulfill this promise because he has "power for ever and ever" (1 Peter 5:10–11).

Throughout his epistle, Peter has sprinkled advice to help his people endure trials. They should avoid trouble by respecting governors and masters (1 Peter 2:13–18). Ordinarily, no trouble should arise for the man or woman who tells the truth, does good, seeks peace, and shows compassion (3:8–11). The church should also stand together, with shepherds overseeing a willing flock (5:1–4). Still, before Peter signs off, he delivers more counsel. His people should humble themselves (5:6), cast their anxieties on God (5:7), be watchful (5:8), and resist the devil (5:8–9), all while trusting God's grace and the power that makes them strong (5:10–11).

As we learned in the previous chapter, the call to humility reads well as a final word for leaders (1 Peter 5:1–6) and the opening of his final counsel for everyone (5:6–14). Young men must submit to the elders, but everyone should wear humility like a garment, for "God opposes the proud but gives grace to the humble" (5:5).

In an essential way, the Christian *must* be humble, for faith begins with repentance. We confess, "I am a sinner, unable to reform myself, and without hope, outside God's sovereign mercy." While there is a definitive, one-time humbling when we repent, we must *remain* humble. Then God promises to exalt us "at the proper time" as he judges it (1 Peter 5:6 esv). Fallen human nature is prone to pride and egocentricity. We often think we *deserve* to be prominent and to excel, so we resent barriers to our ascendance. But if we humble ourselves, we refuse to grumble about adversity. To the question "How are you doing?" we can honestly reply, "Better than I deserve."

Cast Your Anxiety on the Lord

Peter's people had problems, so he urges them, "Cast all your anxiety on him, because he cares for you" (1 Peter 5:7 nrsv). There is an innate antagonism between pagan polytheism and Christianity. The monotheism and exclusivity of the faith were affronts to Rome's religions and way of life. New Christians faced the loss of friends, social status, livelihoods, even life itself—each of which, of course, could induce anxiety.

Notice that *anxiety* (*merimna*) is singular. We normally think of anxieties in the plural. We worry about work, health, relationships, and a too-dense schedule. Problems roll in like waves, but they can congeal into one mass of anxiety. If we pay attention, we sense the big Anxiety in our friends—and our friends can see it in us. We can weather modest problems, arriving singly, but when one great problem falls on us, or a cluster arrives, we feel it differently.

Peter commands us to take our anxiety and throw, toss, or cast it onto God. As we throw a bag of gym clothes into a car or hoist a saddle onto a horse, so we should toss our anxiety on the Lord.[1] He is mighty and he will exalt us at the right time, because *our* cares are *his*.

Jesus tells us not to be anxious: "Do not worry about your life." Pagans constantly worry, asking what they will eat, drink, or wear. If we trust God, we don't wear ourselves out chasing these things, for we know that our Father will feed and clothe us (Matt. 6:25–32). We should not indulge our worries.

Yet Paul admits that he has anxiety (*merimna* again). He lists his troubles as an apostle—the beatings and jails, the hunger, thirst, cold, and shipwreck—and then concludes, "And, apart from other things, there is the daily pressure on me of my *anxiety* for all the churches" (2 Cor. 11:28 ESV). So Paul has anxiety and apparently sees it as a *problem* but not as a *sin*.

From this we conclude that anxiety is normal in some circumstances and that it's possible to be anxious and yet not sin, if we address it properly. Specifically, we neither panic nor attempt to solve our problems autonomously. Suppose someone is anxious about his or her inability to find a job or to conceive a child. We should do what we can to solve the problem and ask God to bless our actions (Ps. 90:17). Yet even as we act, we should pray, "Lord, I've done what I can; now I leave the results to you. My fears weigh me down, and I give them to you."

Grammatically, 1 Peter 5:7 is subordinate to 5:6, and it's easy to see how that subordination works.[2] We humble ourselves before God, in part, by giving our cares to him. We do that by remembering what Peter just said: God is mighty, he exalts us in his time, and he cares for us (5:6–7).

RESIST THE DEVIL

But God isn't the only spiritual being who takes interest in us. An evil foe stands behind our visible enemies. Peter warns, "Be sober-minded; be watchful. Your adversary the devil prowls around like a roaring lion, seeking someone to devour" (1 Peter 5:8 ESV).

---

1. See Luke 19:35, where the disciples *cast* (using the same Greek word, *epiripto*) their cloaks onto a donkey so that Jesus could ride it.

2. The verb *cast* is not an imperative, but a participle (*epiripsantes*). Participles that follow imperatives are commonly imperatival—this one follows the command to "humble yourselves"—so the translation is good. Still, a participial clause is subordinate to the main clause. Thus, "cast all your anxiety" is subordinate to "humble yourselves," so that Peter presents "cast all your anxiety" as one way in which we humble ourselves.

Conventional Christian wisdom rightly observes that we make two mistakes regarding Satan. We can take him too seriously, as if he possessed God's omnipotence, omniscience, and omnipresence. But he is an angel, and like all other creatures, he is in one place at a time, has areas of ignorance (see notes on 1 Peter 3:19), and has finite power. Indeed, Michael the archangel is presented as his peer in Revelation 12:7ff. On the other hand, we can fail to take him seriously enough, reducing him to a cartoon villain. First Peter states the essentials.

First, the term *devil* translates a Greek word meaning "deceiver," for he does seek to deceive (Zech. 3; Rev. 20:2). Second, he is dangerous. Hungry and wounded lions attack, and Satan, whose name means "adversary" in Hebrew, is both.[3] His power is limited, but he walks around, looking for victims. Because the devil aims to deceive and then to devour, Peter warns us twice, "Be sober-minded; be watchful" (1 Peter 5:8 ESV).

Satan operates by tempting or enticing people to sin. One classic case is Satan's attempt to persuade Jesus to use his powers selfishly. After Jesus fasted forty days, he was hungry, and Satan invited him to turn nearby stones to bread (Matt. 4:2–3). We can imagine his words: "You're hungry, aren't you? You have the power, so why not? What's the harm? Who gets hurt?" We guess at these lines because we have heard them ourselves. "Why not? Take what's yours. You deserve it. No one will suffer and no one will know."

Satan has additional tactics. He incites idolatry, the worship of anything but the true God (Matt. 4:8–9). He also tempts us to doubt our standing with God (Rev. 12:10). He confuses or blinds people so that they cannot see the truth (2 Cor. 3:14–16). Today it seems that he has blinded Western societies ethically. Notice how we talk about ethics. People are no longer evil or perverse; they adopt alternative lifestyles. Deeds are no longer right or wrong; they are appropriate or inappropriate. That implies that wicked acts are nothing worse than breaches of etiquette. If someone offers us a chance to do evil, we don't say, "That's wrong"; we say, "I'm not comfortable with that," as if comfort were a moral category. But the right course of action is often intensely uncomfortable, and the path to evil will be comfortable if habit makes it familiar. Satan is probably quite pleased when we do what is

3. The lion metaphor might also suggest that the devil is frightening. Lions are large predators, known to threaten humans, and at close range their roar, in decibels, nearly matches that of a jet airplane. Also, note the flexibility of biblical metaphors, for Jesus is also called a Lion in Revelation 5:5.

comfortable and shun what is not. How readily our essential but difficult duties would fall away.

"Resist him, standing firm in the faith," Peter commands (1 Peter 5:9). James adds, "Resist the devil, and he will flee from you" (James 4:7). It's hard to resist the devil, and at first, the longer we resist, the harder it feels. Suppose you accidentally start to divulge something before you recall that it's confidential. You pause, and a friend begins to plead, "Come on, tell me! I can keep a secret, I promise."[4] As he begs and guesses, the pressure builds. It eases if you break your silence. Yet if the intensity of the temptation increases as we resist it in the short term, it falls off in the long term, as we keep resisting sin. Most addicts see this when they break with addictive use of alcohol, drugs, or tobacco. The longer we break with lying or the use of pornography, the easier it is to stay away from those sins.

One way to resist sin is to flee temptation. Paul advised, "Flee from sexual immorality" (1 Cor. 6:18) and "flee from idolatry" (10:14). He told Timothy to flee from love of money, to "flee the evil desires of youth," and to "pursue righteousness" (1 Tim. 6:11; 2 Tim. 2:22).

When we resist Satan, he must seek *another* opportune moment to tempt us, as Luke 4:13 points out. But when we capitulate to temptation, we offer him *more* time to do his will with us. When we succumb once, it's easier to sin again, as we form sinful habits. We form pathways and gain skill at sinning, since practice, even at sin, makes us more efficient.

Resistance to temptation should be both individual and communal. God's grace trains us to "renounce worldly passions," so that we are responsible, as individuals, to monitor our internal life. Each individual is responsible to say No when sin presents itself (Titus 2:11–12). Yet the command to resist the devil is, like the other commands here, addressed to *you*, plural. We are part of the church, and together we strive to live faithfully.

Let me illustrate the individual and communal aspects of resistance of Satan. A friend of mine is both a dedicated disciple and an alcoholic. He has stayed clear of alcohol *almost* continually for twenty years. Sadly, he has strayed a couple of times, when alone and under great pressure. As an *individual*, he is responsible to recognize moments of weakness. When alone, he must resist the temptation to sneak a drink. But he is not funda-

---

4. The immortal reply is: "I know *you* can keep a secret; it's the people you tell that I worry about."

mentally alone. He is in community with other sober alcoholics. He has friends who pray for him and ask him about his faithfulness. If a group of men is having a beer, some will drink water or juice with him as a sign that they stand with him. In this way he resists Satan both as an individual and as a member of God's family.

Peter shows his interest in Christian solidarity when he says that we know that our "brothers throughout the world are undergoing the same kind of sufferings" (1 Peter 5:9b). Because we face the same sorts of trouble, we should be more resolute to resist temptations. This is essential, since there is no reason to think persecution will cease, as Paul Achtemeier observes:

> The opposition the Christians face from their non-Christian contemporaries is not something they can avoid by modifying their behavior or adapting their beliefs . . . to escape such opposition. Only by completely abandoning the gospel and the community shaped by it, only by submitting to the satanic forces that stand in total opposition to God, can they escape the persecutions they otherwise face.[5]

By God's Grace

Peter closes his epistle with the assurance that the outcome of our life rests more on God's power and grace than on our labors: "And the God of all grace, who called you to his eternal glory in Christ, after you have suffered a little while, will himself restore you and make you strong, firm and steadfast" (1 Peter 5:10). This is good news. God, the source of all grace, has called us to "eternal glory." Still, suffering precedes glory (4:13), so we must suffer "a little while" before he restores and strengthens us. Peter uses four nearly synonymous verbs, all in the future tense, to emphasize God's promise. The four promises rise in "a rhetorical crescendo."[6] God himself will restore us, establish us, strengthen us, and set us on a firm foundation. All of this happens "in Christ," that is, through our union with him, and by God's eternal power. Thus, as God one day sets creation right and removes the sin that drives all suffering, he pledges to restore us, too.

5. Paul J. Achtemeier, *1 Peter* (Minneapolis: Fortress, 1996), 341.
6. Karen H. Jobes, *1 Peter* (Grand Rapids: Baker Academic, 2005), 316.

The promise of saving grace applies to many things. For example, if *God* calls his people to glory, then parents do not issue that call. That is a helpful antidote to what Scotty Smith has called "Messianic parenting." Messianic parents dream that if we do everything right—live well, love well, tell Bible stories well, and stay cool with our teens—all will *be* well in the end. But our performance, which is more flawed than we like to admit, doesn't save our children. God does, and he can accomplish all he wills and promises, because his is "the power for ever and ever" (1 Peter 5:11).

GREETINGS AND BLESSINGS

Since Peter often tells his people to stand together (1 Peter 5:1–3, 5, 9), it is fitting that he mention his colaborers, Silvanus and Mark, as he closes: "By Silvanus, a faithful brother as I regard him, I have written briefly to you, exhorting and declaring [or *testifying*] that this is the true grace of God. Stand firm in it" (5:12 ESV).

The phrase "by Silvanus" means either that the epistle was delivered by Silvanus or that Peter wrote through him. *Silas* and *Silvanus* are probably variant forms of one name, like *Pete* and *Peter*. Most scholars believe the Silvanus mentioned here is the Silas mentioned seventeen times from Acts 15 to 18.[7] That is why some translations (e.g., NIV) render the name *Silas* and others render it *Silvanus* (e.g., ESV; the Greek letters in 5:12 are closer to *Silvanus*).

In the short phrase "by Silvanus," the word *by* translates the Greek word *dia*, which can mean "by" or "through." If Peter wrote *through* Silvanus, then Silvanus wrote the actual words of the letter. He might have taken dictation as Peter spoke. But that seems unlikely, since the letter has complex and elegant sentences, suggesting skillful, painstaking composition. Others think Peter wrote through Silvanus because he was an amanuensis, a literary secretary who had freedom to express Peter's thoughts as he judged appropriate. Some scholars are drawn to this idea, since they wonder how Peter, a Galilean fisherman, could acquire the substantial literary skill that the epistle displays. The NIV translation seems to support the view that Silas/

---

7. Yet it is not certain that this Silvanus is the Silas of Acts. The name was fairly common, and Peter is traditionally dated at A.D. 65–70, that is, twenty to twenty-five years after the events recorded in Acts 15, so that Silas might easily have already died.

Silvanus aided the composition of 1 Peter when it translates our phrase "with the help of Silas" in 5:12.

But the notion of a literary secretary has flaws. First, it is speculative; there is no evidence that Silvanus had literary training. Second, talent can surface outside schools; many great writers have no formal training.[8] Third, if Silvanus did compose 1 Peter, it seems boastful that he would call himself "a faithful brother as I regard him" (5:12 ESV). And who would be the *I* in the sentence "With the help of Silas, whom *I* regard as a faithful brother, *I* have written to you" (NIV)? For him to promote himself in that way would clash with Peter's teaching on humility.

Some say that it hardly matters who wrote the words of 1 Peter, since we know the essence is Peter's and since the Holy Spirit is the animating and guiding Author (cf. 1 Peter 1:10–12). But there is reason to believe that Silvanus delivered the letter, so that it came *by* his hand. In the Greek, the phrase "by Silvanus" resembles Acts 15:22–23, where the Jerusalem Council appointed respected messengers, including Silvanus himself, to deliver a letter to the entire church. Finally, it makes sense to call Silvanus a "faithful brother" if he delivered the letter. The messenger might need to explain aspects of its contents, and Peter's commendation would lend him authority to do so.[9] We also see Peter's interest in securing a good reception for his letter when he says that he has written "briefly," for brevity was considered good form and length a burden in that day.

Peter also describes the letter itself, asserting that it exhorts and testifies that this is the true grace of God. "This is the true grace" (1 Peter 5:12b) refers to the whole letter, which began with God's election, moved to Jesus' atoning death, resurrection, and ascension, and closed with God's promise of "eternal glory in Christ" (5:10). The gospel, Peter declares, is true, and trust in Jesus is trust in the living God. Jesus is no mere man, the gospel no mere story. It is the truth about the eternal and gracious God. None of this

8. See Randolph Richards, "Silvanus Was Not Peter's Secretary: Theological Bias in Interpreting δία Σιλουανοῦ . . . ἔγραψα in 1 Peter 5:12," *Journal of the Evangelical Theological Society* 43 (2000): 417–32. Richards points out that Ignatius and Polycarp use the same formula that is in Peter—"I write through"—to indicate the letter carrier.

9. J. Ramsey Michaels, *1 Peter*, Word Biblical Commentary 49 (Nashville: Thomas Nelson, 1988), 306–7. See also Achtemeier, *1 Peter*, 348–52. Both argue persuasively against the notion that Silvanus was an amanuensis. Peter H. Davids, *The First Epistle of Peter* (Grand Rapids: Eerdmans, 1990), 198, argues that Silvanus wrote the letter, although the thoughts behind it are Peter's. He believes Peter's Silvanus must be the Silas of Acts 15–18 and of Paul's letters.

is in doubt, but humans are fickle, so Peter commands his people to "stand fast" in this grace (5:12).[10]

Next, Peter, along with Mark, the longtime companion of Paul and Barnabas before he joined Peter (Acts 12:12, 25; Col. 4:10; Philem. 24), sends a greeting. "She who is in Babylon, chosen together with you, sends you her greetings, and so does my son Mark" (1 Peter 5:13). As we have noted, "Babylon" is not the literal city, but code for "Rome." If the gods that oppose the faith are oppressive power, materialism, and false religion, Rome and Babylon are two cities that offered both power and wealth, both violence and sensual indulgence (Isa. 46–47; Rev. 17–18). If Peter dwells in Rome/Babylon, his flock should see that he stands with them. Even if many miles separate the apostle and the churches, they live in the same setting.

Finally, Peter commands his people to stay together locally: "Greet one another with a kiss of love" (1 Peter 5:14). The kiss of love meant the ritual touch of cheeks, not lips. Further, the kiss was given from man to man or woman to woman, not man to woman.

In the empire, the kiss of greeting was common when friends or family reunited. But not everyone kissed. The kiss demonstrated friendship, kinship, and affection. The Ephesian elders kissed Paul when they saw him for the last time (Acts 20:37). In Jesus' parable, the father kisses the prodigal son (Luke 15:20). But a Pharisee proves that he has no love for Jesus when he offers no kiss (7:45).

The command to "greet one another with a kiss of love" reminds us of Peter's emphasis on love in God's household. Love is our prime disposition and main action, our sign of solidarity. First Peter 1:22 said, "Love one another deeply, from the heart." We also notice the phrasing of 2:17, "Show proper respect to everyone: love the brotherhood of believers." So we *respect* everyone, but we *love* the brotherhood. Since love must show itself in unity, we should "live in harmony with one another; . . . love as brothers, be compassionate and humble" (3:8). Love also heals breaches: "love each other deeply, because love covers over a multitude of sins" (4:8). Peter also sprinkles family metaphors through his letter. God is our Father, and we are "obedient children" (1:14) who have been "born again" (1:23). Since we belong to a new and loving family (1:17–18, 22; 5:9), we should seal our ties with "a kiss of love."

10. C. E. B. Cranfield, *I & II Peter and Jude* (London: SCM Press, 1960), 138–39.

Joel Green says that the kiss of love has traits that shape the Christian's world. The kiss generated a sense of identity and focused attention on believers' shared life. The visual, tactile act sealed "the community's essential commitments with physical demonstration." They had suffered hostility and alienation from the pagan world; now the kiss affirmed that they belonged in a loving family. The kiss of love strengthened "patterns of thinking and feeling" and a "quality of life, determined by the merciful initiative of God who brings liberation in Christ and creates a household structured around his grace."[11]

The kiss of love is still known in many cultures, but where the practice is alien, we find other ways to demonstrate our affection. That could be a handshake or a hug. Physical affection is important, as the fivefold command to greet with a kiss shows (Rom. 16:16; 1 Cor. 16:20; 2 Cor. 13:12; 1 Thess. 5:26; 1 Peter 5:14; cf. Luke 7:45; Acts 20:37). But the custom must be grounded in reality. We need genuine ties for the *signs* of affection to carry weight. It's awkward, not helpful, to hug a stranger. We need relationships and must take time to form them.

Even the great apostles Peter and Paul never wanted to be alone; they needed loving relationships, too. As Peter wrote, Silvanus and Mark were with him. He wanted the whole church and each church to know the benefits of familial love. At the least, we more richly experience grace when we are together. We help each other stand in God's grace. This is one way that Jesus, the Chief Shepherd, cares for us as we move toward the eternal glory that God promises us. All of this allows Peter to conclude with a simple but profound benediction: "Peace to all of you who are in Christ" (1 Peter 5:14).

CLOSING THOUGHTS

So we have finished our journey through 1 Peter. How beautiful to receive God's peace at its conclusion. How fitting that Peter, who betrayed the Lord and received the grace of forgiveness, closes his epistle by offering his churches the grace of God. His letter began, "Grace and peace be yours in abundance" (1 Peter 1:2). He concludes, "I have written to you briefly, encouraging you and testifying that this is the true grace of God. Stand fast

11. Joel B. Green, *1 Peter* (Grand Rapids: Eerdmans, 2007), 185. See also William E. Paden, *Religious Worlds: The Comparative Study of Religion* (Boston: Beacon, 1994).

in it" (5:12). The apostle's talk of grace is not formulaic. Peter denied Jesus three times, swearing on oath that he did not even know him. Yet when Peter repented, Jesus both forgave him and reinstated him as an apostle. Because of the depth of his sin, Peter loved the grace of God.

But Peter offered no cheap grace. He called the church to a holiness grounded in the work of Christ. Because God is holy, we are holy. Because Jesus ransomed us, we put away sin (1 Peter 1:13–2:3). Because we are God's holy nation, we abstain from sin and live honorably, even if slandered (2:4–12). Holiness manifests itself socially, in submission to governors and masters (2:13–25), and it shows itself in the home (3:1–7). Peter says that disciples can ordinarily expect to "see good days," living in substantial peace, if we live well, treat others well, and seek peace (3:8–13). Still, it is possible to suffer for doing good (3:13–17). Jesus did so when he died for us and so liberated us from death (3:18–22). Jesus' example prepares us for opposition from the Gentiles (4:1–6). Nonetheless, the disciples' eyes are not always on possible troubles. We are self-controlled, loving, hospitable, and quick to use God's gifts to administer God's grace (4:7–11). The elders of the church lead God's flock in all this, setting an example and watching over all (5:1–5). So we hope to stand firm in God's grace and enjoy the peace of Christ (5:7–14).

SELECT COMMENTARIES ON 1 PETER

Achtemeier, Paul J. *1 Peter*. Minneapolis: Fortress, 1996.

Calvin, John. *Calvin's Commentaries*. Translated by John Owen. Vol. 22, *The First Epistle of Peter*. Grand Rapids, Baker, 1999.

Cranfield, C. E. B. *I & II Peter and Jude*. London: SCM Press, 1960.

Davids, Peter H. *The First Epistle of Peter*. Grand Rapids: Eerdmans, 1990.

Goppelt, Leonhard. *A Commentary on 1 Peter*. Translated by John E. Alsup. Grand Rapids: Eerdmans, 1993.

Green, Joel B. *1 Peter*. Grand Rapids: Eerdmans, 2007.

Jobes, Karen H. *1 Peter*. Grand Rapids: Baker Academic, 2005.

Kelly, J. N. D. *A Commentary on the Epistles of Peter and Jude*. New York: Harper & Row, 1969.

McKnight, Scot. *1 Peter*. NIV Application Commentary. Grand Rapids: Zondervan, 1996.

Michaels, J. Ramsey. *1 Peter*. Nashville: Thomas Nelson, 1988.

Stibbs, Alan M. *The First Epistle General of Peter*. London: Tyndale, 1959.

Index of Scripture

APOCRYPHA

Ecclesiasticus

OLD TESTAMENT PSEUDEPIGRAPHA

1 Enoch

Index of Subjects and Names

reverent fear, 46–47, 52, 65, 75, 145
reward, 47, 216–17
Richards, Randolph, 235n8
Robert the Monk, 43
rock, 68
role, 185–86
Roman Empire, 5, 7, 10, 12, 92, 125, 137, 189, 193, 236
romantic marriage, 122
Rome, as Babylon, 24n1
royal priesthood, 72
ruling elders, 173
Russell, Bertrand, 58, 60
Russian Orthodox Church, 150–51

salvation, 16
    ready to be revealed in the last time, 18
    as theme of Scriptures, 26
salvation by works, 47
same–sex marriage, 48
Sarah, 116–17
Satan, 231
Saul, 215
Schrage, Wolfgang, 86
Schuurman, Douglas, 96
Scripture
    dual authorship of, 28
    as God–breathed, 29
    inerrancy of, 29
    infallibility of, 29, 151
    inspiration of, 26–29
    private reading of, 29–30
    in public worship, 29–30
    reading of, 34–35
    and salvation, 25–27
second exodus, 228
Second Helvetic Confession, 174
self–assertion, 129
self–control, 13, 38, 109n4, 171–72, 238

self–denial, 128–29, 179
self–fulfillment, 96, 179
self–indulgence, 80, 89
selfish ambition, 80
selfishness, 162, 225
self–preservation, 163
self–reliance, 222
self–righteousness, 63
Seneca, 19n7, 93
Septuagint, 16n2
Servant of the Lord, 66
servants, Christians as, 88–89, 186
service to God, 89
serving, 173–75, 182, 209–10
sexual ethics, 125
sexual immorality, 80, 89, 193
sexual relations, 117–18
shepherds, 203, 207–8, 213–14
Silas, 234
Silvanus, 234–35, 237
sin, 79–81, 225
    break with, 162, 168
skepticism, 21
skills, 178
slander, 61–62, 82
slaves
    endure mistreatment, 101
    in Roman Empire, 92–94
    submission to masters, 99, 117, 125
Smith, Scotty, 234
social ethics, 92
sojourners, 47, 77, 161
sola Scriptura, 155
solidarity, 236
souls, 22, 152
Spanish Armada, 36–37
speaking gifts, 182
spirit, 148
spirits in prison, 151–53, 167